CHRISTIAN HERITAGE CLASSICS

The Eighteenth Century

Sherwood Eliot Wirt, Editor

Spiritual Awakening

*Classic Writings of the
18th Century to Inspire the
20th Century Reader*

Sherwood Eliot Wirt, editor

CROSSWAY BOOKS • WESTCHESTER, ILLINOIS 60153
A DIVISION OF GOOD NEWS PUBLISHERS

To my granddaughter
Bree Anna Wirt

Contents

Foreword

The favorable reception accorded the first volume in our Christian Heritage Classics series, *Spiritual Disciplines* (Crossway, 1983), both in America and the British Commonwealth, has encouraged us to bring out a second volume containing devotional classics of the eighteenth century. Our principle remains the same: we chose these selections not because they are necessarily representative of the authors, or even their finest literary work. Rather, we chose them because spiritually they have helped thousands, perhaps millions of believers in the past, and can be expected to help us as well.

Apart from changing the old English "thee" and "thou," and introducing some paragraphing, the editor has made practically no changes in the text. As in the earlier volume on the seventeenth century, an attempt was made at geographical representation. In Volume I selections were included from two Frenchmen and one Frenchwoman, a Scot, an American, a German, and seven Englishmen. In this volume we have chosen from one Frenchman, one German, five Americans (including an American Indian), six Englishmen, and one Englishwoman.

Five of the present selections are taken from works that are recognized today as all-time devotional classics: the *Journal* of Woolman, Edwards' description of the Northampton revival, Brainerd's diary, Massillon's famous sermon, and Law's "Serious Call." The other nine represent some of the hidden gold of the eighteenth century that we have enjoyed bringing to light. Why they were popular in their day, you will soon discover.

Again I would like to thank the board of editorial advisers who have provided me with invaluable assistance in putting together this volume. Dr. Geoffrey W. Bromiley is the distinguished professor of church history and historical theology at Fuller Theological Seminary, Pasadena, California. Helga Bender Henry is an author, teacher, and editor living in Arlington, Virginia. She is perhaps best known as the wife of Dr. Carl F. H. Henry, dean of American evangelical theologians. Dr. Calvin D. Linton is professor emeritus of English literature and emeritus dean of the College of Arts and Sciences at The George Washington University, Washington, D.C. D. Bruce Lockerbie, M.A., editor, author, educational consultant, and popular lecturer, is Staley Scholar-in-Residence and former dean of the faculty at The Stony Brook School, Stony Brook, New York.

A fifth member of our board, Dr. Frank E. Gaebelein, author, alpinist, musician, educator, and general editor of *The Expositor's Bible,* was of generous help in preparing Volume I. The first headmaster of The Stony Brook School, he passed away just before the first volume went to press, and his counsel is missed in the present work.

It is worthy of mention that two selections in Volume II, from the writings of Woolman and Newton, deal with the issue of Negro slavery which was just beginning to awaken the conscience of England and America. Frank Gaebelein, who was one of the few northern evangelicals to join the Selma, Alabama march of 1967, would have warmly endorsed their inclusion.

And now, welcome to the eighteenth century—not to its wars, its politics, its intellectual "enlightenment," or its scientific or industrial advances, but to another side of it—which, in all the depth and variety of its devotion to Almighty God, is for some of us the best side.

S.E.W.

John Wesley

To attempt to capture John Wesley (1703-1791) on a page or two is to pursue an eagle with a butterfly net. Some say Wesley saved England from the horrors of a French Revolution. Others say he gave birth to Methodism at a time when English Christianity seemed to have no power to lift the people; when social conditions were insufferable; when dram-drinking was an epidemic, and freethinkers' clubs were flourishing. Whatever the assessment of this godly man's life, it is certain that once he became convinced he had received salvation from sin, he set his goal (in his own words) "to promote so far as I am able vital, practical religion; and by the grace of God to beget, preserve, and increase the life of God in the souls of men."

John Wesley was born in the rectory at Epworth, Lincolnshire, England, the fifteenth of nineteen children. He was educated at Oxford University, and was elected to a fellowship at Lincoln College at age twenty-three. In 1728 he was ordained a priest of the Church of England. Soon after, his younger brother Charles (child number eighteen) organized some Oxford undergraduates into what became laughingly known as the "Holy Club." John was the leader. The club was strong on method (its members were called "Methodists"), but short on evangelism. In later years Wesley said of those days, "I preached much, but saw no fruit to my labor."

In 1735 John and Charles accepted an assignment to the colony of Georgia as missionaries. John sailed back two years later, writing in his Journal: "I went to America to convert the Indians; but oh, who will convert me?" On shipboard and in Georgia he had been deeply impressed by some Moravian missionaries, and in 1738 he visited their colony at Herrnhut, Germany. He returned to London and underwent a genuine conversion experience during a Moravian meeting at a chapel in Aldersgate street.

Now sensing his call to be an evangelist, Wesley discovered that the Anglican churches were closed to him. Following his younger colleague George Whitefield's suggestion, he began field-preaching to the miners around Bristol with remarkable success. He had found a way to reach *the masses that the church had missed. To conserve the gains of his evangelism, Wesley began forming societies in the wake of his preaching missions. This was the beginning of what became the worldwide Methodist movement.*

Much of the impetus came from Wesley himself. During his lifetime he crossed the Irish Sea forty-two times to preach in Ireland, paid twenty-two visits to Scotland, traveled eight thousand miles per year on horseback through England, and preached an average of fifteen sermons a week wherever he was. As a social reformer he broke new ground, providing work for the poor and supplying them with clothes and food. He created a taste for good reading and supplied books at the lowest prices. He established credit to help struggling businessmen and relieved debtors who had been thrown into prison. He opened medical dispensaries in London and Bristol, established schools, and preached against the slave trade.

Wesley opposed the American Revolution, but had already established Methodism in the colonies through appointed preachers whom he ordained. At his death there were 294 Methodist preachers and 71,668 members in Great Britain, nineteen missionaries and five thousand three hundred members on mission stations, and 198 preachers and 43,265 members in America. Wesley has been called "one of the greatest Christians of his age."

This sermon has been taken from a volume entitled Selections from the Writings of the Rev. John Wesley, M.A., *edited by Herbert Welch and published in 1901 by Eaton and Mains, New York.*

ONE

Genuine Christianity
by John Wesley

We have long been disputing about Christians, about Christianity, and the evidence whereby it is supported. But what do these terms mean? Who is a Christian indeed? What is real, genuine Christianity? And what is the surest and most accessible evidence (if I may so speak) whereby I may know that it is of God?

I would consider, first, who is a Christian indeed? What does that term properly imply? It has been so long abused, I fear, not only to mean nothing at all, but, what was far worse than nothing, to be a cloak for the vilest hypocrisy, for the grossest abominations and immoralities of every kind, that it is high time to rescue it out of the hands of wretches who are a reproach to human nature; to show determinedly what manner of man he is, to whom this name of right belongs.

A Christian cannot think of the Author of his being without abasing himself before Him. In His presence he sinks into the dust, so that he can only cry out from the fullness of his heart, "O God! what is man? what am I?" He has a continual sense of his dependence on the Parent of good for his being and all the blessings that attend it. To Him [God] he refers every natural and every moral endowment; and hence he acquiesces in whatsoever appears to be His will, not only with patience, but with thankfulness.

And as he has the strongest affection for the Fountain of all good, so he has the firmest confidence in Him; a confidence which neither pleasure nor pain, neither life nor death, can shake. But yet this, far from creating sloth or indolence, pushes him on to the most vigorous industry. It causes him to put forth all his strength, in obeying Him in whom he confides. He knows the most acceptable worship of God is to imitate Him he worships; in particular, His justice, mercy, and truth, so eminently displayed in all His creatures.

Above all, remembering that God is love, he is conformed to the same likeness. He is full of love to his neighbor; of universal love; not confined to one sect or party; not restrained to those who agree with him in opinions or in outward modes of worship; or to those who are allied to him by blood, or recommended by nearness of place. Neither does he love those only that love him, or that are endeared to him by intimacy of acquaintance.

But his love resembles that of Him whose mercy is over all His works. It soars above all these scanty bounds, embracing neighbors and strangers, friends and enemies; yea, not only the good and gentle, but also the froward, the evil and unthankful. For he loves every soul that God has made; every child of man, of whatever place or nation. And yet this universal benevolence does in no wise interfere with a peculiar regard for his relations, friends and benefactors; a fervent love for his country; and the most endeared affection to all men of integrity, of clear and generous virtue.

[The Christian's] love, as to these, so to all mankind, is in itself generous and disinterested, springing from no view of advantage to himself, from no regard to profit or praise; no, nor even the pleasure of loving. This is the daughter, not the parent, of his affection. By experience he knows that social love, if it mean the love of our neighbor, is absolutely different from self-love, even of the most allowable kind; just as different as the objects at which they point.

And this universal, disinterested love is productive of all right affections. It is fruitful of gentleness, tenderness, sweetness; of humanity, courtesy, and affability. It makes a Christian rejoice in the virtues of all, and bear a part in their happiness, at the same time that he sympathizes with their pains and [feels] compassion [for] their infirmities. It creates modesty, condescension, prudence, together with calmness and evenness of temper. It is the parent of generosity, openness, and frankness, void of jealousy and suspicion. It begets candor, and willingness to believe and hope whatever is kind and friendly of every man; and invincible patience, never overcome of evil, but overcoming evil with good.

The same love constrains him to converse, not only with a strict regard to truth, but with artless sincerity and genuine simplicity, as one in whom there is no guile. And, not content with abstaining from all such expressions as are contrary to justice or truth, he endeavors to refrain from every unloving word, either to a present or of an absent person. In all his conversation he aims either to improve himself in knowledge or virtue, or to make those with whom he converses some way wiser, or better, or happier than they were before.

The same love is productive of all right actions. It leads him into an earnest and steady discharge of all social offices, of whatever is due to relations of every kind; to his friends, to his country, and to any particular community whereof he is a member. It prevents his willingly hurting or grieving any man. It guides him into a uniform practice of justice and mercy, equally extensive with the principle whence it flows. It constrains him to do all possible good, of every possible kind, to all men; and makes him invariably resolved in every circumstance of life to do that, and that only, to others which, supposing he were himself in the same situation, he would desire they should do to him.

And as he is easy to others, so he is easy in himself. He is free from the painful swellings of pride, from the flames of anger, from the impetuous gusts of irregular self-will. He is no longer tortured with envy or malice, or with unreasonable and hurtful desire. He is no more enslaved to the pleasures of sense, but has the full power over his mind and body, in a continued cheerful course of sobriety, of temperance and chastity. He knows how to use all things in their place, and yet is superior to them all. He stands above those low pleasures of imagination which captivate vulgar minds, whether arising from what mortals term greatness, or from novelty, or beauty. All these too he can taste, and still look upward; still aspire to nobler enjoyments. Neither is he a slave to fame; popular breath affects not him; he stands steady and collected in himself.

And he who seeks no praise, cannot fear dispraise. Censure gives him no uneasiness, being conscious to himself that he would not willingly offend, and that he has the approbation of the Lord of all. He cannot fear want, knowing in whose hand is the earth and the fullness thereof, and that it is impossible for Him to withhold from one who fears Him any manner of thing that is good. He cannot fear pain, knowing it will never be sent unless it be for his real advantage; and that then his strength will be proportioned to it, as it has always been in times past. He cannot fear death, being able to trust Him he loves with his soul as well as his body; yea, glad to leave the corruptible body in the dust, till it is raised incorruptible and immortal. So that in honor or shame, in abundance or want, in ease or pain, in life or in death, always, and in all things, he has learned to be content, to be easy, thankful, happy.

He is happy in knowing there is a God, an intelligent Cause and Lord of all, and that he is not the product either of blind chance or inexorable necessity. He is happy in the full assurance that this Creator and End of all things is a Being of boundless wisdom, of infinite power to execute all the designs of His wisdom, and of no less infinite goodness to direct all His power to the advantage of all His creatures. Nay, even the consideration of His immutable justice, rendering to all their due, of His unspotted holiness, of His all-sufficiency in Himself, and of that immense ocean of all perfections which center in God from eternity to eternity, is a continual addition to the happiness of a Christian.

In contemplating the things that surround him, he takes knowledge of the invisible things of God, even His eternal power and wisdom in the things that are seen, the heavens, the earth, the fowls of the air, the lilies of the field; and the thought strikes warmly upon his heart. While rejoicing in the constant care which he still takes of the work of his own hand, he breaks out in a transport of love and praise, "O Lord our Governor, how excellent are Thy ways in all the earth! Thou that hast set Thy glory above the heavens!"[1]

While he as it were sees the Lord sitting upon His throne and ruling all things well; while he observes the general providence of God, coextended with His whole creation, and surveys all the effects of it in the heavens and earth as a well-pleased spectator; while he sees the wisdom and goodness of His general government descending to every particular, so presiding over the whole universe as over a single person, so watching over every single person as if he were the whole universe; how does he exult when he reviews the various traces of the Almighty goodness in what has befallen himself, in the several circumstances and changes of his own life!

He is peculiarly and inexpressibly happy in the clearest and fullest conviction that "this all-powerful, all-wise, all-gracious Being, this Governor of all loves me. This Lover of my soul is always with me, is never absent, no, not for a moment. And I love Him. 'There is none in heaven but Thee, none on earth that I desire beside Thee!'[2] And He has given me to resemble Himself; He has stamped His image on my heart. And I live unto Him. I do only His will. I glorify Him with my body and my spirit. And it will not be long before I shall die unto Him; I shall die into the arms of God. Then farewell sin and pain; then it only remains that I should live with Him forever."

This is the plain, naked portraiture of a Christian. But be not prejudiced against him for his name. Forgive his peculiarities of opinion and (what you think) superstitious modes of worship. These are circumstances but of small concern, and do not enter into the essence of his character. Cover them with a veil of love and look at the substance—his tempers, his holiness, his happiness.

Can calm reason conceive either a more amiable or a more desirable character? Is it your own? Away with names! Away with opinions! I care not what you are called. I ask not (it does not deserve a thought) what opinion you are of, so that you are conscious to yourself that you are the man whom I have been (however faintly) describing.

Do you not know you ought to be such? Is the Governor of the world well pleased that you are not? Do you (at least) desire it? I would to God that desire may penetrate your inmost soul; and that you may have no rest in your spirit till you are not only almost, but altogether a Christian!

* * *

The second point to be considered is, what is real, genuine Christianity? Whether we speak of it as a principle in the soul or as a system of doctrine. Taken in the latter sense, Christianity is that system of doctrine which describes the character above recited, and which promises it shall be mine, and tells me how I may attain it, provided I will not rest till I attain. It describes this character in all its parts in the most lively and affecting manner. The main lines of this picture are beautifully drawn in many passages of the Old Testament. These are filled up in the New, retouched and finished with all the art of God.

Christianity promises this character shall be mine, both in the Old Testament and the New. Indeed the New is in effect all a promise. Every description of the servants of God mentioned therein has the nature of a command. Thus: "Be ye followers of me, as I am of Christ."[3] "Be ye followers of them who through faith and patience inherit the promises."[4] And every command has the force of a promise. "A new heart will I give you . . ., and I will put my Spirit within you, and cause you to walk in My statutes."[5] "I will put My laws into their minds, and write them in their hearts."[6] Accordingly when it is said, "Thou shalt love the Lord thy God with all thy heart, and with all thy soul, and with all thy mind,"[7] it is not only a direction of what I shall do, but a promise of what God will do in me.

Christianity tells me how I may attain the promise, namely, by faith. But what is faith? Not an opinion, no more than it is a form of words. Not any number of opinions put together, be they ever so true. A man may assent to three, or twenty-three creeds. He may assent to all the Old and New Testaments (at least as far as he understands them) and yet have no Christian faith at all. The faith by which the promise is attained is a power wrought by the Almighty in an immortal spirit, inhabiting a house of clay, to see through that veil into the world of spirits; a power to discern those things which with eyes of flesh and blood no man hath seen or can see. More particularly, Christian faith is a divine evidence or conviction wrought in the heart that God is reconciled to me through His Son, and inseparably joined with a confidence in Him, as a gracious reconciled Father, as for all things, so especially for all those good things which are invisible and eternal.

To believe in the Christian sense is, then, to walk in the light of eternity, and to have a clear sight of and confidence in the Most High, reconciled to me through the Son of His love.

Now, how highly desirable is such a faith, were it only on its own account! Is it not so? Let impartial reason speak. Does not every thinking man want a window, not so much in his neighbor's as in his own breast? He wants an opening there of whatever kind, that might let in light from eternity. He is pained to be thus feeling after God so darkly, so uncertainly; to know so little of God. What he sees, he sees in the dim, sullied glass of sense. It is all a mere enigma.

Now, these very desiderata faith supplies. It gives a more extensive knowledge of things visible, showing what eye had not seen, nor ear heard, neither could it before enter into our heart to conceive. And all these it shows in the clearest light, with the fullest certainty and evidence. It resolves a thousand enigmas. O, who would not wish for such a faith, were it only on these accounts! How much more, if by this I may receive the promise, I may attain all that holiness and happiness!

So Christianity tells me; and so I find it. I am assured these things are so because I experience them in my own breast. What Christianity promised is accomplished in my soul. It is the completion of all those promises; a fountain of peace and love springing up into everlasting life.

This I conceive to be the strongest evidence of the truth of Christianity. I do not undervalue traditional evidence. Let it have its place and its due honor. It is highly serviceable in its kind and in its degree. And yet I cannot set it on a level with this. It is generally supposed that traditional evidence is weakened by length of time; as it must necessarily pass through so many hands, in a continued succession of ages. But no length of time can possibly affect the strength of this internal evidence. It is equally strong, equally new, through the course of seventeen hundred years. It passes now, even as it has done from the beginning, directly from God into the believing soul. Do you suppose time will ever dry up this stream? O no! It shall never be cut off.

Traditional evidence is of an extremely complicated nature, so that only men of a strong and clear understanding can be sensible of its full force. On the contrary, how plain and simple is this, and how level to the lowest capacity! "One thing I know; I was blind, but now I see."[8] An argument so plain that a peasant, a child, may feel all its force.

The traditional evidence of Christianity stands, as it were, a great way off, and therefore, although it speaks loud and clear, yet makes a less lively impression. It gives us an account of what was transacted long ago, in far distant times as well as places. Whereas the inward evidence is intimately present to all persons, at all times, and in all places. It is nigh thee, in thy mouth, and in thy heart, if thou believest in the Lord Jesus Christ. This, then, is the record, this is the evidence, emphatically so-called, "that God hath given unto us eternal life; and this life is in His Son."[9]

Every true believer hath the witness or evidence in himself. If then it were possible (which I conceive it is not) to shake the traditional evidence of Christianity, still he who has the internal evidence would stand firm and unshaken.

May I be permitted to speak freely [to the nominal Christians of England]? Though you bear the name, you are not Christians; you have neither Christian faith nor love. You have no divine evidence of things unseen; you have not entered into the holiest by the blood of Jesus. You do not love God with all your heart; neither do you love your neighbor as yourself. You are neither happy nor holy. You have not learned in every state therewith to be content; to rejoice evermore, even in want, pain, death; and in everything to give thanks. You are not holy in heart;

superior to pride, to anger, to foolish desires. Neither are you holy in life; you do not walk as Christ also walked. As to morality, even honest, heathen morality (O let me utter a melancholy truth!) there is reason to fear that many of those whom you style Deists have far more of it than you.

O, how do I long for you to be partakers of the exceeding great and precious promise! How am I pained when I hear any of you using those silly terms which the men of form have taught you, calling the mention of the only thing you want, *cant!* The deepest wisdom, the highest happiness, *enthusiasm!* What ignorance is this! What reasonable assurance can you have of things whereof you have not personal experience? Suppose the question were, can the blind be restored to sight? This you have not yourself experienced. How then will you know that such a thing ever was? Can there be an easier or surer way than to talk with men who were blind, but are now restored to sight? If they are honest men, they will not deceive you.

Now transfer this to the case before us, and [it] will afford you a very strong evidence of the truth of Christianity: as strong as can be in the nature of things, till you experience it in your own soul.

*   *   *

We know "all Scripture is given by inspiration of God,"[10] and is therefore true and right concerning all things. But we know likewise that there are some Scriptures which more immediately commend themselves to every man's conscience. In this rank we may place the passage before us:

> "Though I speak with the tongues of men and of
> angels, and have not love, I am become as sounding
> brass, or a tinkling cymbal. And though I have the gift
> of prophecy, and understand all mysteries and all
> knowledge, and though I have all faith, so as to remove
> mountains, and have not love, I am nothing. And
> though I bestow all my goods to feed the poor, and
> give my body to be burned, and have not love, it
> profiteth me nothing." (1 Corinthians 13:1-3)

There are scarce any that object to this passage. On the contrary, the generality of men very readily appeal to it. Nothing is more common than to find even those who deny the authority of the Holy Scriptures, yet affirming, "This is my religion: that which is described in the thirteenth chapter of the Corinthians." Nay, even a Jew, Dr. Nunes, a Spanish physician then settled at Savannah, Georgia, used to say with great earnestness that "Paul of Tarsus was one of the finest writers I have ever read. I wish the thirteenth chapter of his first letter to the Corinthians were wrote in letters of gold, and I wish every Jew were to carry it with him wherever he went." He judged (and herein he certainly judged right) that this single chapter contained the whole of true religion. It contains "whatsoever things are just, whatsoever things are pure, whatsoever things are lovely, if there be any virtue, if there be any praise"[11]—it is all contained in this.

St. Paul's word is *agape*, exactly answering to the plain English word *love*. It is so rendered in all the old translations of the Bible. So it stood in William Tyndale's Bible, which I suppose was the first English translation of the whole Bible.[12] So it was also in the Bible published by the authority of King Henry VIII. So it was likewise in all the editions of the Bible that were successively published in England during the reign of King Edward VI, Queen Elizabeth, and King James I. Nay, so it is found in the Bibles of King Charles the First's reign.

The first Bibles I have seen wherein the word was changed were those printed by Roger Daniel and John Field, printers to the Parliament, in the year 1649. Hence it seems probable that the alteration was made during the sitting of the Long Parliament. Probably it was then that the Latin word *charity* was put in place of the English word *love*. It was in an unhappy hour this alteration was made. The ill effects of it remain to this day; and these may be observed not only among the poor and illiterate—thousands of common men and women no more understand the word *charity* than they do the original Greek—but the same miserable mistake has diffused itself among men of education and learning.

Thousands of these are misled thereby, and imagine that the "charity" treated of in this chapter refers chiefly, if not wholly, to outward actions, and means little more than almsgiving. I have heard many sermons preached upon this chapter, particularly before the University of Oxford, and I never heard more than one in which the meaning of it was not totally misrepresented. But had the old and proper word *love* been retained, there would have been no room for misrepresentation.

But what kind of love is that whereof the apostle is speaking throughout the chapter? Many persons of eminent learning and piety apprehend that it is the love of God. But from reading the whole chapter numberless times, and considering it in every light, I am thoroughly persuaded that what St. Paul is here directly speaking of is the love of our neighbor. I believe whoever carefully weighs the whole tenor of his discourse will be fully convinced of this. But it must be allowed to be such a love of our neighbor as can only spring from a love of God. And whence does this love of God flow? Only from that faith which is of the operation of God. Whoever has it, has a direct evidence that "God was in Christ reconciling the world unto Himself."[13]

When this is particularly applied to his heart, so that he can say with humble boldness, "The life which I now live, I live by faith in the Son of God who loved me and gave Himself for me," then, and not till then, "the love of God is poured out into his heart."[14] And this love sweetly constrains him to love every child of man with the love which is here spoken of; not with a love of esteem or of complacence, for this can have no place with regard to those who are (if not his personal enemies, yet) enemies to God and their own souls; but with a love of benevolence, of tender goodwill to all the souls that God has made.

But it may be asked, "If there be no true love of our neighbor but that which springs from the love of God; and if the love of God flows from no other fountain than faith in the Son of God, does it not follow that the whole heathen world is excluded from all possibility of salvation? Seeing they are cut off from faith, for faith cometh by hearing; and how shall they hear without a preacher?"[15]

I answer that St. Paul's words, spoken on another occasion, are applicable to this: "What the law speaketh, it speaketh to them that are under the law."[16] Accordingly that sentence, "He that believeth not shall be damned"[17] is spoken of them to whom the gospel is preached. Others it does not concern, and we are not required to determine anything touching their final state. How it will please God, the Judge of all, to deal with them, we may leave to God Himself. But this we know, that He is not the God of the Christians only, but the God of the heathen also; that he is "rich in mercy to all that call upon Him"[18] according to the light they have, and that "in every nation he that feareth God and worketh righteousness is accepted of Him."[19]

This is the nature of that love whereof the apostle is here speaking. But what are the properties of it? The fruits which are inseparable from it? The apostle reckons up many of them, but the principal of them are these:

First, *love is not puffed up.* As is the measure of love, so is the measure of humility. Nothing humbles the soul so deeply as love. It casts out all "high conceits, engendering pride," all arrogance and overweening; makes us little, and poor, and base, and vile in our own eyes. It abases us both before God and man; makes us willing to be the least of all, and the servants of all, and teaches us to say, "A mote in the sunbeam is little, but I am infinitely less in the presence of God."

Second, *love is not provoked.* Our present English translation renders it, "is not easily provoked." But how did the word *easily* come in? There is not a tittle of it in the text. The words of the apostle are simply these, *ou paroxunetai.* Is it not probable that it was inserted by the translators with a design to excuse St. Paul, for fear his practice should appear to contradict his doctrine? For we read in Acts 15, "And some days after, Paul said unto Barnabas, Let us go again and visit our brethren in every city where we have preached the word of the Lord, and see how they do. And Barnabas determined to take with them John, whose surname was Mark. But Paul thought it not good to take with them one who departed from the work. And the contention was so sharp between them that they departed asunder one from the other. And so Barnabas took Mark and sailed unto Cyprus, and Paul chose Silas and departed, being recommended by the brethren unto the grace of God. And he went through Syria and Cilicia, confirming the churches."

Would not anyone think on reading these words that they were both equally sharp? That Paul was just as hot as Barnabas, and as much wanting in love as he? But the text says no such thing, as will be plain, if we consider first the occasion. When St. Paul proposed that they should "again visit the brethren in every city where they had preached the word," so far they were agreed. "And Barnabas determined to take with them John," because he was his sister's son, without receiving or asking St. Paul's advice. "But Paul thought it not good to take with them him who had departed from them from Pamphylia," whether through sloth or cowardice; "and went not with them to the work."[20] And undoubtedly he thought right; he had reason on his side.

The following words are, *egeneto oun paroxusmos,* literally, "and there was a fit of anger." It does not say, in St. Paul.

Probably it was Barnabas alone, who thus supplied the want of reason with passion, "so that they parted asunder." And Barnabas, resolved to have his own way, did as his nephew had done before. He "departed from the work," "took Mark with him and sailed to Cyprus." But Paul went on in his work, "being recommended by the brethren to the grace of God," which Barnabas seems not to have stayed for. "And he went through Syria and Cilicia, confirming the churches." From the whole account it does not appear that St. Paul was in any fault; that he either felt any temper or spoke any word contrary to the law of love. Therefore, not being in any fault, he does not need any excuse.

Certainly he who is full of love is "gentle towards all men." He "in meekness instructs those that oppose themselves," that oppose what he loves most, even the truth of God, or that holiness without which no man shall see the Lord. How does he know but that "God, peradventure, may bring them to the knowledge of the truth"?[21] However provoked, he does not "return evil for evil, or railing for railing."[22] Yea, he "blesses those that curse him, and does good to them that despitefully use him and persecute him."[23] He is "not overcome of evil," but always "overcomes evil with good."[24]

Third, *love is long-suffering.* It endures not just a few affronts, reproaches, injuries, but *all things,* which God is pleased to permit either men or devils to inflict. It arms the soul with inviolable patience, not harsh, stoical patience, but yielding as the air. It makes no resistance to the stroke and receives no harm thereby. The lover of mankind remembers him who suffered for us, "leaving us an example that we might tread in his steps."[25] Accordingly if his enemy hunger, he feeds him; if he thirst, he gives him drink, and by so doing, he heaps coals of fire of melting love upon his head.[26] Many waters cannot quench this love, neither can the floods of ingratitude drown it.[27]

We are now to inquire what those things are which, it is commonly supposed, will supply the place of love? And the first of these is eloquence: a faculty for talking well, particularly on religious subjects. Men are generally inclined to think well of one who talks well. If he speaks properly and fluently of God, and the things of God, who can doubt of his being in God's favor? And it is very natural for him to think well of himself—to have as favorable an opinion of himself as others have.

But men of reflection are not satisfied with this. They are

not content with a flood of words. They prefer thinking before talking, and prefer one that knows much to one that talks much. And it is certain, knowledge is an excellent gift of God, particularly knowledge of the Holy Scriptures, in which are contained all the depths of divine knowledge and wisdom. Hence it is generally thought that a man of much knowledge—knowledge of Scripture in particular—must not only be in the favor of God, but likewise enjoy a high degree of it.

But men of deeper reflection are apt to say, "I lay no stress upon any other knowledge of God than by faith. Faith is the only knowledge which, in the sight of God, is of great price. We are saved by faith alone; this is the one thing needful." There is much truth in this. It is unquestionably true that we are saved by faith. But some men will say with the Apostle James, "Show me thy faith without thy works" (if thou canst; but indeed it is impossible) "and I will show thee my faith by my works."[28] And many are induced to think that good works, works of piety and mercy, are of far more consequence than faith itself, and will supply the want of every other qualification for heaven. Indeed, this seems to be the general sentiment, not only of the church of Rome, but of Protestants also; not of the giddy and thoughtless, but the serious members of our own church.

And this cannot be denied. Our Lord Himself hath said, "Ye shall know them by their fruits."[29] But yet it may be doubted whether there is not a surer proof of the sincerity of our faith than even our works, and that is our willingness to suffer for righteousness' sake—especially if, after suffering reproach and pain and loss of friends and substance, a man gives up life itself, rather than give up faith and a good conscience.

What a beautiful gradation there is, each step rising above the other, of those things which some of those who are called Christians, and are usually accounted so, really believe will supply the absence of love. St. Paul begins at the lowest point, *talking well,* and advances step by step, till he comes to the highest of all. A step above eloquence is *knowledge; faith* is a step above this. *Good works* are a step above that faith, and even above this is *suffering for righteousness' sake.* Nothing is higher than this but *Christian love:* the love of our neighbor, flowing from the love of God.

Whatever passes for religion in any part of the Christian world (whether it be part of religion, or no part at all) may with very little difficulty be reduced to one or other of these heads. I am now to demonstrate to all who have ears to hear that neither any one of these five qualifications, nor all of them together, will avail anything before God without the love above described. In order to do this in the clearest manner we may consider them one by one.

First, though I speak with an eloquence such as never was found in men, concerning the nature, attributes, and works of God, whether of creation or providence; though I were not a whit behind the chief of the apostles, preaching like St. Peter and praying like St. John, yet unless humble, gentle, patient love be the ruling temper of my soul, I am no better in the judgment of God "than sounding brass or a rumbling cymbal."[30] Therefore the brightest talents either for preaching or prayer, if they were not joined with humble, meek, and patient resignation, might sink me the deeper into hell, but will not bring me one step nearer heaven.

Second, though I have the gift of foretelling those future events which no creature can foresee, and though I understand all the mysteries of nature, of providence, and the Word of God, and have all knowledge of things divine or human that any mortal ever attained to; though I can explain the most mysterious passages of Daniel, of Ezekiel, and the Revelation, yet if I have not humility, gentleness, and resignation, "I am nothing" in the sight of God.[31]

And what would it profit a man to "have all knowledge," even that which is infinitely preferable to all other, the knowledge of the Holy Scripture? I knew a young man about twenty years ago who was thoroughly acquainted with the Bible. Such a master of Biblical knowledge I never saw before and never expect to see again. Yet if with all his knowledge he had been void of love; if he had been proud, passionate or impatient, he and all his knowledge would have perished together, as sure as ever he was born.

"And though I have all faith, so that I could remove mountains . . ." Yet if this faith does not work by love, if it does not produce universal holiness, if it does not bring forth lowliness, meekness and resignation, it will profit me nothing. All faith that is, ever was, or ever can be, apart from tender benevolence to every child of man, friend or foe, Christian, Jew, heretic, or pagan; apart from gentleness to all men; apart from resignation in all events, and contentedness in all conditions—is not the faith of a Christian, and will stand us in no stead before the face of God.

"Although I give all my goods to the poor . . ." Though I divide all my real estate and my personal estate into small portions (so the original word properly signifies) and diligently bestow it on those who, I have reason to believe, are the most proper subjects—yet if I am proud, passionate, or discontented; if I give way to any of these tempers; whatever good I may do to others, I do none to my own soul. Oh, how pitiable a case is this! Who would not grieve, that these beneficent men should lose all their labor! Oh, that they were wise!

But stranger still is that assertion of Paul which comes in the last place: "Although I give my body to be burned, and have not love, it profiteth me nothing." Although rather than deny the faith, rather than commit a known sin or omit a known duty, I voluntarily submit to a cruel death, yet if I am under the power of pride, or anger, or fretfulness, "it profiteth me nothing."

The sum of all that has been observed is this: whatever I speak, whatever I know, whatever I believe, whatever I do, whatever I suffer; if I have not the faith that worketh by love; that produces love to God and all mankind, I am not in the narrow way which leadeth to life, but in the broad road that leadeth to destruction. In other words, whatever eloquence I have, whatever natural or supernatural knowledge; whatever faith I have received from God; whatever works I do, whether of piety or mercy; whatever sufferings I undergo for conscience' sake, even though I resist unto blood: all these things put together, however applauded of men, will avail nothing before God unless I am meek and lowly in heart, and can say in all things, "Not as I will, but as Thou wilt!"

We conclude from the whole (and it can never be too much inculcated, because all the world votes on the other side) that true religion, in the very essence of it, is nothing short of holy tempers. Consequently all other religion, whatever name it bears, whether pagan, Mohammedan, Jewish, or Christian; and whether Popish or Protestant, Lutheran or Reformed; without these, is lighter than vanity itself.

Let every man therefore who has a soul to be saved, see that he secure this one point. With all his eloquence, his knowledge, his faith, works, and sufferings, let him hold fast this "one thing needful."[32] He that through the power of faith endureth to the end in humble, gentle, patient love; he, and he alone shall, through the merits of Christ, "inherit the kingdom prepared from the foundation of the world."[33]

NOTES

1. Psalm 8:1.
2. Psalm 73:25.
3. 1 Corinthians 11:1.
4. Hebrews 6:12.
5. Ezekiel 36:26, 27.
6. Hebrews 8:10.
7. Deuteronomy 30:6.
8. John 9:25.
9. 1 John 5:11.
10. 2 Timothy 3:16.
11. Philippians 4:8.
12. The first English translation of the whole Bible was made from the Latin Vulgate under the sponsorship of John Wycliffe (1320-1384). William Tyndale (1492-1536) translated the New Testament and the Pentateuch from the Greek and Hebrew originals.
13. 2 Corinthians 5:19. Cf. Zinzendorf's comments on 1 Corinthians 13 on page 239.
14. Cf. Galatians 2:20; Romans 5:5.
15. Cf. Romans 10:14.
16. Romans 3:19.
17. Mark 16:16.
18. Cf. Ephesians 2:4; Psalm 103:8-11.
19. Acts 10:35.
20. Cf. Acts 15:38.
21. Cf. 2 Timothy 2:25.
22. 1 Peter 3:9.
23. Matthew 5:44.
24. Cf. Romans 12:21.
25. 1 Peter 2:21.
26. Cf. Romans 12:20.
27. Cf. Song of Solomon 8:7.
28. James 2:18.
29. Matthew 7:16.
30. 1 Corinthians 13:1.
31. Cf. 1 Corinthians 13:2.
32. Luke 10:42.
33. Matthew 25:24.

George Whitefield

After more than two centuries people are still talking about George Whitefield (1714-1770), the extraordinary evangelist who was once a bartender and busboy at the Bell Inn in Gloucester, England. Many are saying that he became the greatest gospeler of them all, excepting only the Apostle Paul himself.

From the time when, as a twenty-one-year-old ordinand, Whitefield (pronounced Whitfield) first stepped into the pulpit of St. Mary de Crypt, Gloucester, on June 27, 1736, until the September day in 1770 when he preached his life away in Exeter, New Hampshire, and Newburyport, Massachusetts, he seems to have lived for one consuming purpose: to preach Jesus Christ and to bring men and women into a saving relationship with him. "God forbid," he once said, "that I should travel with anybody a quarter of an hour without speaking of Christ to them." Again he declared in a sermon, "Believe me, I am willing to go to prison and to death for you, but I am not willing to go to heaven without you."

Whitefield tells us that as a boy he ran wild, but with adolescence his mind turned to serious thoughts. In 1732 his mother arranged for him to matriculate at Pembroke College, Oxford, where in exchange for free tuition he became a "servitor," or lackey, to older students. He soon heard of the popularly derided "Holy Club" and its leaders, John and Charles Wesley, but as a servitor he was not allowed to speak to them. They, however, could speak to him. He was invited into the club, and thus began a lifelong friendship which, though interrupted by theological quarrels about Calvinism and Arminianism, was renewed and continued warm until Whitefield's death.

In the spring of 1735 Whitefield went through a seven-week illness and spiritual crisis, and emerged on fire for the Lord. For the next thirty-five whirlwind years he left his impress on the destinies of Great Britain and the American colonies. When the Great Awakening came to America in 1740, Whitefield being then twenty-five years of age, he became a torch to kindle spiritual revival from Georgia to New England. He established the first charity in America, an orphanage near

Savannah, and was involved in the beginnings of half a dozen American colleges. (His statue stands today on the campus of the University of Pennsylvania.) He spent two years at sea, crossing the Atlantic thirteen times in flimsy ships in the interest of the gospel. He introduced open-air preaching to Britain when the churches were denied him. In Scotland they speak to this day of "the preaching braes of Cambuslang," where Whitefield's message drew thousands.

Despite his tremendous popularity, Whitefield was slandered in his homeland as perhaps no other figure of his era. Many attempts were made to murder him. His enemies blew horns to drown out his message. They sent an army recruiter drumming through his crowds. They hired merry-andrews to dress like the Devil and mimic him. The aristocracy, with the exception of the Countess of Huntingdon and a few of her friends, heaped scorn on him. The Christian clergy on both sides of the Atlantic resented him. The entire Harvard College faculty signed a petition against him. Scores of pamphlets were published by eminent churchmen denouncing him.

Through it all, Whitefield kept on preaching and showed surprising mildness in the face of his attackers. He established friendships with people outside the church—with Lord Chesterfield, David Garrick, Lord Bolingbroke, and Benjamin Franklin. He also preached to plantation slaves, Welsh miners, shipboard passengers, and the vast multitudes of London's poor.

The sermon "Soul Dejection" was one of eighteen taken down in shorthand by Joseph Gurney in London about the year 1766, and later published. They were criticized by many, including Whitefield himself, who faulted the transcription; but here we have the true Whitefield. I have expanded it with brief excerpts from two other Gurney renditions. The volume is titled Eighteen Sermons Preached by the Late Rev. George Whitefield, A.M., Taken Verbatim in Shorthand and Faithfully Transcribed by Joseph Gurney, Revised by A. Gifford, D.D., *and was published in 1809 by John Tiebout, New York.*

Soul Dejection
by George Whitefield

"Why art thou cast down, O my soul? and why art thou disquieted in me? hope thou in God: for I shall yet praise him for the help of his countenance" (Psalm 42:5).

I have often told you, in my plain way of speaking, that grace is very frequently grafted on a crab-stock; that the Lord Jesus picks out persons of the most peevish, churlish disposition, and imparts to them the largest measure of grace. For want of a better natural temper, a great deal of grace does not shine so bright in them, as a small degree in those who are constitutionally good-natured. Persons of this disposition are generally complaining, and are not only tormentors of themselves, but are great plagues to those about them. You will hear them always complaining something or other is the matter.

What a pity it is we cannot all agree on one thing, to leave off chiding others to chide our own selves, till we can find nothing in ourselves to chide for. This we shall find will be a good way to grow in the divine life, when by constant application to the Lamb of God, we get a mastery over those things which hitherto have had the mastery over us.

But are these the only people that complain? Are people of a melancholy disposition only subject to a disquietude of heart? I will venture to affirm that the greatest, the dearest children of God have got their complaining and their dreary hours. Those who have been favored with large measures of grace, even those who have been wrapped up as it were to the third heavens, basking on the mount in the sunshine of redeeming grace, and crying out in raptures of love, "It is good for us to be here,"[1] even these must go down to Gethsemane. If they would not be scorched with a strong burning fever from the sun of prosperity, they shall find clouds from time to time overshadowing them, not to burn, but to keep them low.

It is on this account that you see good men in different frames [of mind] at different times. Our Lord Himself was so. He rejoiced sometimes in Spirit, but at other times you find Him, especially near the last, crying out, "My soul is exceeding sorrowful even unto death: tarry you here and watch."[2] And I am going to tell you of one tonight who had the honor of being called "the man after God's own heart,"[3] and who, though an Old Testament saint, was greatly blessed with a New Testament spirit, and had the honor of composing Psalms. [These] in past ages of the church have been, and in future ones will be, a rich magazine and storehouse of spiritual experience, from which the children of God may draw spiritual armor for fighting the good fight of faith until God shall call them to life eternal. May this be your happy lot!

What frame was this good man in when he composed this Forty-second Psalm? The Psalm itself can best tell. It seems composed when he was either persecuted by Saul, or driven from his own court by his fondling, beloved son, Absalom. Then David appeared truly great. I honor him when I see him yonder, attending a few sheep. I admire the young stripling when I see him come out with his sling and stone, and aiming at the head of Goliath, the enemy of God; or when exalted and filling the seat of justice. But to me he never appears greater than when he is bowed down in low circumstances, beset on every side, struggling between sense and faith; and then, like the sun after an eclipse, breaking forth with greater luster to all the spectators. In this view we must consider this great, this good man, when he cries out, "Why art thou cast down, O my soul? and why art thou disquieted within me? hope thou in God!"[4]

Supposing you understand the words as a question: why art thou cast down, O my soul, though thou art in such circumstances? Pray now, what is the cause of your being so dejected? The word implies that he was sinking under the weight of his present burden, like a person stooping under a load that lies upon his shoulder. The consequence of this outside pressure was disquietude, uneasiness, and anxiety within. For say what you will to the contrary, there is such a connection between soul and body that when one is disordered, the other must sympathize with its ever-loving friend.

Or you may understand it as chiding himself. "How foolish

it is to be thus drooping and dejected. How improper for one favored of God with so many providences and special, particular privileges—for such a one as you are to stoop and be made subject to every temptation. Why do you give your enemies such room to find fault with your religion on account of your gloomy looks and the disquietude of your heart? It is a yoke that you will find to be lined with love, and God will keep it from galling your shoulders."

You see, David speaks not to others, but to himself; would to God we did thus learn that charity begins at home. Then he goes to God with his case. "O my God," says he, "my soul is cast down within me."[5] O that we could learn when in these moods to go more to God and less to man! We should find more relief, and religion would be less dishonored.

But see how faith triumphs in the midst of all. No sooner does unbelief pop up its head, but faith immediately knocks it down. A never-failing maxim is there proposed: "Hope thou in God." Trust in God, believe in God; for I am sure, and all of you that know Jesus Christ are persuaded of it too, that all our troubles arise from our unbelief. O unbelief, injurious bar to comfort, force of tormenting fear! On the contrary, faith bears everything.

"Put thy trust in God," as in the old translation; "Hope in God," as in the new. "I shall now praise Him." The Devil tells me my trouble is so great, I shall never lift up my head again; but unbelief and the Devil are liars. *I shall yet praise Him.* My God will carry me through all. I shall yet praise Him, even for casting me down. I shall praise Him even for that which is the cause of my disquietude. He will be "the health of my countenance."[6] Though my afflictions have now made my body low, have sucked up my spirits, and hurt my animal frame, He will be the help of my countenance. I shall by and by see Him again, and will be favored with those transforming views which my God has favored me with in times past.

He is the health of my countenance, and my God, though the Devil tempts me, and my evil neighbors say, "Where is now thy God? Do you think you are a child of God, and your Father suffers you to be cast down?"

I tell you, O Satan, that God whom I have been so vilely tempted to believe has forsaken me, will come over the mountains of my guilt, and will forgive my backslidings against Himself. My unbelief shall not make His promises of none effect. I shall praise Him even while I live. I shall praise Him before I die. I shall praise Him forever in Heaven, where He will be after death "the health of my countenance, and my God." Thus faith will get the better in a saint.

David was sometimes left to say, in effect, that all things are against me. Yet still in the Psalms, in this text, in Psalm 113, and in many of the rest, he triumphs in God. And he composed very few without praising at the end, though he complains at the beginning. God helps us thus to do!

But it is time to leave off speaking particularly of David, and turn to you to whom these words, I pray God, may prove salutary and useful. I have had a great struggle in my mind this afternoon what I should preach from. I have been praying and looking up to God, and could not preach for my life on any other text. This has often been the case before, and whenever it was, some poor soul has been comforted and raised up.

Among such a mixed multitude there are some, no doubt, come to this poor despised place cast down and disquieted within. I shall endeavor to enquire what you are cast down for, and then I shall propose a great cure for you, namely, trust in God; and I pray that what was David's comfort may be yours. Why should not we expect an answer when we pray that God, before you go home, may make you leave your burdens behind you, whether you will or no? And that God keep you from taking them up as you go home!

Probably there may be some of you that are real believers. Perhaps I ought to ask your pardon. Where am I preaching? In the Tabernacle![7] The most despised place in London! So scandalous a place that many of the children of God would rather go elsewhere. God help us to keep up our scandal!

But yet I believe there are many King's daughters here— many of you whom God enabled in this place first to say, "My Lord and my God!"[8] When you put your fingers, as it were, on the print of Christ's nails, and put your hands into His side, and were no longer faithless, but believing, you thought you should never be cast down any more. But now you have found yourselves mistaken; and I shall endeavor, in the prosecution of this text, to speak to all that are cast down, whether before or after conversion; and then to such that were never cast down at all. And if you were never cast down before, God cast you down now!

What are persons cast down for? What are some of you

disquieted within for? I have reason to believe, from the notes put up at both ends of the town, that there are many of you that have arrows of conviction stuck fast in your souls. I have taken in near two hundred at the other end of the town within a fortnight. If this be the case, that God is thus at work, let the Devil roar, and we will go on in the name of the Lord.

And what are you cast down for? Some poor soul will say, with a sense of sin, the guilt of it, the enmity of it, the very aggravated circumstances that attend it, appear and set themselves as in battle array before me. Once I thought I had no sin; at least, I thought that sin was not so exceeding sinful. But I now find it such a burden, I could almost say with Cain, "It is greater than I can bear."[9] And perhaps some of you are so cast down as Colonel Gardiner. That great man of God told me himself [that he] had said when under conviction, "I believe God cannot be just unless He damns my wicked soul."

Is this your case? Are you wicked, are you so cast down, so disquieted, that you cannot rest night or day? Shall I send you away without any comfort? Shall I send you away as the legal [i.e., legalistic] preachers do? As a minister did some time ago, when a man told him how wicked he had been. "O," says he, "if you are so wicked you are damned to be sure; I shall not trouble myself with you."

When a poor Negro was taken up for thieving, another went to him and said, "You are so bad I must turn my back to you." That is the law; but the gospel is, "Turn your face to God." Think not that God is dealing with you as an absolute God, a God out of Christ. "I would have nothing to do," says Luther, "with an absolute God; as such He is a consuming fire." Trust God in Christ! Throw yourself upon Him. Throw yourself on the Son of God. Cry with your brother, and now that you are in that temper, you will not be ashamed to call the thief your brother. Say with him, "Lord, remember me when you are in your Kingdom."[10]

You shall yet praise Him. The Spirit of God is engaged to train up the souls of His people. All that are given to Jesus Christ shall come. He will not lose one of them. This is food for the children of God. A bad mind will turn everything to poison, so that if it were not for this, that God had promised to keep them, my soul within these thirty years would have sunk a thousand times over. Come, then, O suffering saints; to you the word of this salvation is sent. I don't know who of you are followers of the Lamb, [but] may the Spirit of the living God point them out; may every one be enabled to say, "I am the man!"

You shall yet have the forgiveness of your sins. Your pardon shall not only be sealed in Heaven, but you shall have it in your heart. These are only the pangs of the new birth, the first strugglings of the soul immersing into the divine life. He shall yet be the "health of your countenance." These poor cheeks, though bedewed with tears, shall by and by have a fine blush, when a pardoning God comes with His love. It shall even make a change in your countenance, for as a heavy heart makes a man's countenance sad, so a cheerful heart makes the countenance pleasant. You shall know Him to be your God. You shall say, "My Lord and my God."

Lord Jesus grant this may be the happy moment. Were Jesus here, were the Redeemer now in this metropolis, I am sure He would go about the streets. He would be a field-preacher. He would go out into the highways and hedges. He would invite, He would run after them. O, may God bless this foolishness of preaching to some of God's poor, and perhaps doubting, beloved ones. Come, you poor souls. I often think that field-preaching is particularly comfortable to the poor. Whenever field-preaching is stopped, farewell to the power of religion. When poor people have been working hard all day, how sweet must it be for them to come to a place of worship, and get a lift for tomorrow. May the Lord God bless His barley bread! Lord Jesus, take the veil from our hearts, and let us see tonight Your loving heart as the Son of God!

"Trust in God!" you will say. "It is very easy for you to say so, but I cannot trust in God." Can't you? Who told you that? That is the work of God. You are not far from the Kingdom of God. Who convinced you of your inability to believe? Do you think the Devil did? No, it was the Spirit of God procured by the blood of the Lamb, that was come to convince the world of sin. If you cannot trust as you would, say, "Lord, I believe, help my unbelief." Stretch out your poor hand. Blessed be God that there is yet a day of grace. Oh! that this might prove the accepted time. Oh! that this might prove the day of salvation. Oh! angel of the everlasting covenant, come down. Thou blessed, dear Comforter, have mercy, mercy, mercy upon the unconverted, upon our unconverted friends, upon the unconverted part of this auditory. Speak, and it shall be done. Command, O Lord, and it shall come to pass. Who knows but God may hear our prayer? Who knows but God may hear this cry? "I have seen, I have seen the afflictions of My people. The cry of the children of Israel is come up to me, and I am come down to deliver them." God grant this may be His word to you under all your trouble. God grant he may be your Comforter.

I am thinking of Sunday last, when I was giving the sacrament [the Lord's Supper]. I observed there was one blind communicant who could not see, but he thrust out his hand. I observed several lame persons, but there were enough [helping] to give it to them. I saw also a poor barrow-woman, and I took particular care to give the cup to her; so I put it up to the mouth of the poor blind man. If that is the case, what love must there be in God to the poor soul!

But I hear some poor soul say, "That is not my case. I am not cast down for that, but I am cast down because after that I knew God to be my God; after I knew Jesus to be my King, and after I had mounted upon my high places, the Devil and my unbelieving heart threw me down again. Would you not have me cast down? Would you not have me disquieted?

A person of Antinomian [i.e., above-the-law] spirit would say, "Don't tell me of your frames [i.e., state of mind]. I have learned to live by faith. I don't care whether Christ manifests Himself to me or no; I have got the Word and the promise. I am content with a promise now." These poor creatures go on without any frame, because they will not live in it.

From such Antinomianism, good God, deliver me. How? How? How? Not cast down at an absent God? Not disquieted when God withdraws? Where are you gone? You are gone from your Father's house. If nothing else will do, may your Father whip you home again! But tender hearts, when they reflect how it was once, are cast down.

David says, "My tears have been my meat day and night, for I had gone with a multitude to the house of God."[11] Here he looks back upon his former enjoyments, his spiritual prosperity, as Job looked back upon his temporal; and David says, "Why are you cast down, O my soul?" It is because I don't meet God in his ordinances as I used to do. Poor, deserted, panting soul! Poor disquieted soul! He must be the help of your countenance; He will yet be your God. Who was it sought Jesus sorrowing? What would you have thought of the Virgin Mary if she had said, "I don't care whether I see my son or not"? She sought Him and found Him in the temple. God grant [that] every poor deserted soul may find Him tonight: I mean in the temple of his heart. In the case of Mary [Magdalene], she says, "They have taken away my Lord, and I know not where they have laid Him."[12] If they had not taken away her Lord, Mary would have been rich. So you may say that your corruptions, your backslidings and ingratitude have taken away your Lord. The Lord grant that you may find Him tonight. He that said, "Mary!" can call you tonight, and can make you say, "My dear Lord, I come tonight." He can call you by your name.

But, say you, "I am cast down because I am wearied with temptation. Not only my God is departed from me, but an evil spirit is come upon me to torment me. I am haunted with this and that evil suggestion, [so] that I am a terror to myself." Come, come, hear what David says in the beginning of the Psalm: "As the hart panteth after the water-brooks, so panteth my soul after Thee, O God."[13] What say you to that? Well, is it the case that unbelief dogs you, go where you will? Still trust in God! "Thou shalt yet praise Him for the help of His countenance. He will command His lovingkindness in the day, and His song shall be with you in the night."[14]

Though it be night, there is some moon, blessed be God, or some stars; and if there is a fog [so] that you cannot see, God can quiet His people in the dark. He will make the enemy flee. Fear him not; God will comfort you if you trust in Him.

But, say you, "I am cast down and disquieted within me. Why? Because I have one affliction after another. No sooner is one trial gone, but another succeeds. Now I think I shall have a little rest; the tormenter will not come nigh me today." But no sooner has the Christian so said, but another storm comes, and the clouds return after the rain.

I have a number of bills[15] here tonight. One says, "If I am beloved of the Lord, why am I so afflicted?" Another says, "If I am beloved of the Lord, why am I so poor?" Says another, "If I am beloved of the Lord, why am I left to starve? Can I think God loves, when I see thousands and thousands squandered away every day, and yet my poor babes groaning, my poor children quite emaciated, for want only of a little bread that I see in the baker's shop as I go along?" "If I am beloved of the Lord, how is it that my poor children are ready to cry for bread, and I have none to give them? That others are adorned with diamonds, but I have not so much as a rag to put on my little one's back?" "If I am beloved of the Lord, how is it that my friends are against me; my children, instead of being a blessing, are a curse, and break my heart?"

"If I am beloved of the Lord, how is it that I have so many domestic trials that cause me to cry out, 'Woe is me that I sojourn in Mesech, that I dwell in the tents of Kedar!' "[16] "If I am beloved of the Lord, how is it that I am harassed with blasphemous thoughts thus—the trials I meet within bringing down the outward man?" "If I am beloved of the Lord, how is it that instead of living in plenty, I now want bread to eat, and should be glad to have it from those 'I would have disdained to set with the dogs of my flock'?"[17]

Our dear Jesus was never more beloved of His Father than when He cried out, "My God! My God! Why hast thou forsaken Me?"[18] Never more beloved of His Father than when He was sweating great drops of blood, when He cried, "Father, if it be possible, let this cup pass from Me."[19] I remember a dear minister of Christ, now in Suffolk, telling me that when he was in Scotland, going to receive the sacrament, he was so dry and dark and benumbed and tempted that he thought he would go away. As he was going, this word came to his mind: When was Jesus Christ most acceptable to His Father? When did He give the greatest trial of His love? When He cried out, "My God! My God! Why hast thou forsaken Me?" "Why, then," says he, "upon this I will venture; if I perish, I perish at Christ's feet." And he came away filled with comfort from his blessed God and Father in Christ.

Well, then, what is to be done to those who are beloved of the Lord? Here's for you: "They shall dwell in safety." Why? "He shall dwell between His shoulders."[20] Note the expression: the prophet says they shall dwell in love. "Will God indeed dwell on earth?" asks Solomon.[21] Yes! God, says he, dwells in my earthly heart, made heavenly by the grace of God. Amazing! I [used to think] God dwelt in Heaven; but as a poor woman said who was once in darkness fourteen years before she was brought out of it, "God has two homes, one in Heaven, the other in the lowest heart."

Did ever any of you hear such an expression from the mouth of God: "I will be thy God; I am thy shield and thy exceeding great reward"?[22] He does not say an angel shall go. If God had said in His Word that I was to be kept only by angels, I am sure my wicked heart would despair, because it would deceive all the angels in Heaven. But God says, "I will be thy keeper,"[23] so that they that would hurt His people must go through God Himself. "He shall dwell on high. Bread shall be given him; his waters shall be sure."[24] We are "kept by the power of God through faith unto salvation."[25]

But David was cast down and disquieted; that was his case. What does he say? "All thy waves and thy billows are gone over me."[26] I believe he found after that, there were more waves to come than he had yet felt. Says a poor distressed soul, "I have been so long in Christ, and have got these cursed corruptions yet within. I thought I had no corruptions left thirty-three years ago, and that the Canaanites were all rooted out of the land; that Pharaoh and his host were all drowned in the Red Sea; but I find the old man is strong in me. I look upon myself to be less than the least of all saints, God knows. And you that walk near God [the soul continues] and have made greater advances in the divine life, if you are honest [you] must say, 'O, this body of sin and death, if I shut this old man out of the fore-door he comes in at the back door.' "

Come, come, come, soul, trust in God. He will give power to the faint, He will give strength, and in due time deliver you. Go to God, tell Him of them; beg your Redeemer to take His whip into His hand, either of small or large cords, and use it, rather than [that] your corruption should get head again.

Time would fail to mention all that are cast down on these accounts, but I must mention one more. Perhaps some of you may be cast down with the fear not of death only, but of judgment. I believe there are thousands of people [who] die a thousand times for fear of dying once. Dr. Mather[27] and Mr. Pemberton[28] of New England were always afraid of dying, but when they came to die, one or both of them said to some that were intimate with them, "Is this all? I can bear this very well."[29] I have generally found that a poor soul that cannot act that faith on God it once did (as in old age when the body grows infirm), yet it goes off rejoicing in God, as a good soul said that was buried at the Chapel the other day, "I am going over Jordan."

Leave this to God. He will take care of your dying hour. If any of you here are poor, and I was to promise to give you a coffin and a shroud, you would be easy. Now, can you trust the word of a man, and not that of God? Well, the Lord help you to trust in Him. "Having loved His own, He loved them unto the end."[30]

He is a faithful, unchangeable friend that sticketh closer than a brother.

Who would not be a Christian, who would but be a believer, my brethren? See the preciousness of a believer's faith! The quacks will say, "Here, buy this packet which is good for all diseases"—and it is really worth nothing. But this will never fail the soul.

Now I wish I could make you all angry. (I am a sad mischief-maker.) But I will assure you, I don't want to make you angry with one another. Some people that profess to have grace in their hearts seem resolved to set all God's people at variance. They are like Samson's foxes with firebrands in their tails, setting fire to all about them.[31] Are any of you come from the Foundery[32] or any other place tonight? I do not care where you come from, I pray you may all quarrel tonight. I want you to fall out with your own hearts. If we were employed as we ought to be, we should have less time to talk about vain things that are the subjects of conversation. God grant your crosses may be left at the cross of the Lamb of God this night.

And if there be any of you here, as no doubt there are many, that are crying, "What nonsense he is preaching tonight!" I should not wonder if they were to mimic me when they go home. If they should say, "I thank God, I was never cast down"— the very answer you have given makes me cast down for you. Why so? Why, as the Lord liveth (I speak out of compassion) there is but one step between you and death.

Don't you know the [court] sessions began at the Old Bailey today? If there were any capitally convicted, what would you think to see them playing at cards, or go on rattling and drinking and swearing? Would not you yourself cry, and if it were a child of your own, would it not break your heart? Yet *you* are that wretch. I must weep for you, my brother-sister. We had both one father and mother, Adam and Eve; this was our sad original.

Lord, search us; Lord, try us; Lord God Almighty, help us to examine ourselves, that we may know whether we are beloved of the Lord or not. "Oh," says one, "I have been watching and very attentive tonight. Thank God, I have no pride at all." Like the bishop of Cambray, as mentioned by Dr. Watts, who said he had received many sins from his father Adam, but thank God, he had no pride. Alas! Alas! We are all as proud as the Devil. Pray, what do you think of passion, that burns not only themselves, but all around them? What do you think of enmity? What do you think of jealousy? There are some people that pride themselves [claiming] they have not got so much of the beast about them. They never got drunk, [they] scorn to commit murder, and at the same time are as full of enmity, of envy, malice, and pride as the devil. The Lord God help such to see their condition!

I remember once I was preaching in Scotland, and saw ten thousand affected in a moment, some with joy, others crying, "I cannot believe," others [saying], "God has given me faith," some fainting in their friends' arms. [I remember] seeing two stout creatures upon a tombstone, hardened indeed. I cried out, "You rebels, come down!" and down they fell directly, and cried before they went away, "What shall we do to be saved?"

Have any of you got apprentices whom you have brought from time to time to the Tabernacle, but now will not let them come because you think they grow worse and worse, and you will be tempted to leave off praying for them? Don't do that. Who knows but this may be the happy time! Children of godly parents, apprentices of godly people, servants of people who fear the Lord, that hear gospel preachers, that are on the watch for every infirmity, that go to their fellow-servants and say, "These saints love good eating and drinking, they are only gospel-gossips"—is this the case with any of you? If it is, you are in a deplorable condition, under the gospel and not convinced thereby. O, may God bring down you rebels tonight. May this be the happy hour [when] you may be cast down and disquieted within you.

There are very few Christians [who] can live together. Very few relations can live together under one roof. We can take that from other people that we can't bear from our own flesh and blood; and if God did not bear with us more than we bear with one another, we should all have been destroyed every day. Does the Devil make you say that you will give [it] all up? "I will go to the Tabernacle no more; I will lay on my couch and take my ease." Oh! If this is the case of any tonight, thus tempted by Satan, may God rescue their souls!

Oh, poor, dear soul, whatever your trials are, our suffering times will be our best times. I know we had more comfort in Moorfields, on Kennington Common, and especially when the rotten eggs, the cats and dogs were thrown upon me, and my gown was filled with clods of dirt [so] that I could scarce move it. I have had more comfort in this . . . than when I have been in ease.

I remember when I was preaching at Exeter, a stone came and made my forehead bleed. I found at that very time the Word came with double power to a laborer that was gazing at me, who was wounded at the same time by another stone. I felt for the lad more than for myself. I went to a friend [for help], and the lad came to me. "Sir," says he, "the man gave me a wound, but Jesus healed me. I never had my bonds broke till I had my head broke!"

I appeal to you whether you were not better when it was colder than now, because your nerves were braced up. You have a day like a dog-day now, [and] you are weak and are obliged to fan yourselves. Thus it is prosperity lulls the soul, and I fear Christians are spoiled by it.

What can I say more? I would speak till I burst. I would speak till I could say no more. O poor souls, that have never yet been cast down, I will tell you that if you die without being cast down, however you may die and have no pangs in your death (and your carnal relations may thank God that you died like lambs), but no sooner will your souls be out of your bodies, but God will cast you down to Hell. You will be lifting up your eyes in yonder place of torment. You will be disquieted, and there will be nobody there to say, "Hope thou in God, for I shall yet praise Him."³³

O my God, when I think of this, I could go to the very gates of Hell to preach. I thought the other day, O if I had my health, I would stand on the top of every hackney coach and preach Christ to those poor creatures. Unconverted old people, unconverted young people, will you have no compassion on your own souls? If you will damn yourselves, remember I am free from the blood of you all.

O if it be Your will, Lord most holy, O God most mighty, take the hearts of these sinners into Your hand. Methinks I see the heavens opened, the Judge sitting on his throne, the sea boiling like a pot, and the Lord Jesus coming to judge the world. Well, if you are damned, it shall not be for want of calling after. O come, come, God help you to come, whilst Jesus is standing ready to receive you. O fly to the Savior this night for refuge! Remember, if you die in an unconverted state you must be damned forever.

O that I could persuade but one poor soul to fly to Jesus Christ, make Him your refuge; and then however you may be cast down, *hope in God, and you shall yet praise Him.* God help those who have believed to hope more and more in his salvation, till faith be turned into vision, and hope into fruition. Even so, Lord Jesus. Amen and Amen.

NOTES

1. Mark 9:5.
2. Mark 14:34.
3. 1 Samuel 13:14.
4. Psalm 42:5.
5. Psalm 42:6.
6. Psalm 42:11.
7. The first "tabernacle" was a huge wooden shed erected by Whitefield's followers in the Moorfields district of London in 1741, and was replaced by a brick building twelve years later. Prior to 1741 he preached outdoors.
8. John 20:28.
9. Genesis 4:13.
10. Luke 23:42.
11. Psalm 42:3, 4.
12. John 20:13.
13. Psalm 42:1.
14. Psalm 42:5, 8.
15. It would seem, from this reference and an earlier one to "notes put up at both ends of the town," that Whitefield encouraged his hearers to respond in writing to his messages at the Moorfields Tabernacle.
16. Psalm 120:5.
17. Job 30:1.
18. Mark 15:34.
19. Matthew 26:39.
20. Deuteronomy 33:12.
21. 1 Kings 8:27.
22. Genesis 15:1.
23. Cf. Psalm 121:5; Isaiah 41:10.
24. Isaiah 33:16.
25. 1 Peter 1:5.
26. Psalm 42:7.
27. Cotton Mather (1663-1728), famed colonial Puritan minister and writer.
28. Rev. Ebenezer Pemberton (1704-1777) for twenty years pastor of Old South Church, Boston, and a close friend of Whitefield.
29. It must have been Mather, as Pemberton did not die until seven years after Whitefield.
30. John 13:1.
31. Cf. Judges 15:3-5.
32. The Foundery was John Wesley's chapel, located not far from Whitefield's tabernacle.
33. Psalm 43:5.

John Woolman

The true measure of Christian faith, according to the New Testament, is neither fame nor miracle nor erudition, but the quality of character it produces in its adherents. That being the case, it could be said that John Woolman (1720-1772) is standing tall. The Quaker poet John Greenleaf Whittier, in his 1871 introduction to Woolman's Journal, wrote, "I have been awed and solemnized by the presence of a serene and beautiful spirit redeemed of the Lord from all selfishness, and I have been made thankful for the ability to recognize and the disposition to love him."

John Woolman was not considered an important person in his century. He was a modest, devout, largely self-taught shopkeeper and tailor; but his concern for the poor whites, the Indians, and especially the Negro slaves in colonial America made him an outspoken champion of the underprivileged. Regardless of what his century thought of him, Woolman is honored today as one of the greatest Americans for his early advocacy of the abolition of slavery and the slave trade.

Two years after Woolman died of smallpox in York, England, the Philadelphia Yearly Meeting of Friends, with which he was associated, voted to abolish slave-owning among Quakers. It was a tribute to the continuing influence of the man's testimony. It took nearly another century and a bloody civil war before the rest of America caught up with him.

Woolman did not spare other social abuses. He criticized the sale of rum to Indians, the seizing of Indian lands by the whites, and the conscription of soldiers and taxes for military supplies. Finery of all kinds he avoided; he almost canceled his transatlantic crossing because he didn't like the scrollwork on the ship's housing.

But the chief concern of his heart, and the burden Christ laid upon it, was the condition of the enslaved black people around him. By quiet persuasion he talked many Quaker owners into freeing their slaves when they came asking him to make out their wills. Woolman's travel in many colonies north and south was principally in the interest of setting slaves free. It was said that he hated the institution so much he *could not taste food provided by the labor of slaves. Even when he was unsuccessful in remonstrating with slave owners, his gentle rebuke was not forgotten.*

John Woolman was born in Northampton township, Burlington County, New Jersey, as he tells in his Journal. *He grew up on a plantation, and embellished his early education with wide reading. Some frolicsomeness in his youth soon gave over to a serious frame of mind, and he became active in the Quaker movement. He loved the silent meeting, though his convictions often prompted him to speak. His humanitarian spirit was of a different stripe from that of George Fox, the founder of the Quakers. Fox was an evangelist who enthusiastically sought confrontations. Woolman was often labeled a mystic.*

There was no mysticism, however, in his indignation over the way Negroes were brutally mistreated on the plantations he visited. Says Whittier, "Sin was not to him an isolated fact, the responsibility of which began and ended with the individual transgressor. He saw it as a part of a vast network and entanglement, and traced the lines of influence converging upon it in the underworld of causation. In his lifelong testimony against wrong he never lost sight of the oneness of humanity, its common responsibility, its fellowship of suffering. The first inquiry which [it] awakened was addressed to his own conscience. How far am I responsible for this?"

While he was unknown outside the Society of Friends during his lifetime, after his death Woolman's writings were widely circulated. A century later they became ammunition in the hands of Horace Greeley and the abolitionists, and helped create the climate of the future.

These excerpts are taken from The Journal, with Other Writings of John Woolman, *Everyman edition, published in London by J. M. Dent, no date.*

THREE

From the Journal of John Woolman

I was born in Northampton, in Burlington County, West Jersey, in the year 1720; and before I was seven years old I began to be acquainted with the operations of divine love. Through the care of my parents I was taught to read nearly as soon as I was capable of it. As I went from school one seventh day [Saturday] I remember, while my companions went to play by the way, I went forward out of sight, and sitting down I read the twenty-second chapter of Revelation: "He shewed me a pure river of water of life, clear as crystal, proceeding out of the throne of God and of the Lamb," etc. And in reading it, my mind was drawn to seek after that pure habitation which, I then believed, God had prepared for His servants. The place where I sat, and the sweetness that attended my mind, remain fresh in my memory.

My parents, having a large family of children, used frequently, on First Days [Sundays] after Meeting, to put us to read in the Holy Scriptures or some religious books, one after another, the rest sitting by without much conversation; which, I have since thought, was a good practice. About the twelfth year of my age, my father being abroad, my mother reproved me for some misconduct, to which I made an undutiful reply; and the next First Day, as I was with my father returning from Meeting, he told me he understood I had behaved amiss to my mother, and advised me to be more careful in future. I knew myself blameable, and in shame and confusion remained silent. Being thus awakened to a sense of my wickedness, I felt remorse in my mind, and getting home, I retired, and prayed to the Lord to forgive me; and do not remember that I ever after that spoke unhandsomely to either of my parents, however foolish in some other things.

Having attained the age of sixteen years, I began to love wanton company, and though I was preserved from profane language or scandalous conduct, still I received a plant in me which produced much wild grapes. Yet my merciful Father forsook me not utterly, but at times, through His Grace, I was brought seriously to consider my ways, and the sight of my backslidings affected me with sorrow. But for want of rightly attending to the reproofs of instruction, vanity was added to vanity, and repentance to repentance. Upon the whole, my mind was more and more alienated from the truth, and I hastened toward destruction. While I meditate on the gulf toward which I traveled, and reflect on my youthful disobedience, for these things I weep; mine eyes run down with water.

Thus time passed on: my heart was replenished with mirth and wantonness, and pleasing scenes of vanity were presented to my imagination, till I attained the age of eighteen years; near which time I felt the judgments of God in my soul, like a consuming fire. Looking over my past life, the prospect was moving. I was often sad, and longed to be delivered from those vanities. Then again, my heart was strongly inclined to them, and there was in me a sore conflict. At times I turned to folly, and then again, sorrow and confusion took hold of me. In a while I resolved totally to leave off some of my vanities; but there was a secret reserve in my heart of the more refined part of them, and I was not low enough to find true peace.

Thus for some months I had great troubles, there remaining in me an unsubjected will, which rendered my labors fruitless, till at length, through the merciful continuance of heavenly visitations, I was made to bow down in spirit before the Lord. I remember one evening I had spent some time in reading a pious author; and walking out alone, I humbly prayed to the Lord for His help, that I might be delivered from all those vanities which so ensnared me. Thus being brought low, He helped me; and as I learned to bear the Cross, I felt refreshment to come from His presence. But, not keeping in that strength which gave victory, I lost ground again. I sought deserts and lonely places and there, with tears, did confess my sins to God, and humbly craved help of Him. And I may say with reverence, He was near to me in my troubles, and in those times of humiliation opened my ear to discipline.

I was now led to look seriously at the means by which I was drawn from the pure Truth, and learned this, that, if I would live in the Life which the faithful servants of God lived in, I must not go into company as heretofore in my own will; but all the cravings of sense must be governed by a divine principle. In times of sorrow and abasement these instructions were sealed upon me, and I felt the power of Christ prevail over selfish desires, so that I was preserved in a good degree of steadiness.

I kept steadily to Meetings; spent First Day afternoons chiefly in reading the Scriptures and other good books; and was early convinced in mind that true religion consisted in an inward life, wherein the heart doth love and reverence God the Creator, and learns to exercise true justice and goodness, not only toward all men, but also toward the brute creatures. I found no narrowness respecting sects and opinions; but believed that sincere upright-hearted people in every society, who truly love God, were accepted of Him.

While I silently ponder on that change wrought in me, I find no language equal to it, nor any means to convey to another a clear idea of it. I looked on the works of God in this visible creation, and an awfulness covered me. My heart was tender and often contrite, and universal love to my fellow-creatures increased in me. This will be understood by such as have trodden the same path. Some glances of real beauty may be seen in their faces who dwell in true meekness. There is a harmony in the sound of that voice to which divine love gives utterance, and some appearance of right order in their temper and conduct, whose passions are regulated. Yet all these do not fully shew forth that inward life to such as have not felt it. But this white stone and new name[1] is known rightly to such only as have it.

All this time I lived with my parents and wrought on the plantation, and having had schooling pretty well for a planter, I used to improve it in winter evenings and other leisure times. Being now in the twenty-first year of my age, a man in much business at shopkeeping and baking asked me if I would hire with him to tend shop and keep books. I acquainted my father with the proposal, and after some deliberation it was agreed for me to go. After a while my former acquaintances gave over expecting me as one of their company, and I began to be known to some whose conversation was helpful to me.

About the twenty-third year of my age I had many fresh and heavenly openings [personal revelations] in respect to the care and providence of the Almighty over His creatures in general, and over man as the most noble amongst those which are visible. My employer having a Negro woman, sold her, and desired me to write a bill of sale, the man being waiting who bought her. The thing was sudden; and though the thoughts of writing an instrument of slavery for one of my fellow-creatures felt uneasy, yet I remembered I was hired by the year. It was my master who directed me to do it, and it was an elderly man, a member of our [Quaker] Society, who bought her. So through weakness I gave way and wrote; but at the executing of it I was so afflicted in my mind that I said, before my master and the Friend, that I believed slave-keeping to be a practice inconsistent with the Christian religion.

This in some degree abated my uneasiness. Yet as often as I have reflected seriously upon it, I thought I should have been clearer, if I had desired to have been excused from it as a thing against my conscience; for such it was. And some time after this a young man of our Society spoke to me to write a conveyance of a slave to him, he having lately taken a Negro into his house. I told him I was not easy to write it; for though many of our Meeting and in other places kept slaves, I still believed the practice was not right, and desired to be excused from it. I spoke to him in goodwill, and he told me that keeping slaves was not altogether agreeable to his mind, but that the slave being a gift to his wife, he had accepted of her.

My employer, though now a retailer of goods, was by trade a tailor, and kept a servant-man at that business. I began to think about learning the trade, expecting that I might by this trade and a little retailing of goods get a living in a plain way, without the load of great business. I mentioned it to my employer, and we soon agreed on terms, and when I had leisure from the affairs of merchandise, I worked with his man. I believed the hand of Providence pointed out this business for me, and was taught to be content with it, though I felt at times a disposition that would have sought for something greater. But through the revelation of Jesus Christ I had seen the happiness of humility, and there was an earnest desire to me to enter into it.

After some time my employer's wife died. Soon after this he left shop-keeping and we parted. I then wrought at my trade as a tailor, carefully attended Meetings for worship and discipline, and found an enlargement of gospel-love in my mind, and therein a concern to visit Friends in some of the back-settlements of Pennsylvania and Virginia. Being thoughtful about a companion, I expressed it to my beloved Friend, Isaac Andrews, who then told me that he had drawings to the same places; also to go through Maryland and Carolina. We obtained certificates from the Friends to travel as companions.

In our journeying to and fro we found some honest-hearted Friends who appeared to be concerned for the cause of Truth amongst a backsliding people. We reached home the sixteenth day of the sixth month, in the year 1746; and I may say that through the assistance of the Holy Spirit, my companion and I traveled in harmony and parted in the nearness of true brotherly love.

Two things were remarkable to me in this journey. First, in regard to my entertainment, when I ate, drank, and lodged at free-cost with people who lived in ease on the hard labor of their slaves, I felt uneasy. Where the masters bore a good share of the burden, and lived frugally, so that their servants were well provided for, and their labor moderate, I felt more easy; but where they lived in a costly way, and laid heavy burdens on their slaves, my exercise was often great, and I frequently had conversation with them in private concerning it.

Secondly, this trade of importing slaves from their native country being much encouraged amongst them, and the white people and their children so generally living without much labor, was frequently the subject of my serious thoughts. I saw in these southern provinces so many vices and corruptions, increased by this trade and this way of life, that it appeared to me as a gloom over the land; and though now many willingly run into it, yet in future the consequence will be grievous to posterity. I express it as it has appeared to me, not at once nor twice, but as a matter fixed on my mind.

* * *

About this time, believing it good for me to settle, and thinking seriously about a companion, my heart was turned to the Lord with desires that He would give me wisdom to proceed therein agreeable to His will; and He was pleased to give me a well-inclined damsel, Sarah Ellis, to whom I was married the eighteenth day of the eighth month, in the year 1749.

In the year 1753, a person at some distance was lying sick and his brother came to me to write his will. I knew he had slaves, and asking his brother, was told he intended to leave them as slaves to his children. As writing is a profitable employ, and as offending sober people was disagreeable to my inclination, I was straitened in my mind. But as I looked to the Lord, He inclined my heart to His testimony, and I told the man that I believed the practice of continuing slavery to this people was not right. I told him I had a scruple in my mind against doing writings of that kind; that though many in our Society kept them as slaves, still I was not easy to be concerned in it, and desired to be excused from going to write the will.

* * *

About this time an ancient man, of good esteem in the neighborhood, came to my house to get his will written. He had young Negroes, and I asked him privately how he purposed to dispose of them. He told me. I then said, I cannot write thy will without breaking my own peace, and respectfully gave him my reasons for it. And so he got it written by some other person. A few years after, there being great alterations in his family, he came again to get me to write his will. His Negroes were still young. We had much friendly talk on the subject, and then deferred it. A few days after, he came again, and directed their freedom; and then I wrote his will.

Having found drawings in my mind to visit Friends on Long Island, after obtaining a certificate from our monthly Meeting, I set off in the year 1756. My mind was deeply engaged in this visit, both in public and private; and at several places, observing that they had slaves, I found myself under a necessity in a friendly way to labor with them on that subject; expressing, as the way opened, the inconsistency of that practice with the purity of the Christian religion, and the ill effects of it manifested amongst us.

The latter-end of the week, their Yearly Meeting began. The exercise of my mind at this meeting was chiefly on account of those who were considered as the foremost rank in the Society. In a meeting of ministers and elders, way opened that I expressed in some measure what lay upon me. At a time when Friends were met for transacting the affairs of the Church, having sat a while silent, I felt a weight on my mind, and stood up; and through the gracious regard of our Heavenly Father, strength was given fully to clear myself of a burden which, for some days, had been increasing upon me.

Through the humbling dispensations of divine Providence, men are sometimes fitted for His service. The messages of the prophet Jeremiah were so disagreeable to the people and so reverse to the spirit they lived in, that he became the object of their reproach. In the weakness of nature, he thought of desisting from his prophetic office; but, saith he, "His Word was in my heart as a burning fire shut up in my bones; and I was weary with forbearing, and could not stay."[2] I saw at this time that if I was honest in declaring that which truth opened in me, I could not please all men; and labored to be content in the way of my duty, however disagreeable to my own inclination.

Until this year I continued to retail goods, besides following my trade as a tailor. About this time I grew uneasy on account of my business growing too cumbersome. Having got a considerable shop of goods, my trade increased every year, and the road to large business appeared open; but I felt a stop in my mind. Through the mercies of the Almighty I had in a good degree learned to be content with a plain way of living. I had but a small family,[3] and on serious consideration I believed truth did not require me to engage in much cumbering affairs.

There was now a strife in my mind between the two; and in this exercise my prayers were put up to the Lord, who graciously heard me, and gave me a heart resigned to His holy will. Then I lessened my outward business, and as I had opportunity, told my customers of my intention, that they might consider what shop to turn to. In a little while I wholly laid down merchandise, following my trade as a tailor, myself only, having no apprentice. In merchandise it is the custom where I lived to sell chiefly on credit, and poor people often get in debt. Creditors then often sue for it at law. Having often observed occurrences of this kind, I found it good for me to advise poor people to take such goods as were most useful and not costly.

On the eleventh day of the fifth month in the year 1757, we crossed the rivers Potomac and Rappahannock and lodged at Port Royal. On the way, we happening in company with a colonel of the militia who appeared to be a thoughtful man, I took occasion to remark on the difference in general betwixt a people used to labor moderately for their living, training up their children in frugality and business, and those who live on the labor of slaves. The former, in my view, I felt was the most happy life; with which he concurred. He mentioned the trouble arising from the untoward, slothful disposition of the Negroes, adding that one of our laborers would do as much in a day as two of their slaves.

I replied that free men, whose minds were properly on their business, found a satisfaction in improving, cultivating, and providing for their families; but Negroes, laboring to support others who claim them as their property, and expecting nothing but slavery during life, had not the like inducement to be industrious. After some further conversation, I said that men having power too often misapplied it; that though we made slaves of the Negroes, and the Turks made slaves of the Christians, I believed that liberty was the natural right of all men equally. Which he did not deny, but said the lives of the Negroes were so wretched in their own country that many of them lived better here than there. I only said there are great odds in regard to us, on what principle we act; and so the conversation on that subject ended.

And I may here add that another person, some time afterward, mentioned the wretchedness of the Negroes, occasioned by their intestine wars, as an argument in favor of our fetching them away for slaves. To which I replied, if compassion on the Africans, in regard to their domestic troubles, were the real motive of our purchasing them, that spirit of tenderness being attended to, would incite us to use them kindly, so that as strangers brought out of affliction, their lives might be happy among us. As they are human creatures whose souls are as precious as ours, and who may receive the same help and comfort from the Holy Scriptures as we do, we could not omit suitable endeavors to instruct them therein.

But while we manifest by our conduct that our views in purchasing them are to advance ourselves; and while our buying captives taken in war animates those parties to push on that war and increase desolation amongst them, to say they live unhappy in Africa is far from being an argument in our favor. And I further said that the slaves look like a burdensome stone to such who burden themselves with them; and that if the white people retain a resolution to prefer their outward prospects of gain to all other considerations, and do not act conscientiously toward them as fellow creatures, I believe the burden will grow heavier and heavier, till times change in a way disagreeable to us.

As I was riding along in the morning in company with several Friends to Camp Creek in Virginia, my mind was deeply affected in a sense I had of the want of divine aid to support me in the various difficulties which attended me. In an uncommon distress of mind, I cried in secret to the Most High, O Lord, be merciful, I beseech Thee, to Thy poor afflicted creature. After some time I felt inward relief; and soon after, a Friend in our company began to talk in support of the slave trade, and said the Negroes were understood to be the offspring of Cain, their blackness being the mark God set upon him after he murdered Abel his brother. He said it was the design of Providence they should be slaves, as a condition proper to the race of so wicked a man as Cain was. Then another spake in support of what had been said.

To all which, I replied in substance as follows: that Noah and his family were all who survived the flood, according to Scripture; and as Noah was of Seth's race, the family of Cain was wholly destroyed. One of them said that after the flood Ham went to the Land of Nod and took a wife; that Nod was a land far distant, inhabited by Cain's race, and that the flood did not reach it; and as Ham was sentenced to be a servant of servants to his brethren, these two families, being thus joined, were undoubtedly fit only for slaves.

I replied, the flood was a judgment upon the world for its abominations, and it was granted that Cain's stock was the most wicked and was unreasonable therefore to suppose they were spared. As to Ham's going to the Land of Nod for a wife, no time being fixed, Nod might be inhabited by some of Noah's family before Ham married a second time. Moreover the text saith "that all flesh died that moved upon the earth" (Genesis 7:21). I further reminded them how the prophets repeatedly declare "that the son shall not suffer for the iniquity of the father; but every one be answerable for his own sins."[4]

I was troubled to perceive the darkness of their imaginations; and in some pressure of Spirit said that the love of ease and gain is the motive in general for keeping slaves, and men are wont to take hold of weak arguments to support a cause which is unreasonable. I added that I have no interest on either side, save only the interest which I desire to have in the truth. And as I believe liberty is their right, and observe that they are not only deprived of it, but treated in other respects with inhumanity in many places, I believe that He who is a refuge for the oppressed will, in His own time, plead their cause; and happy will it be for such as walk in uprightness before Him. And thus our conversation ended.

* * *

When we love the Lord with all our hearts, and His creatures in His love, we are then preserved in tenderness both toward mankind and the animal creation; but if another spirit gets room in our minds, and we follow it in our proceedings, we are then in the way of disordering the affairs of society.

I have felt great distress of mind, since I came on this island,[5] on account of the members of our Society being mixed with the world in various sorts of business and traffic, carried on in impure channels. Great is the trade to Africa for slaves! And in loading these ships, abundance of people are employed in the factories; amongst whom are many of our Society. Friends in early times refused on a religious principle to make, or trade in, superfluities, of which we have many large testimonies on record. But for want of faithfulness, some gave way—even some whose examples were of note in our Society; and from thence others took more liberty. Members of our Society worked in superfluities, and bought and sold them, and thus dimness of sight came over many. At length Friends got into the use of some superfluities in dress and in the furniture of their houses, and this hath spread from less to more, till superfluity of some kinds is common amongst us.

Of late years a deep exercise hath attended my mind, that Friends may dig deep, may carefully cast forth the loose matter, and get down to the Rock, the sure Foundation, and there hearken to that divine Voice which gives a clear and certain sound. I have felt in that which doth not deceive that if Friends who have known the Truth keep in that tenderness of heart, where all views of outward gain are given up, and their trust is only on the Lord, He will graciously lead some to be patterns of deep self-denial in things relating to trade and handicraft labor. Some, who have plenty of the treasures of this world, will example in a plain frugal life, and pay wages to such as they may hire more liberally than is now customary in some places.

If a man successful in business expends part of his income in things of no real use, while the poor employed by him pass through great difficulties in getting the necessaries of life, this requires his serious attention. If several principal men in business unite in setting the wages of those who work for hire, and therein have a regard to profit to themselves, while the wages of the other on a moderate industry will not afford a comfortable living for their children, this is like laying a temptation in the way of some to strive for a place higher than they are in, when they have not stock sufficient for it.

Now I feel a concern in the spring of pure love, that all who have plenty of outward substance may example others in the right use of things; may carefully look into the condition of poor people, and beware of exacting on them with regard to their wages. While hired laborers by moderate industry, through the divine blessing, may live comfortably, raise up families, and give them suitable education, it appears reasonable for them to be content with their wages.

If they who have plenty love their fellow creatures in that Love which is divine, and in all their proceedings have an equal regard to the good of mankind universally, their place in society is a place of care, an office requiring attention, and the more we possess, the greater is our trust. When our will is subject to the will of God, and in relation to the things of this world we have nothing in view but a comfortable living equally with the rest of our fellow creatures, then outward treasures are no further desirable than as we feel a gift in our minds equal to the trust. A desire for treasures on any other motive appears to be against the command of our blessed Savior. In great treasure there is a great trust. A great trust requires great care. Here we see that man's happiness stands not in great possessions, but in a heart devoted to follow Christ, in the use of things where customs contrary to universal love have no power over us.

Through departing from the truth as it is in Jesus, through introducing ways of life attended with unnecessary expenses, many wants have arisen, the minds of people have been employed in studying to get wealth, and in this pursuit some departing from equity have retained a profession of religion. Others have looked at their example and thereby been strengthened to proceed further in the same way. Thus many have encouraged the trade of taking men from Africa and selling them as slaves. It has been computed that near one hundred thousand Negroes have of late years been taken annually from that coast by ships employed in the English trade.

As I have traveled on religious visits in some parts of America, I have seen many of these people under the command of overseers, in a painful servitude. I have beheld them as Gentiles under people professing Christianity, not only kept ignorant of the Holy Scriptures, but under great provocations to wrath. Where children are taught to read the Sacred Writings while young, and exampled in meekness and humility, it is often helpful to them. But where youth are pinched for want of the necessaries of life, forced to labor hard under the harsh rebukes of rigorous overseers, and many times endure unmerciful whippings—in such an education, how great are the disadvantages they lie under! And how forcibly do these things work against the increase of the government of the Prince of Peace!

Under the sense of a deep revolt and an overflowing stream of unrighteousness, my life has been often a life of mourning, and tender desires are raised in me, that the nature of this practice may be laid to heart. From all accounts it appears evident that great violence is committed, and much blood shed in Africa in getting slaves. And the professed followers of Christ joining in customs evidently unrighteous, which manifestly tend to stir up wrath and increase wars and desolations, hath often covered my mind with sorrow.

If we bring this matter home, and as Job proposed to his friends, "put our soul in their soul's stead";[6] if we consider ourselves and our children as exposed to the hardships which these people lie under; had we none to plead our cause, nor any hope of relief from man; and if they who thus afflicted us continued to lay claim to religion; when we were wearied with labor, denied the liberty to rest, and saw them spending their time at ease; when garments answerable to our necessities were denied us, while we saw them clothed in that which was costly and delicate; under such affliction, how would these painful feelings rise up as witnesses against their pretended devotion! And if the name of their religion was mentioned in our hearing, how would it sound in our ears like a word which signified self-exaltation and hardness of heart!

In procuring slaves on the coast of Africa, many children are stolen privately. Wars are also encouraged amongst the Negroes, but all is at a great distance. Many groans arise from dying men, which we hear not. Many cries are uttered by widows and fatherless children, which reach not our ears. Many cheeks are wet with tears, and faces sad with unutterable grief, which we see not.

Cruel tyranny is encouraged. The hands of robbers are strengthened, and thousands reduced to the most abject slavery who never injured us. Were we for the term of one year only to be an eyewitness to what passeth in getting these slaves; was the blood which is there shed to be sprinkled on our garments; were the poor captives bound with thongs to pass before our eyes on their way to the sea; were their bitter lamentations day after day to ring in our ears, and their mournful cries in the night to hinder us from sleeping; were we to hear the sound of the tumult when the slaves on board the ships attempt to kill the English, and behold the issue of those bloody conflicts—what pious man could be a witness to these things, and see a trade carried on in this manner, without being deeply affected with sorrow?

To relate briefly how these people are treated [in the southern colonies of America] is no agreeable work; yet, after often reading over the notes I made as I traveled, I find my mind engaged to preserve them. Many of the white people in those provinces take little or no care of Negro marriages; and when Negroes marry after their own way, some make so little account of those marriages that, with views of outward interest, they often part men from their wives by selling them far asunder, which is common when estates are sold by executors.

Many whose labor is heavy are followed at their business in the field by a man with a whip, hired for that purpose. They have in common little else allowed but one peck of Indian corn and some salt for one week, with a few potatoes—the potatoes they commonly raise by their labor on the first day of the week [Sunday]. The correction ensuing on their disobedience to overseers, or slothfulness in business, is often very severe and sometimes desperate.

The men and women have many times scarce clothes enough to hide their nakedness, and boys and girls ten and twelve years old are often quite naked amongst their master's children. Some of our Society and some of the Society called New Lights use some endeavors to instruct those they have in reading; but in common this is not only neglected but disapproved. These are the people by whose labor the other inhabitants are in a great measure supported, and many of them in the luxuries of life. These are the people who have made no agreement to serve us, and who have not forfeited their liberty that we know of. These are souls for whom Christ died, and for our conduct toward them we must answer before Him who is no respecter of persons.

They who know the only true God, and Jesus Christ whom He hath sent, and are thus acquainted with the merciful, benevolent Gospel Spirit, will therein perceive that the indignation of God is kindled against oppression and cruelty; and in beholding the great distress of so numerous a people, will find cause for mourning.

* * *

[Written on board the sailing ship *Mary and Elizabeth,* en route from Chester, Pennsylvania, to London in 1772.]

On the seventeenth day of the month, and first of the week, we had a Meeting in the cabin, to which the seamen generally came. My spirit was contrite before the Lord, whose love, at this time, affected my heart. This afternoon I felt a tender sympathy of soul with my poor wife and family left behind. My heart was enlarged in desires that they may walk in that humble obedience wherein the everlasting Father may be their guide and support through all the difficulties in this world. A sense of that gracious assistance through which my mind hath been strengthened to take up the Cross and leave them, to travel in the love of Truth, hath begotten thankfulness in my heart to our great Helper.

The twenty-eighth day of the month. Wet weather of late, small winds inclining to calms. Our seamen have cast a lead, I suppose about one hundred fathoms, but find no bottom. Foggy weather this morning. Through the kindness of the great Pre-server of men, my mind remains quiet. A degree of exercise attends me from day to day, that the pure peaceable government of Christ may spread and prevail amongst mankind.

The leading on of a young generation in that pure way in which the wisdom of this world has no place; where parents and tutors, humbly waiting for the heavenly Counselor, may example them in the Truth as it is in Jesus—this for several days has been the exercise of my mind. O! how safe, how quiet is that state, where the soul stands in pure obedience to the voice of Christ, and a watchful care is maintained not to follow the voice of the stranger!

Here Christ is felt to be our Shepherd, and under His leading, people are brought to a stability. Where He does not lead forward we are bound, in the bonds of pure love, to stand still and wait upon Him. In the love of money and in the wisdom of this world, business is proposed. Then the urgency of affairs pushes forward; nor can the mind in this state discern the good and perfect will of God concerning us.

The love of God is manifested in graciously calling us to come out of that which stands in confusion. But if we bow not in the Name of Jesus; if we give not up those prospects of gain which, in the wisdom of this world, are open before us, but say in our hearts, I must needs go on and, in going on, I hope to keep as near to the purity of Truth as the business before me will admit of—here the mind remains entangled, and the shining of the Light of Life into the soul is obstructed.

In an entire subjection of our wills the Lord graciously opens a way for His people, where all their wants are bounded by His wisdom. Here we experience the substance of what Moses the prophet figured out in the Water of Separation as a purification from sin.[7] Though we have been amongst the slain through the desire of gain, yet in the purifying love of Christ we are washed in the Water of Separation. We are brought off from that business, from that gain, and from that fellowship, which was not agreeable to His holy will.

I have felt a renewed confirmation in the time of this voyage, that the Lord in His infinite love is calling to His visited children, so to give up all outward possessions and means of getting treasures, that His Holy Spirit may have free course in their hearts, and direct them in all their proceedings. I am confirmed in a belief that if all inhabitants lived according to sound wisdom, laboring to promote universal love and righteousness, and ceasing from every inordinate desire after wealth, and from all customs which are tinctured with luxury, the way would be easy to live comfortably on honest employments. To be redeemed from that wisdom which is from beneath, and walk in the Light of the Lord, is a precious situation. Thus His people are brought to put their trust in Him; and in this humble confidence in His wisdom, goodness and power, the righteous find a refuge in adversities superior to the greatest outward helps, and a comfort more certain than any worldly advantages can afford.

NOTES

1. Revelation 2:17.
2. Jeremiah 20:9.
3. Elsewhere Woolman mentions a daughter.
4. Jeremiah 31:30; Ezekiel 18:20.
5. England, 1772.
6. Job 16:4.
7. Numbers 19:13.

Hannah More

At a time when the evangelical churches are being penetrated by the "self-concept" movement, and preachers are going so far as to maintain that Christ died for our self-esteem, this essay on "Self-Love" by Hannah More (1745-1833) has become highly relevant. In these pages of flowing English prose we are given a fresh, microscopic look at ourselves. Few writings lay bare the subtle motives of the human heart as cleverly as does Miss More's assessment of the devious workings of self-love.

She begins her examination of our protean nature with quotations taken from the poetry of Alexander Pope, who informed us that "the proper study of mankind is man," and that "self-love but serves the virtuous mind to wake." Such claims she challenges with elegant warmth, if not heat, declaring that self-love is a "malignant distemper" that is the root cause of all social corruption and disorder. As she analyzes the way the self uses everything it comes across to further its own end—including the reading of pious books—she lays bare the real weakness of those who insist unduly on the value of self-worth, self-fulfillment, and self-realization: they treat human sin too lightly. They seem to forget that pride enters into and corrupts all self-evaluations, using everything it can get its hands on to make us look better than we are.

Hannah More herself was a witty, vivacious Englishwoman who never married, but who won distinction in many fields and became one of the outstanding women of her time. After a betrothal failed to result in marriage, she moved from Bristol to London and became part of the literary scene. She was a much-admired associate of Samuel Johnson, Sir Joshua Reynolds, Edmund Burke, and David Garrick. She published poems and wrote highly successful dramas.

In a move to be emulated more recently by Dorothy L. Sayers, Miss More in the 1780s began writing on spiritual topics. She became a friend of John Newton and William Wilberforce and joined the Clapham Sect, which was the vital center of the evangelical community in London. She began producing spirited rhymes, prose tales, and "cheap repository tracts" which sold two million copies. Aimed at the lower classes, these tracts taught their readers to rely on (and here I quote from a twentieth-century critic) "the virtues of contentment, sobriety, humility, industry, reverence for the British Constitution, hatred of the French, trust in God and in the kindness of the gentry."

Hannah More also engaged in philanthropy, a lifelong interest in which she was joined by her four sisters. Backed by private evangelical sponsorship, she centered her work in the Mendip hills and started a school and Sunday school at Cheddar, teaching children to read and also to spin, thereby incurring opposition from farmers and clergy alike. The work expanded into the mining districts where the government had yet to start an educational program.

Miss More's literary efforts included books of essays on Christian morals, on female education, and on religion in the fashionable world. The force and originality of her style are still felt, although the rhetoric is of an earlier day. She was called an "old bishop in petticoats," but her writings continued to be enormously popular, while her philanthropy made her internationally famous. She is virtually unknown to the twentieth century.

The essay on "Self-Love" is taken from her volume on Practical Piety, *which is found in her* Collected Works *(in eleven volumes!) published in London in 1830.* Practical Piety *appeared shortly after the turn of the century; this essay was written sometime earlier.*

FOUR

Self-Love
by Hannah More

"The idol Self," says an excellent old divine,[1] "has made more desolation among men than ever was made in those places where idols were served by human sacrifices. It has preyed more fiercely on human lives than Moloch or the Minotaur."

To worship images is a more obvious, but scarcely a more degrading idolatry, than to set up self in opposition to God. To devote ourselves to this service is as perfect slavery as the service of God is perfect freedom. If we cannot imitate the sacrifice of Christ in His death, we are called upon to imitate the sacrifice of Himself in His will. Even the Son of God declared, "I came not to do My own will, but the will of Him who sent Me."[2] This was His grand lesson, this was His distinguishing character.

Self-will is the ever-flowing fountain of all the evil tempers which deform our hearts, of all the boiling passions which inflame and disorder society, the root of bitterness on which all its corrupt fruits grow. We set up our own understanding against the wisdom of God, and our passions against the will of God. If we could ascertain the precise period when sensuality ceased to govern in the animal part of our nature, and pride in the intellectual, that period would form the most memorable era of the Christian's life. From that moment he begins a new date of liberty and happiness; from that stage he sets out on a new career of peace, liberty, and virtue.

Self-love is a Proteus of all shapes, shades, and complexions. It has the power of dilation and contraction, as best serves the occasion. There is no crevice so small through which its subtle essence cannot work its way, no space so ample that it cannot stretch itself to fill. It is of all degrees of refinement, so coarse and hungry as to gorge itself with the grossest adulation; so fastidious as to require a homage as refined as itself; so artful as to elude the detection of ordinary observers; so specious as to escape the observation of the very heart in which it reigns paramount; yet though so extravagant in its appetites, it can adopt a moderation which imposes a delicacy which veils its deformity, an artificial character which keeps its real one out of sight.

We are apt to speak of self-love as if it were only a symptom, whereas it is the distemper itself; a malignant distemper which has possession of the moral constitution, of which malady every part of the system participates. In direct opposition to the effect produced by the touch of the fabled king,[3] which converted the basest materials into gold, this corrupting principle pollutes by coming into contact with whatever is in itself great and noble.

Self-love is the center of the unrenewed heart. This stirring principle, as has been observed,[4] serves indeed "the virtuous mind to wake"; but it disturbs it from its slumber to ends and purposes directly opposite to those assigned to it by our incomparable bard. Self-love is by no means "the small pebble which stirs the peaceful lake." It is rather the pent-up wind within, which causes the earthquake; it is the tempest which agitates the sleeping ocean. Had the image been as just as its clothing is beautiful; or rather had Mr. Pope been as sound a theologian as he was an exquisite poet, the allusion in his hands might have conveyed a sounder meaning without losing a particle of its elegance. This might have been effected by only substituting the effect for the cause; that is, by making benevolence the principle instead of the consequence, and by discarding self-love from its central situation in the construction of the metaphor.

But by arraying a beggarly idea in princely robes, he [Pope] knew that his own splendid powers could at any time transform meanness into majesty, and deformity into beauty.

After all, however, *le vrai est le seul beau* [only the true is beautiful]. Had [Pope] not blindly adopted the misleading system of the noble skeptic, "his guide, philosopher, and friend,"[5] he might have transferred the shining attributes of the base-born thing which he has dressed out with so many graces, to the legitimate claimant, benevolence—of which self-love is so far from being, as he claims, the moving spring, that they are both working in a course of incessant counteraction, the Spirit striving against the flesh, and the flesh against the Spirit.

To Christian benevolence all the happy effects attributed to self-love might have been fairly traced. It needed only to dislodge the idol and make the love of God the center, and the poet's delightful numbers might have conveyed truths worthy of so perfect a vehicle. Pope writes:

"Self-love thus pushed to social, to divine,
gives thee to make thy neighbor's blessing thine.
Self-love but serves the virtuous mind to wake,
as the small pebble stirs the peaceful lake.
The center moved, a circle straight succeeds,
another still, and still another spreads;
Friend, parent, neighbor, first it will embrace,
his country next, and next all human race."[6]

The "center moved" does indeed extend its pervading influence in the very manner ascribed to the opposite principle. It does indeed spread from its throne in the individual breast to all these successive circles, "wide and more wide," of which the poet makes self-love the first mover.

The Apostle James appears to have been of a different opinion from the ethic bard; he speaks as if he suspected that the pebble stirred the lake a little too roughly. He traces this mischievous principle from its birth to the largest extent of its malign influence. The question, "Whence come wars and fightings among you?" he answers by another question, "Come they not hence, even of your lusts that war in your members?"[7]

The same pervading spirit which creates hostility between nations, creates animosity among neighbors and discord in families. It is the same principle which, having in the beginning made Cain, the first male child, a murderer in his father's house, has been ever since in perpetual operation. This principle has been transmitted in one unbroken line of succession through that long chain of crimes of which history is composed, to the late triumphant spoiler of Europe.[8] In cultivated societies, laws repress by punishing the overt act in private individuals, but no one thing but the Christian faith has ever been devised to cleanse the spring.

"The heart is deceitful above all things, and desperately wicked; who can know it?"[9] This proposition, this interrogation, we read with complacency, and both the aphorism and the question being a portion of Scripture, we think it would not be decent to controvert it. We read it, however, with a secret reservation, that it is only the heart of all the rest of the world that is meant, and we rarely make the application which the Scripture intended.

Each hopes that there is *one* heart which may escape the charge, and he makes the single exception in favor of his own. But if the exception which everyone makes were true, there would not be a deceitful or wicked heart in the world.

As a theory we are ready enough to admire self-knowledge; yet when the practice comes in question we are as blindfold as if our happiness depended on our ignorance. To lay hold on a religious truth, and to maintain our hold, is no easy matter. Our understandings are not more ready to receive than our affections to lose it. We like to have an intellectual knowledge of divine things, but to cultivate a spiritual acquaintance with them cannot be effected at so cheap a rate. We can even more readily force ourselves to believe that which has no affinity with our understanding, than we can bring ourselves to choose that which has no interest in our will, no correspondence with our passions.

One of the first duties of a Christian is to endeavor to conquer this antipathy to the self-denying doctrines against which the human heart so sturdily holds out. The learned take incredible pains for the acquisition of knowledge. The philosopher cheerfully consumes the midnight oil in his laborious pursuits; he willingly sacrifices food and rest to conquer a difficulty in science. Here the labor is pleasant, the fatigue is grateful, the very difficulty is not without its charms. Why do we feel so differently in our religious pursuits? Because in the most laborious human studies there is no contradiction to self, there is no opposition to the will, there is no combat of the affections. If the passions are at all implicated, if self-love is at all concerned, it is rather in the way of gratification than of opposition.

There is such a thing as a mechanical Christianity. There are good imitations of faith, so well executed and so resembling as not only to deceive the spectator but the artist. Self-love, in its various artifices to deceive us to our ruin, sometimes makes use of a means which, if properly used, is one of the most beneficial that can be devised to preserve us from its influence—the perusal of pious books.

But these very books in the hands of the ignorant, the indolent, and the self-satisfied, produce an effect directly contrary to that which they were intended to produce, and which they actually do produce on minds prepared for the perusal. They inflate where they were intended to humble. As some hypochondriacs, who amuse their melancholy hours with consulting indiscriminately every medical book which falls in their way, fancy they find their own case in every page, their own ailment in the ailment of every patient, till they believe they actually feel every pain of which they read, though the work treats of cases diametrically opposite to their own; so the religious valetudinarian, as unreasonably elated as the others are depressed, reads books descriptive of a high state of devotion with the same unhappy self-application. He feels his spiritual pulse by a watch that has no movements in common with it, yet he fancies that they go exactly alike. He dwells with delight on symptoms, not one of which belongs to him, yet flatters himself with their supposed agreement. He observes in these books what are the signs of grace, and he observes them with complete self-application; he traces what are the evidences of being in God's favor, and these evidences he finds in himself.

Self-ignorance appropriates truths faithfully stated, but wholly inapplicable. The presumption of the novice arrogates to itself the experience of the advanced Christian. He is persuaded that it is his own case, and seizes on the consolations which belong only to the most elevated piety. Self-knowledge would correct this false judgment. It would teach us to use the pattern held out as an original to copy, instead of leading us to fancy that we are already wrought into the assimilation. It would teach us when we read the history of an established Christian to labor after a conformity to it, instead of mistaking it for the delineation of our actual character.

Human prudence, daily experience, self-love, all teach us to distrust others; but all motives combined do not teach us to distrust ourselves. We confide unreservedly in our own heart, though as a guide it misleads, as a counselor it betrays. It is both party and judge. As the one, it blinds through ignorance; as the other, it acquits through partiality.

Though we value ourselves upon our discretion in not confiding too implicitly in others, yet it would be difficult to find any friend, any neighbor, or even any enemy who has deceived us so often as we have deceived ourselves. If an acquaintance betray us, we take warning, are on the watch, and are careful not to trust him again. But however frequently the bosom traitor [the self] deceive and mislead, no such determined stand is made against his treachery; we lie as open to his next assault as if he had never betrayed us. We do not profit by the remembrance of the past to guard against the future.

Yet if another deceive us, it is only in matters respecting this world; but we deceive ourselves in things of eternal moment. The treachery of others can only affect our fortune or our fame, or at worst our peace; but the internal traitor may mislead us to our everlasting destruction. We are too much disposed to suspect others who probably have neither the inclination nor the power to injure us, but we seldom suspect our own heart, though it possesses and employs both.

We ought, however, fairly to distinguish between the simple vanity and the hypocrisy of self-love. Those who content themselves with talking as if the praise of virtue implied the practice, and who expect to be thought good because they commend goodness, only propagate the deceit which has misled themselves, whereas hypocrisy does not even believe herself. She has deeper motives, she has designs to answer, competitions to promote, projects to effect. But mere vanity can subsist on the thin air of the admiration she solicits, without intending to get anything by it. She is gratuitous in her loquacity, for she is ready to display her own merit to those who have nothing to give in return, whose applause brings no profit and whose censure no disgrace.

It is not strange that we should judge of things not according to truth, but according to the opinion of others, in cases foreign to ourselves, cases on which we have no correct means of determining. But we do it in things which relate immediately to ourselves, thus making not truth but the opinion of others our standard in points which others cannot know, and of which we ought not to be ignorant.

We are as fond of the applause even of the upper gallery as the dramatic poet. Like him, we affect to despise the mob considered as individual judges; yet as a mass we covet their applause. Like him, we feel strengthened by the number of voices in our favor, and are less anxious about the goodness of the work than the loudness of the acclamation. Success is merit in the eye of both.

But even though we may put more refinement into our self-love, it is self-love still. No subtlety of reasoning, no elegance of taste, though it may disguise the radical principle, can destroy it. We are still too much in love with flattery, even though we may profess to despise that praise which depends on the acclamations of the vulgar. But if we are anxious only for the admiration of the better born and the better bred, this by no means proves that we are not vain. It only proves that our vanity has a better taste. Our appetite is not coarse enough, perhaps, to relish that popularity which ordinary ambition covets; but do we never feed in secret on the applause of more distinguishing judges? Is not their having extolled *our* merit a confirmation of their discernment, and the chief ground of our high opinion of *theirs?*

But if any circumstance arise to induce them to change the too favorable opinion which they had formed of us, though their general character remain unimpeachable, and their general conduct as meritorious as when we most admired them, do we not begin to judge them unfavorably? Do we not begin to question their claim to that discernment which we had ascribed to them? To suspect the soundness of their judgment which we had so loudly commended? It is well if we do not entertain some doubt of the rectitude of their principles, as we probably do of the reality of their friendship. We do not candidly allow for the effect which prejudice, which misrepresentation, which party may produce, even on an upright mind. Still less does it enter into our calculation that we may actually have deserved their disapprobation, that something in our conduct may have incurred the change in theirs.

It is no low attainment to detect this lurking injustice in our hearts, to strive against it, to pray against it, and especially to conquer it. We may reckon that we have acquired a sound principle of integrity when prejudice no longer blinds our judgment, nor resentment biases our justice; when we do not make our opinion of another depend on the opinion which we conceive he entertains of us.

We must keep a just measure, and hold an even balance in judging of ourselves as well as of others. We must have no false estimate which shall incline to condemnation without, or to partiality within. The examining principle must be kept sound, as our determination will not be exact. It must be at once a testimony of our rectitude and an incentive to it.

In order to improve this principle, we should make it a test of our sincerity to search out and commend the good qualities of those who do not like us. But this must be done without affectation and without insincerity. We must practice no false candor. If we are not on our guard, we may be laying out for the praise of generosity, while we are only exercising a simple act of justice. These refinements of self-love are the dangers only of spirits of the higher order, but they are dangers.

The ingenuity of self-deceit is inexhaustible. If people extol us, we feel our good opinion of ourselves confirmed. If they dislike us, we do not think the worse of ourselves, but of them; it is not we who lack merit, but they who lack penetration. If we cannot refuse them discernment, we persuade ourselves that they are not so much insensible to our worth as envious of it. There is no shift, stratagem, or device which we do not employ to make us stand well with ourselves.

We are too apt to calculate our own character unfairly in two ways, by referring to some one signal act of generosity, as if such acts were the common habit of our lives, and by treating our habitual faults not as common habits but occasional failures. There is scarcely any fault in another which offends us more than vanity, though perhaps there is none that really injures us so little. We have no patience that another should be as full of self-love as we allow ourselves to be; so full of himself as to have little leisure to attend to us. We are particularly quick-sighted to the smallest of his imperfections which interferes with our self-esteem, while we are lenient to his more grave offenses, which, by not coming into contact with our vanity, do not shock our self-love.

Is it not strange that though we love ourselves so much better than we love any other person, yet there is hardly one, however little we value him, that we had not rather be alone with, than ourselves? Scarcely anyone that we had not rather converse with, that we had not rather come to close quarters with, whose private history, whose thoughts, feelings, actions, and motives we had not rather pry into than our own? Do we not use every art and contrivance to avoid getting at the truth of our own character? Do we not endeavor to keep ourselves ignorant of what everyone else knows respecting our faults? And do we not account that man our enemy who takes on himself the best office of a friend—that of opening to us our real estate and condition?

The little satisfaction people find when they faithfully look within, makes them fly more eagerly to things without. Early practice and long habit might conquer the repugnance to look at home, and the fondness for looking abroad. Familiarity often makes us pleased with the society which, while strangers, we dreaded. Intimacy with ourselves might produce a similar effect.

We might perhaps collect a tolerably just knowledge of our own character, if we could ascertain the *real* opinion of others respecting us. But that opinion, being, except in a moment of resentment, carefully kept from us by our own precautions, profits us nothing. We do not choose to know their secret sentiments, because we do not choose to be cured of our error, and because we "love darkness rather than light,"[10] and because we conceive that in parting with our vanity we should part with the only comfort we have, that of being ignorant of our own faults.

Self-knowledge would materially contribute to our happiness, by curing us of that self-sufficiency which is continually exposing us to mortifications. The hourly rubs and vexations which pride undergoes are far more than an equivalent for the short intoxications of pleasure which it snatches.

The enemy within is always in a confederacy with the enemy without, whether that enemy be the world or the Devil. The domestic foe accommodates itself to their allurements, flatters our weaknesses, throws a veil over our vices, tarnishes our good deeds, gilds our bad ones, hoodwinks our judgment, and works hard to conceal our internal springs of action. We are all too much disposed to dwell on that smiling side of the prospect which pleases and deceives us, and to shut our eyes upon that part which we do not choose to see, because we are resolved not to quit. Self-love always holds a screen between the superficial self-examiner and his faults. The nominal Christian wraps himself up in forms which he makes himself believe are "religion." He exults in what he does, overlooks what he ought to do, and never suspects that what is done at all can be done amiss.

Self-love has the talent of imitating whatever the world admires, even though it should happen to be the Christian virtues. It leads us, from our regard to reputation, to avoid all vices, not only those which would bring punishment and discredit. It can even assume the zeal and copy the activity of Christian charity. It communicates to our outward conduct the same proprieties and graces manifested in the conduct of those who are actuated by a sounder motive. The difference lies in the ends proposed. The object of the one is to please God, of the other to obtain the praise of man.

A person who has left off some notorious vice, who has softened some shades of a glaring sin, or substituted some outward forms in the place of open irreligion, looks on his change of character with pleasure. He compares himself with what he was, and views the alteration with complacency. He deceives himself by taking his standard from his former conduct, or from the character of still worse men, instead of taking it from the unerring rule of Scripture. He looks rather at the discredit than the sinfulness of his former life; and being more ashamed of what is disreputable than grieved at what is vicious, he is, in this state of shallow reformation, more in danger in proportion as he is more in credit. He is not aware that it is not having a fault or two less that will carry him to Heaven, while his heart is still glued to the world and estranged from God.

If we ever look into our hearts at all, we are naturally most inclined to it when we think we have been acting right. Here inspection gratifies self-love. We have no great difficulty in directing our attention to an object, when that object presents us with pleasing images. But it is a painful effort to compel the mind to turn in on itself, when the view only presents subjects for regret and remorse. This painful duty, however, must be performed, and will be more salutary in proportion as it is less pleasant. Let us establish it into a habit to ruminate on our faults. With the recollection of our virtues we need not feed our vanity. They will, if that vanity does not obliterate them, be recorded elsewhere.

We are also most disposed to look at those parts of our character which will best bear it, and which, consequently, least need it. We look at those parts which afford most self-gratulation. If a covetous man, for instance, examines himself, instead of turning his attention to this fault, he applies the probe where he knows it will not go very deep. He turns from his avarice to his sobriety. Another, who is the slave of passion, fondly rests upon some act of generosity.

It is only by scrutinizing the heart that we can know it. It is only by knowing the heart that we can reform the life. Self-examination, by detecting self-love, turns the temper of the soul from its natural bias, controls the disorderly appetite, and, under the influence of divine grace, restores in a good measure to a person that dominion over himself which God gave him at first over the inferior creatures. But in our self-inquisition let us fortify our virtue by a rigorous exactness in calling things by their proper names. Self-love is particularly ingenious in inventing disguises of this kind. Let us lay them open, strip them bare, face them, and give them as little quarter as if they were the faults of another. Self-love is made up of soft and sickly sensibilities. It is alive in every pore where self is concerned. A touch is a wound. It is careless in inflicting pain, but exquisitely awake in feeling it. It defends itself before it is attacked, revenges affronts before they are offered, and resents as an insult the very suspicion of an imperfection.

Being a very industrious principle, self-love has generally two concerns in hand at the same time. It is as busy in concealing our own defects as in detecting those of others, especially those of the wise and good. We lessen our respect for pious characters when we see the infirmities which are blended with their fine qualities, and we turn their failings into a justification of our own. When we are compelled by our conscience to acknowledge and regret any fault we have recently committed, this fault so presses upon our recollection that we seem to forget that we have any other. This single error fills our mind, and we look at it as through a telescope. Thus, while the object in question is magnified, the others are as if they did not exist.

Self-love, judging of the feelings of others by its own, is aware that nothing excites so much odium as its own character would do if nakedly exhibited. We feel, by our own disgust at its exhibition in others, how much disgust we ourselves should excite, did we not invest it with the soft garb of gentle manners and a polished address. When, therefore, we would not condescend "to take the lowest place, to think ourselves better than ourselves, to be courteous and pitiful" on the true Scripture ground, politeness steps in as the accredited substitute of humility, and the counterfeit brilliant is willingly worn.

There is a certain elegance of mind which will often restrain a well-bred man from sordid pleasures and gross voluptuousness. He will be led by his good taste, perhaps, not only to abhor the excesses of vice, but to admire the theory of virtue. But it is only the surfeit of vice which he will abhor. Exquisite gratification, sober luxury, incessant but not unmeasured enjoyment, form the principle of his plan of life. If he observes a temperance in his pleasures, it is only because excess would take off the edge, destroy the zest, and abridge the gratification. By resisting gross vice he flatters himself that he is a temperate man, and that he has made all the sacrifices which self-denial imposes. Inwardly satisfied, he compares himself with those who have sunk into coarser indulgences, enjoys his own superiority in health, credit, and unimpaired faculties, and triumphs in the dignity of his own character.

There is, if the expression may be allowed, a sort of religious self-deceit, an affectation of humility which is in reality full of self. It resolves all importance into what concerns self, and looks only at things as they refer to self. This religious vanity operates in two ways. We not only fly out at the imputation of the smallest individual fault, while at the same time we affect to charge ourselves in general with more corruption than is attributed to us. But on the other hand, while we are lamenting our general want of all goodness, we fight for every particle that is disputed. The one quality that is in question always happens to be the very one to which we *must* lay claim, however deficient in others. Thus while renouncing the pretension to every virtue, "we depreciate ourselves unto all." We had rather talk even of our faults than not occupy the foreground of the canvas.

Humility does not consist in telling our faults, but in bearing to be told of them, in hearing them patiently and even thankfully, in correcting ourselves when told, and in not hating those who tell us of them. If we were little in our own eyes, and felt our real insignificance, we should avoid false humility as much as more obvious vanity; but we seldom dwell on our faults except in an indefinite way, and rarely on those of which we are really guilty. We do it then in the hope of being contradicted, and thus of being confirmed in the secret good opinion we entertain of ourselves.

It is not enough that we inveigh against ourselves; we must in a manner forget ourselves. This oblivion of self from a pure principle would go farther toward our advancement in Christian virtue than the most splendid actions performed on the opposite ground.

Self-acquaintance will give us a far more deep and intimate knowledge of our own errors than we can possibly have, with all the inquisitiveness of an idle curiosity, of the errors of others. We are eager enough to blame them without knowing their motives. We are no less eager to vindicate ourselves. When we hear others commend our charity, which we know is so cold; when others extol our piety, which we feel to be so dead; when they applaud the energies of our faith, which we must know to be so faint and feeble; we cannot possibly be so intoxicated with the applause which never would have been given, had the applauder known us as we know or ought to know ourselves.

If we contradict him, it may be only to draw on ourselves the imputation of a fresh virtue, humility, which perhaps we as little deserve to have ascribed to us, as that which we have been renouncing. If we kept a sharp lookout, we should not be proud of praises which cannot apply to us. To be delighted at finding that people think so much better of us than we are conscious of deserving, is in effect to rejoice in the success of our own deceit.

Did we turn our thoughts inward, it would abate much of the self-complacency with which we receive the flattery of others. Flattery hurts not him who flatters not himself. If we examined our motives keenly, we should frequently blush at the praises our actions receive. Let us then conscientiously inquire not only what we do, but whence and why we do it, from what motive and to what end.

Is it not astonishing that we should go on repeating periodically, "Try me, O God!" while we are yet neglecting to try ourselves? Is there not something more like defiance than devotion to invite the inspection of Omniscience to that heart which we ourselves neglect to inspect? How can a Christian solemnly cry out to the Almighty, "Seek the ground of my heart, prove me, and examine my thoughts, and see if there be any way of wickedness in me,"[11] while he himself neglects to "examine his heart," is afraid of "proving his thoughts," and dreads to inquire if "there be any way of wickedness" in himself, knowing that the inquiry ought to lead to the expulsion?

That self-knowledge which teaches us humility teaches us compassion also. The sick pity the sick. They sympathize with the disorder of which they feel the symptoms in themselves. Self-knowledge also checks injustice, by establishing the equitable principle of showing the kindness we expect to receive. It represses ambition by convincing us how little we are entitled to superiority. It renders adversity profitable, by letting us see how much we deserve it. It makes prosperity safe, by directing our hearts to Him who confers it, instead of receiving it as the consequence of our own desert.

We even carry our self-importance to the foot of the throne of God. When prostrate there, we are not required, it is true, to forget ourselves, but we are required to remember *Him*. We have indeed much sin to lament, but we have also much mercy to adore. We have much to ask, but we have likewise much to acknowledge. Yet our infinite obligations to God do not fill our hearts half as much as a petty uneasiness of our own; nor do we reflect on His infinite perfections as much as on our smallest want.

The great, the only effectual antidote to self-love is to get the love of God and of our neighbor firmly rooted in the heart.

Yet let us ever bear in mind that dependence on our fellow-creatures is as carefully to be avoided as love of them is to be cultivated. There is none but God on whom the principles of love and dependence form but one duty.

Christianity, though the most perfect rule of life that ever was devised, is far from being barely a rule of life. A religion consisting of a mere code of laws might have sufficed for man in a state of innocence. But man who has broken these laws cannot be saved by a rule which he has violated. What consolation could he find in the perusal of statutes, every one of which brings a fresh assurance of his condemnation?

The chief object of the gospel is not to furnish rules for the preservation of innocence, but to hold out the means of salvation to the guilty. It does not proceed upon a supposition, but a fact; not upon what might have suited man in a state of purity, but upon what is suitable to him in the exigencies of his fallen state.

Christianity does not consist in an external conformity to practices which, though right in themselves, may be adopted from human motives and to answer secular purposes. It is not a religion of forms, modes, and decencies. It is being transformed into the image of God. It is being like-minded with Christ. It is considering Him as our sanctification as well as our redemption. It is endeavoring to live to Him here, that we may live with Him hereafter. It is desiring earnestly to surrender our will to His, our heart to the conduct of His Spirit, our life to the guidance of His Word.

If Christianity does not always produce these happy effects, it has always a tendency to produce them. If we do not see progress, it is not owing to any defect in the principle, but to the remains of sin in the heart; to the imperfectly subdued corruptions of the Christian. This Christianity has been the support and consolation of the pious believer in all ages of the church. That it has been perverted makes nothing against the principle itself. But if it has been carried to a blameable excess by the pious error of holy men, it has also been adopted by the less innocent fanatic and abused to the most pernicious purposes.

The enemies of internal Christianity seize every occasion to represent it as if it were criminal, as the foe of morality; ridiculous, as the infallible test of an unsound mind; mischievous, as hostile to active virtue; and destructive, as the bane of public utility. But if these charges be really well founded, then were the brightest luminaries of the Christian church—then were Horne, and Porteus, and Beveridge; then were Hooker, and Taylor, and Herbert; Hopkins, Leighton, and Ussher; Howe, Doddridge, and Baxter; Ridley, Jewel, and Hooper; then were Chrysostom and Augustine, the reformers and the fathers; then were the goodly fellowship of the prophets; then were the noble army of martyrs, then were the glorious company of the apostles, then was the disciple whom Jesus loved, then was Jesus Himself—I shudder at the implication—dry speculatists, frantic enthusiasts, enemies to virtue, and subverters of the public weal.[12]

But when we see how graciously the Almighty has turned the lapse of our natural state into an occasion of improving our condition; how from this evil He was pleased to advance us to a greater good than we had lost; how that life which was forfeited may be restored; how, by grafting the redemption of man on the very circumstance of his fall, He has raised him to the capacity of a higher condition, and to a happiness superior to that from which he fell: what an impression does this give us of the immeasurable wisdom and goodness of God, of the unsearchable riches of Christ!

NOTES

1. John Howe (1630-1705), English Puritan, chaplain to Cromwell.
2. Cf. John 4:34.
3. Midas, a legendary king of Phrygia, Asia Minor (now Turkey).
4. The quotation is from the "Essay on Man" by Alexander Pope (1688-1744), in which the poet extols the love of self.
5. In his poem Pope adopted the philosophy of Henry St. John, Viscount Bolingbroke (1678-1751), English statesman and orator.
6. Pope, *op. cit.*
7. James 4:1.
8. Napoleon.
9. Jeremiah 17:9.
10. John 3:19.
11. Cf. Psalm 139:23, 24.
12. George Horne (1730-1792), bishop of Norwich; Beilby Porteus (1731-1808), bishop of London; William Beveridge (1637-1708), bishop of St. Asaph, Wales; Richard Hooker (1554-1600), English theologian; Jeremy Taylor (1613-1667), preacher and writer; George Herbert (1593-1633), devotional poet; Robert Leighton (1611-1684), archbishop of Glasgow; James Ussher (1581-1656), Bible chronologist; Philip Doddridge (1702-1751), evangelical hymn-writer; Richard Baxter (1615-1691), Puritan leader; Nicholas Ridley (1500-1555), Protestant martyr; John Jewel (1522-1571), bishop and reformer; John Hooper (d. 1555), Protestant martyr; John Chrysostom (347-507), church father, bishop of Constantinople; Augustine (Aurelius Augustinus), (354-430), church father, bishop of Hippo, North Africa.

Rowland Hill

Rowland Hill (1744-1833), the sixth son of Sir Rowland Hill, baronet, was educated at Shrewsbury and Eton before entering St. John's College, Cambridge. He was converted to Christ as a youth, partly through reading Isaac Watts' hymns for children. At Cambridge he joined a group of evangelicals who visited prisons, workhouses, and sick rooms, for which the college severely censured him. After taking his B.A. degree he was denied ordination to the Anglican priesthood by six bishops in turn. Four years later he married a Miss Tudway and was admitted to deacon's orders; the priesthood remained closed.

Hill began preaching to the peasants on his father's estate and soon became an itinerant evangelist, drawing crowds all over England and Wales. On one occasion he drew twenty-thousand persons in south London. On another he preached to an uproarious crowd on a village green in Wiltshire. A listener threw three snakes at him, one of which coiled around his arm, and another fastened on his neck. Seeing they were harmless, Hill threw them off, but attendance picked up and several conversions were reported. As for the prankster, he came back another time and in Hill's words, "He that would have alarmed me by serpents was himself rescued from the old serpent."

The anecdotes about Rowland Hill are endless. To him is attributed the saying, "I don't see any reason why the Devil should have all the good tunes." He also stated, "I like short, ejaculatory prayers, uttered on the spur of the moment, that fly up to Heaven before the Devil can get a shot at them." He was a man of enormous vitality, tall and commanding in appearance, with a powerful, melodious voice and "a singularly fine nose."

In 1783 he opened Surrey Chapel, which he built with funds from his own inherited property, and he became its pastor for nearly fifty years. Built to hold two thousand persons, it often accommodated three thousand with standing room only. It was located amidst the hovels (which he often visited) in Blackfriars, South London. Services at Surrey Chapel usually lasted two and one-half hours, Sunday morning and evening. During the week he was usually out preaching. When *away on his frequent evangelistic trips, he would welcome dissenters (Baptists, Presbyterians, Congregationalists, and others) to his pulpit, thereby incurring the displeasure of his colleagues.* It was said that he preached twenty-three thousand sermons, the Encylopedia Britannica observing that "*his oratory was specially adapted for rude and uncultivated audiences.*"

Scotland responded to Hill's ministry with enthusiasm, and the people loved his anecdotes. Says his biographer, Edward Broome, "The singularity of the stranger's manner, the fervor of his address, and the brilliant powers of his active and energetic mind soon drew vast multitudes around him." *In Edinburgh he addressed eighteen thousand listeners on Calton Hill.* During one visit to Scotland he returned on horseback, preaching along the way in Dunbar, Berwick, Alnick, Newcastle, Durham, Darlington, Leeds, Rotherham, Sheffield, Derby, Coventry, Warwick, Evesham, and Painswick.

Hill was honored not only for his philanthropies, which were many, but for his efforts in the advancement of science; he personally vaccinated the children of his congregation against smallpox. In 1799 he began to write the Village Dialogues, *which appeared in the* Evangelical Magazine *starting in 1801, and proved highly popular. By 1839 they had gone through thirty-nine editions. The present selection from the* Dialogues *has been made from the first, second, and eighth chapters in the first of three volumes of the eighth London edition, published in New York in 1825 by Johnstone & Van Norden.*

Village Dialogues
by Rowland Hill

I. Cottage Piety
Or, The Good Order of Thomas Newman's Family

Farmer Littleworth goes after his laborers, and finds Thomas at his work, singing.

FARMER: Well, Thomas, you seem very merry. What are you singing?

THOMAS: Why, Master, I am singing one of the songs of Zion.

FARMER: What sort of songs can they be? I never heard of such before.

THOMAS: More's the pity, Master. But I am singing His praises who has redeemed me by His blood, sanctified me by His Spirit, and leads me to His glory. And while I am singing I am cheerful, and then I can work the better. Besides, these good songs keep bad thoughts out of my heart.

FARMER: Why, Thomas, I wonder how you can be so merry in these hard times.

THOMAS: Hard, Master! Why, we never mind hard times while we can live with a joyful hope of a happy eternity. We need to be "careful for nothing, while with prayer and thanksgiving we can make our requests known to God."[1]

FARMER: I am sure my wife and I have care enough, what between my son, who is gone to sea, and my three daughters whom I never can keep at home, unless they have twenty gossips and fine misses with them. I have a good farm, and a pretty bit of freehold of my own, yet it almost all goes as fast as it comes in.

THOMAS: Oh, Master! You want a proper housekeeper.

FARMER: Nay, Thomas, you should not say so, for my Dame is as good a housekeeper as any in the parish, if my children did not turn out so untowardly.

THOMAS: The housekeeper I mean is Mr. Godlyfear. By the blessing of God, I know the worth of that gentleman very well. He has lived in my house ever since Mr. Lovegood came to be the vicar of our parish. Mr. Godlyfear charges nothing for his wages, but in these hard times he provides us with more bread and cheese than we ever had when times were better. And, Master, if I may be plain with you, had you and Mistress the same housekeeper, he might have kept your son from running into wickedness, and then he need not have gone to sea, and he would have made your daughters keep at home and mind the business of the house. I beg your pardon, Master, if I say too much.

FARMER: Ah, Thomas! I have many a heartbreaking thought about that boy. But I must confess you are not the worse for hearing your parson. He has made you a better man than when you came home half-drunk with me from Mapleton Fair.

THOMAS: A thousand times I have thought that we were worse than the hogs we went to sell.

FARMER: That was partly my fault, Thomas. But I thought as the hogs went off so well, we might have a cup or two of drink extraordinary.

THOMAS: But Master, if you think I am the better for hearing our minister, why won't you come and hear him too?

FARMER: Why, if I did, I should be jeered at all the market over. You know, Thomas, your cottage is not in our parish; and what would our rector say if I were to leave our church to hear Mr. Lovegood? You know he hates him mortally, calls him all sorts of names, and says he is a " 'thusiast." What he means by it I cannot tell. And I should have as good a peal about my ears from my wife and daughters as ever I should have from the parson.

THOMAS: What of all that, Master, if you could but get good to your soul? For there is no good like it.

FARMER: Ah, Thomas! This is fine talk, for if I were to quarrel with our parson, I should never have any peace in the parish, and he would raise my tithes directly, for he is always after more money.

THOMAS: Why, since I have been blessed with the fear of God, I have been kept from the fear of man, and it has been a thousand times better with me ever since. Now, I am a poor man, and had need fear everybody, and you have a good farm and need fear nobody. If Mr. Godlyfear had lived in your house, he would have kept you far enough from such fears as these.

FARMER: I confess at times I should be glad of such a guest, for he seems to have kept your house very well. How many children have you? I think the last time I was in your house I counted five.

THOMAS: Thank God, Master, I have six, and another a-coming.

FARMER: Why, how do you provide for them all?

THOMAS: By prayer and patience.

FARMER: Is that all? I am sure you must have something better than that.

THOMAS: Better, Master? I am directed to pray for my daily bread, and wait with patience till it comes; and the Lord is as good as His promise. If I am poor, and a little pinched at one time, I have plenty at another. What a sight of things were sent to us when my wife, the fourth time she lay in, was brought to bed of twins. Just as we began to mistrust of what we should do, when the children came so fast, in came Madam Trusty, Squire Worthy's housekeeper, with such a nice bundle of baby-linen and other things for my wife, that she and the children were soon dressed like gentlefolk. Our dear minister also went about and got us money enough to buy coals to serve us all the winter, so that I was never better off in all my life. The faster the children came, the better we were provided for. We had enough to do to praise God for His mercies. And though I say it that

should not, our children look as decent and as
healthy as any children in our parish, or the next
to it.

FARMER: Well, Thomas, you had need mind your hits,[2] to
breed them all up.

THOMAS: Why, Master, I always put the children to work as
soon as they are able. They either spin or knit,
and my second son Billy has got a loom which
our worthy Squire gave him, and he weaves very
tidily, and my wife always keeps us well mended.
But then, Master, we get all this by living in the
fear of God, and that is one of the greatest blessings a man's heart can enjoy.

FARMER: Well I must say, Thomas, you live so orderly that
I should be glad to hear a little about your way of
living.

THOMAS: Why, Master, it would look so much like brag-
ging and boasting, were I to tell you about our
poor way of serving God in our cottage since He
has changed my heart, that I should be quite
ashamed of myself.

FARMER: Nay, but I must hear it.

THOMAS: Well, Master, when I am called to labor, as soon
as my wife and I are out of bed, I kneel down and
go to prayer by the bedside. Then I go to work.
She dresses the children and sets the house in
order. When I come home to breakfast, the milk
porridge, or what my wife can get for us, is all
ready. Next I make my eldest boy ask a blessing,
and then the victuals and drink go down with a
blessing. Then the children say a hymn or some
other good lesson out of the books that our minister gives us. And then one of the other children
returns thanks. After that my wife takes down the
Bible and reads a chapter, for Betty reads bravely,
and I go to prayer. Then I go to work, and as you
know, Master, take my eldest son, Thomas, with
me, and he helps me wonderfully; and I do think
I can do almost double the work since I have had
him with me. I love to work hard for a good
Master.

FARMER: Well, Thomas, I shall have no objection against raising your son's wages, for he is a good lad.

THOMAS: Thank you kindly, Master, for the times are a little sharp, and my son is a growing, hungry boy. But I will tell you what we do next. I come home to [midday] dinner. Now you know, Master, we keep a pig, which we kill for the winter. What between the pickings out of our garden, the acorns which the children pick out of the Squire's park, and a little barley meal, it does not cost us much to keep the pig, so that we can get a slice of bacon that relishes the potatoes and garden stuff. I really think we are as thankful for that as many a lord is for twenty times as much. Then I make one of the children read a bit of the *Pilgrim's Progress,* or some other good book that Mr. Lovegood gives or lends us, and then I go to my work. Master, if you please, I'll tell you the thanksgiving hymn I sing as I walk along.

FARMER: Well, Thomas, let us hear it, for I am told you could sing as merry a song as any of us, before Mr. Lovegood came into your parish.

THOMAS: Ah, Master! That was before the Lord changed my wicked heart. Now He has put a new song in my mouth, and if you choose to hear it, this is my song:

"My heart and my tongue shall unite in the praise
Of Jesus my Savior, for mercy and grace;
He purchased my pardon by shedding His blood,
And bids me inherit the peace of my God.

My lot may be lowly, my parentage mean,
Yet born of my God, there are glories unseen,
Surpassing all joys among sinners on earth,
Prepared for souls of a heavenly birth."

FARMER: I confess, Thomas, you sing better songs than we sing at our Christmas merrymakings. But where did you get it?

THOMAS: Our dear minister brought it one morning while I was at work.

FARMER: I must say your parson teaches you better songs than our parson is apt to sing. When he comes to our house he is mainly fond of singing in his way, "O, the roast beef of old England!" And what a roaring voice he has for sure! But let us hear how you end the day.

THOMAS: After my work I return home. Down I sit, and all my children come around me. I confess, Master, I am a little too fond of the twins. They are a pair of brave children. So I put one on one knee, and the other on the other. Then I give them all a kiss, and my hearty blessing, for I love them dearly and could work my skin to the bones to support them. Next I ask them what work they have done, how they have behaved to their mother and to each other. Then I make the oldest of them read out of some good book, and I tell them what it means, and instruct them as well as I am able. Next we have a bit of supper, as the times afford, and afterward my wife reaches down the Bible and reads a chapter. Then we sing some good hymn, and I go to prayer, after my poor fashion, and then our bed feels sweet to us, for the Lord be praised! We have nothing to fear. Poverty keeps the door from thieves, and a peaceable mind soon sets us all asleep.

FARMER: You have told how you live. I confess I should be ashamed to tell you how we live. But, Thomas, I do not pretend to be a saint. The house would be all in an uproar if I were to call my family to say their prayers as often as you do.

THOMAS: Many a man may say prayers, and never pray!

FARMER: Aye, true, Thomas!

THOMAS: Well, Master, by your desire, I am next to tell you how we spend the Sunday.

FARMER: Why, every day seems to be a Sunday with you, except you do not then go to work.

THOMAS: But, Master, we have something better still on the Sunday. I should be glad if you would walk with me over the next stile, and you will see what a rare plat of ground my boy and I shall make by clearing away that rubbishy hedge, as it was of no use as a fence before.

FARMER: Well, Thomas, let us walk together, and you shall tell me how you spend your Sundays.

THOMAS: See, Master, what a deal of weeds and rubbish we have got together within these few days. All this puts me in mind of the natural heart of man, that there can be nothing done in it till the weeds and filth of sin are got out of it. And sin has taken deeper root in our hearts than these briars and weeds have in this ground. When we have got them all on a heap, we shall burn them out of the way. May the Lord do the same in all our hearts!

FARMER: Why, Thomas, I think Mr. Lovegood will make quite a parson of you soon.

THOMAS: Thank the Lord for His mercy! I hope He has made a Christian of me. That is all I want, till through the Lord's mercy I get safe to Heaven.

FARMER: But, Thomas, you must remember your promise, and tell us how you live on the Sunday.

THOMAS: Well, you must know, my wife always contrives on the Saturday to get our clean linen ready for us, and somewhat a little more decent than our common working dress, to go to church in on a Sunday. The house is always done up neat and clean, and all our clothes got ready against the Sunday morning. Then we get ourselves ready, and begin the Sabbath with a chapter out of the Bible, a hymn or psalm, and a prayer. Then we all eat our breakfast, and afterward send the four eldest of our children to the Sunday school. After this we all go to church, if we can, unless my wife is obliged to stay at home to nurse the little ones, and then we take it by turns.

FARMER: To be sure, Thomas, your wife is a wonderful, notable woman.

THOMAS: Master, everybody in the parish admires our Betty, and I would not part with her for the best duchess in the land. Well, and after church we all come home. Then I ask the children one by one what the text was, and what they can remember of the minister's sermon, and talk with them of the good things we have been hearing. After we have had such a dinner as the mercy of God provides for us (and it is always better than we deserve), then we have another prayer. The children go again to the Sunday school, and we all meet again at church in the afternoon. I think it would do your heart good to hear what pains our dear minister takes with us; how nicely he expounds the chapters, and how he tries from the pulpit to make known to us the way of salvation.

FARMER: Why, the people say he has it all by rote, and that he has no book but the Bible with him in the pulpit. He must have a wonderful memory.

THOMAS: By rote, Master! He has it all in his heart; and by the grace of God he has enough in his heart for a thousand sermons. As it comes from the heart, so it goes to the heart. Blessed be God, it comes to my heart, I am sure of that. Well, after sermon we all go home, and then we treat ourselves, for once in the week, with a dish of tea, and again talk over the good things we heard at church. At seven o'clock we go down to the vicarage. To see how lovingly Madam Lovegood welcomes us would do anyone good—how she helps to bring out the chairs, and seats us all comfortably in the kitchen and hall. When we are ready, our dear minister comes in and repeats to us what he has been preaching before, and exhorts us, and prays, and sings with us so charmingly that it makes us feel like a little Heaven upon earth.

FARMER: Well, Thomas, it is to be hoped you have had enough of religion after all this.

THOMAS: Enough, Master! Why, as we are obliged to keep to very sharp labor through the six days, it would be a thousand pities to lose any part of the only day given us, to seek after our heavenly rest. Blessed be God, we have a little more, after all this. We have some more good talk at supper, a chapter, a psalm or hymn, and a prayer; and then we throw ourselves into the arms of our dear

God and Savior, and sleep on earth as though we were to wake in Heaven.

FARMER: But, Thomas, does God Almighty require all this religion from you? Would not less do?

THOMAS: Why, Master, these things are our delight. We do not serve as slaves, but as sons. We serve, because we love the service. Look into the Bible, Master, and you will find what my wife and I find, that religion is regeneration, and that holiness is Heaven. All the Lord's ways are ways of pleasantness, and all His paths are paths of peace.[3] I wish every family, and all the world, were but as happy as Betty and I.

FARMER: I will look into our great Bible when I get home. But how is it you are so fond of talking about your dear Betty?

THOMAS: Why, she is the joy of my heart and the comfort of my life.

FARMER: Where did you meet with her?

THOMAS: At church.

FARMER: Why, surely you did not go to church to seek a wife?

THOMAS: I only went there to seek for salvation, after I began to know the value of my soul. About half a year after I was converted, I used to see a mighty decent-dressing young woman, and I thought if I married, that the Lord might intend her for my wife. As I used to meet her at Mr. Lovegood's house, I once plucked up courage and plainly told her what I thought about it, but I could get nothing out of her, but that she could not think of it till she had made it a matter of prayer. Then, thought I, this is the damsel that will do for me. I also made it a matter of prayer, and this made me ask her the same question again and again. The young woman went and consulted Mr. Lovegood about my offer. One evening Mr. Lovegood sent for me to his house, while she was there. So down I came, and when I saw her there, my heart went pit-a-pat in a manner I never felt before. We then talked over the matter, and he read to us that wonderful good exhortation in the marriage service, showing the duties there would be between us. Then he went to prayer with us, and after this we promised each other marriage, and we were married accordingly. I have been as happy as a prince ever since. We can praise and bless God for everything.

FARMER: Well, Thomas, I am sure you are a happier man since you have taken to this new religion.

THOMAS: New religion, Master! Why, it is as old as the Bible.

FARMER: Well, I want to know why you changed your religion.

THOMAS: Well then, Master, I'll tell you as near as I can how religion changed me. My father, you know, was a poor working man, and died of consumption. Then my mother went to the workhouse with two children. I was the oldest of them, and was put out apprentice to old James Gripe, who used to work me morning, noon, and night, and half-starved me; and his wife Margery was worse than he. So I ran away from them and went to the Justice about them, and his Worship questioned me very hard and sharp; but when he found how cruelly I was used, he acted very good-naturedly toward me, and said he would not suffer the poor parish 'prentices to be ill-used by anybody. So he got me a better place at Farmer Thrifty's, where I had plenty of work, and good victuals and drink. But the farmer was all for the world, and many of the family were desperate wicked. As I grew up, I wonder they did not make me as wicked as themselves. But wicked enough I was, God knows; for I scarce ever went to church, unless I was to meet someone there, or show my new clothes when I had any. I had no more notion of a Bible, or what it meant, than one of the horses I used to drive at plow.

FARMER: Why, Thomas, you had a good heart at bottom, or you would have followed more of their bad courses.

THOMAS: A good heart indeed! When I never prayed, or read my Bible, or thought of my soul, or anything else but wickedness. I have since found that all our resolutions to mend our ways come to nothing, till God changes the heart; and so it was with me. I am ashamed to think what a fool I used to make myself, especially once at Mapleton Fair, where I was dancing almost all night at the Stag's Head, when I was no more fit for such games than one of our cart horses.

FARMER: But surely, Thomas, there can be no harm in a little innocent mirth now and then.

THOMAS: Why, I'll tell you, Master, I am never afraid of what I do, provided I can but feel prayer while I do it. Well, soon after midsummer our new vicar came, and as it was the first time, many people were there to hear him. Though we had heard nothing of him till we saw him in the church, yet it was to admiration how he read the lessons and prayers. They sounded like new prayers to me, he read them so wonderfully fine. Somehow he seemed to feel every word he read. But when he got into the pulpit, we did not know what to make of it, for he had no book with him, but a little Bible. We thought for sure he had left his sermon book behind him. It is wonderful how lovingly he spoke to us while he preached from this text: "We preach not ourselves, but Christ Jesus the Lord; and ourselves your servants for Jesus' sake."[4] He told us how he hoped he was sent purely for the good of our souls, and how fervently he had prayed to God that he might come with a blessing among us; that his house, his heart was open to us, even the poorest of us; and that all his time and strength should be given up for our good.

FARMER: Well, well, and our minister says he wants to make us good, too, if he can; for he tells us a deal more of our duty than many of us practice; and we have all his sermons round once a year. I have heard them over nineteen times, and he says we shall have no new ones till we practice the old ones better.

THOMAS: Why, I have heard our dear minister these seven

years, and he has his heart full of sermons, and
they are always new.

FARMER: Thomas, I'd give the world to be as good a man
            as you are, and that my wife was as good a wom-
            an as your Betty. Well, well, I will pluck up cour-
            age, and come and hear Mr. Lovegood next Sun-
            day, come what will on it; and I'll try to bring my
            daughter Nancy with me, for she does not seem
            to be so bad set against Mr. Lovegood as the
            others. But I know I shall hear enough of it from
            my minister, Mr. Dolittle, and my neighbors. Oh,
            Thomas, you must be right, and I fear I am
            wrong. Well, I must have another talk with you.
            It begins to threaten rain, and I will come again
            and learn more about why you changed your
            religion.

THOMAS: Master, I will tell you at any time you please, as I
            said, how the Christian religion changed me.

FARMER: Good day, Thomas. Here's a shilling for your
            boy.

THOMAS: Thank you. Your servant, Master.

VIII. The Prodigal's Conversion
[Farmer Littleworth's Son Henry Changes Course]

*Farmer Littleworth comes from his farm near Mapleton, and sits
down in the minister's kitchen, deeply affected. Mr. Lovegood returns from visiting his parishioners.*

LOVEGOOD: Why, Mr. Littleworth, I am sorry to see you so
            much affected. Is all well at home?

FARMER: Oh, Sir! I cannot stand it. It quite overcomes me.

LOVEGOOD: What overcomes you, Sir? We should not be "cast
            down with overmuch sorrow."[5]

FARMER: Oh, Sir! My son! My son!

LOVEGOOD: What then, is poor Henry dead?

FARMER: Dead, Sir? No, blessed be God. "This my son
            was dead, and is alive again."[6] He that was lost,
            and as I thought, forever lost, is found again, and
            I trust found in Christ. Oh, Sir! It so overcomes
            me that I think I never shall be able to outlive it.
            The Lord has not only saved me, a vile old sin-
            ner, and my daughter Nancy, but now, I trust, my

dear Harry is a saved soul. See, Sir, what a sweet letter he has sent to me. Here, Sir, take and read it, if you please, for I cannot read it again, it so affects me. It was above an hour before I could read it through.

LOVEGOOD: *[reads the letter]* "Island of Antigua. Dear and honored Father, it is now full four years since in a most wicked, disobedient, and rebellious state of mind, I left your house and entered as a captain's clerk on board the HMS *Rambler*. I confess you might have heard from me before, but I was ashamed to write. Whenever I thought of it, guilt flew in my face, while I considered how kindly you treated me as your only son. You gave me the best education in your power, and I am sure you did it out of pure love and to the best of your judgment. But in that school, my dearest Father, I met with those who first secretly led me into sin. Even when a schoolboy, none but God knows the wicked devices of my heart.

"I look upon my abominable and cruel conduct to you and my dear Mother with perpetual abhorrence and grief. I pray you both a thousand times to forgive me, as I now trust that, vile as I have been, I myself am forgiven of God. I shall forever bless God if I find you both alive, should I return to my native shore, for again and again have I done enough to bring your gray hairs with sorrow to the grave.

"O my dear parents! I want now only to live, that I may impart to you how I have been converted from my vile ways and have been constrained to live to God. You may rely upon it, while I am enabled to depend on Him, that I shall never grieve your dear hearts any more.

"About three or four years before I went to sea there was much talk about a Mr. Lovegood, who was presented to the living of Lower Brookfield, and was much ridiculed for his religious zeal. I remember we all, especially my sisters, used to join in the general laugh against him. My Father, do for your own soul's sake, for the Lord Jesus

Christ's sake, go and hear him." (Here Mr. Love-good was so affected that he joined with the Farmer and wept. After several attempts he continued the letter.)

"I should be glad, if I had time to write half a volume, to tell you all the most merciful steps in judgment, Providence, and grace that have brought my vile heart to repent and return to God; but the packet is likely to sail every hour which will take this to England. It is supposed in about a fortnight afterward our little fleet will sail for Portsmouth, so that within a month or five weeks after you receive this, you may expect to see your most undutiful and ungrateful child upon his knees before you. And though I shall bring home but a very scanty share of prize money, yet if I can but bring to my dear parents the inestimable prize of the knowledge of Christ, that pearl of great price, how joyful shall I be!

"I hope I shall in a measure earn my daily bread by applying myself diligently to the business of your farm as soon as I shall have my discharge, which is promised me on account of the wound I received in my hip, by a splinter from the ship in an engagement with the enemy. I had nearly been sent to stand before the tribunal of my God, yet I bless God for His most merciful correction; for if I had not been severely wounded, and afterward brought to the gates of death by a fever which attended it, I might have continued the same thoughtless and wicked wretch. I was made willing to attend to the affectionate advice and prayers of some few who are Christians in this floating hell. Though before I could, with others, ridicule them, yet in the time of my danger, when I felt the terrors of the Lord upon my soul, I was made willing to attend to that voice of tender mercy they administered to my desponding heart.

"Since I have been on this island, God has wonderfully preserved my health amidst an abundance of sickness. As soon as I landed I sought after those who knew the converting grace of our Lord Jesus Christ, and found it among the people called Moravians, who came over to this island to instruct the poor Negroes in Christianity. I cannot express with what tenderness and love they carried it toward me. It is wonderful whenever they saw me downcast, how they recommended me to the dying love of the Lord Jesus Christ, that my poor sinful soul might be comforted in Him. I love those good people to the bottom of my heart, and shall love them to the day of my death.

"Present my affectionate love to my sisters; and as we have often joined together in sin, so may we live to pray together. I grieve, dear Father, to think how ignorant we all were before I went to sea, and I write with many tears, while I acknowledge with shame and grief what a sinner I once was. But now I can bless His dear Name, who so mercifully melted down my hardened heart, and changed my polluted nature, so that I can from the bottom of my soul subscribe myself

Your most dutiful
and affectionate son,
Henry Littleworth."

LOVEGOOD: My dear friend, I enter into all the joys you feel and can sympathize with you, knowing how much you need divine support, though the event be so blessed and glorious.

FARMER: Oh, Sir! How can I stand it? And my poor wife was almost as overcome as myself. She says she will never speak against religion any more, since it has done our dear Harry so much good. And if the conversion of my dear child does bring about the salvation of my dear wife and daughters, we shall have quite a heaven upon earth. The hundreds of prayers I have put up for my son since I have been taught to pray for myself! And now I trust they are all answered.

LOVEGOOD: Well, Sir, hope and trust, for nothing is too hard for the Lord. But do you not admire what the grace of God truly is, in that broken and humble spirit the Lord has given to your son?

FARMER: And don't you think that my dear Harry is a partaker of that grace? And that I have also felt something of the same change upon my poor old sinful heart?

LOVEGOOD: Yes, Mr. Littleworth, it is truly glorious—as in your son, so on all the hearts of all wherein the converting grace of God is felt. Sin, however strongly rooted in our corrupted natures, must give way to the omnipotent agency of God's Holy Spirit.

FARMER: And oh! what a wicked blade he was before he went to sea. After he got linked in with Tom Wild, Will Frolic, Sam Blood, and that set, there was no keeping him at home. He would watch every opportunity to be away, and then I should hear of him driving about to every horse race and fair within twenty miles around. One time I would hear that he had been fighting, then that he had been gambling. Twice was he before the Justice for his drunken frolics, and night after night my Dame and I have sat up for him. Sometimes he would be out all the night, and at other times he would come home at twelve or one o'clock, sulky, ill-natured, and half-drunk. And all this was my own doings, for I was foolish enough to send him to that school where there was nothing of the fear of God. Afterward I took him to all sorts of romancing nonsense, such as plays and puppet shows, by way of diverting him, and that led him into company which brought on his ruin.

LOVEGOOD: Yes, Sir, but now a very different scene is before you. Your son, I humbly trust, is "born from above."[7] His hands will no longer be lifted up to strike the angry blow of inward murder and revenge. He will learn to labor as Providence shall direct him. His tongue will no more be employed in the service of folly, blasphemy, and filthy conversation. His conversation will be as becomes the gospel of Christ. Instead of finding him a sulky, ill-natured sot, you will find him sober, temperate in all things, loving and gentle, and easy to be entreated. The lion is already turned into the lamb, and the disposition of the tiger and the bear shall prevail no more. His feet will need no fetters to keep them out of those paths in which he once ran with such eager haste. They will rejoice to walk with you to the house of God, to hear the glad tidings of salvation. No other house like that will his feet now so delight to tread.

FARMER: It quite melts me down. What joy of heart shall I feel the first time he and I shall walk together to your church. Dear child! How grieved I am for the harm I have done to his precious soul. Well, I'll confess it to him with shame, and tell him the fault was mostly mine.

LOVEGOOD: It may be better if neither of you dwell too much on these things. They were done in the "times of ignorance God winked at."[8] You are both, I trust, now arrived in the new world of grace, and your business will be to press forward with him to the eternal world of glory.

SERVANT: Sir, Thomas Newman has brought Mr. Littleworth's horse.

LOVEGOOD: Tell Thomas to put the horse in my stable, and come in and refresh himself.

FARMER: Oh, no, Sir. I thank you, I'll be getting home. I left my wife all in tears, but they were tears of joy. She is mighty fond of Thomas, though she does not like his religion, and always has victuals enough when he comes to our house. It was Thomas' good life that made me think so well of your good sermons.

[Mr. Lovegood goes with Farmer Littleworth to see him mounted, and inquires after Thomas' family. Then:]

LOVEGOOD: Have you heard, Thomas, that Master Harry is coming back from sea?

THOMAS: Why, Sir, I heard that just before I came down,

and that my Master had been most desperately affected at the news. Lord grant he may be brought home, so that he may be brought to God!

FARMER: Oh, Thomas, that is done already! Praise the Lord.

THOMAS: What, has Master Harry felt the converting grace of God?

FARMER: *[Weeps and wipes his eyes.]* I'll tell you as I ride along.

LOVEGOOD: Well, Mr. Littleworth, the Lord bless and support you.

FARMER: And you too, Sir, a thousand times, for the good you have done to my immortal soul. *[To Thomas.]* Oh, Thomas, you will be all amazement to hear how broken and humble and contrite my dear child writes.

THOMAS: Master, that is a blessed sign. Once we are made to hate sin, we may be sure there is a divine change. The Lord be praised if Master Harry has been saved from his wicked state, for wild and wicked for sure he was. But, Master, if you and I but think what we once were, we need not despair of any.

FARMER: But Harry has no notion how the Lord has converted the heart of such a poor old sinner as I have been.

THOMAS: Had we not better contrive to tell him that beforehand?

FARMER: That we have contrived already, and you are to go and meet him at Mapleton, and Mr. Lovegood is to come and sup with us. What a blessed meeting it will be!

THOMAS: But, Master, if I may be so bold, how came it all about?

FARMER: Here, Thomas, *[lending him the letter]* you shall take this home with you, and you and Betty may read it together; but be sure and take care of it, for I value it more than untold gold. I shall count the days till my dear son comes home. And after supper, Mr. Lovegood will give us family prayer, for I am determined in my poor fashion to keep it up. Mr. Lovegood says he will make a hymn on purpose upon the prodigal's return, and a brave hymn I'll warrant it will be. Thomas, you must be there to pitch the tune; and Mr. Lovegood says you shall be clerk at church next, if anything happens to old Andrew Snuffle.

THOMAS: How shall I feel if ever our minister should make such a poor, simple creature clerk of our parish? To be sure it would be a wonderful help to me and my dear Betty, to bring up our children. But I am sadly afraid Mr. Lovegood will not be long minister of our parish.

FARMER: The Lord forbid! But why should you think so, Thomas?

THOMAS: Why, I am told our Squire is to go next winter to London, to put one of his sons in some place of learning. I hope he won't stay long, for all the poor people in our village are in a sad taking when he is away. But I am afraid if he were to tell the Lord Chancellor what a wonderful man our minister is, the King (God bless him) will soon make him Lord Archbishop of Canterbury.

NOTES

1. Cf. Philippians 4:6.
2. "Mind your hits" seems to mean, as we would say, "Watch your P's and Q's."
3. Cf. Proverbs 3:17.
4. 2 Corinthians 4:5.
5. Cf. 2 Corinthians 2:7.
6. Cf. Luke 15:32.
7. John 3:3.
8. Acts 17:30.

Jonathan Edwards

Jonathan Edwards (1703-1758) was profoundly esteemed, deeply beloved, and cordially hated in his lifetime as perhaps no other American of his day. More than two centuries later the same feelings persist; little has changed. The paradoxical issue of freewill vs. determinism, on which he took such a strong stand, remains unsettled and shrouded in mystery. Who, except God, knows the answer? Dr. Johnson's remark is still apposite: "All theory is against the freedom of the will, all experience for it."

Few today can challenge the intellectual stature of the New Englander who led the Great Awakening of 1735. Perry Miller, the late Harvard scholar who can hardly be considered in the Puritan camp, has described Edwards as "the greatest philosopher-theologian yet to grace the American scene." But the discernment, or lack of it, that the man showed during the revival that swept through his Northampton congregation is still a topic of fierce discussion. His rigid Calvinistic viewpoint has alienated all but a tiny segment of the contemporary church. Edwards will always be respected for his faith, but not many are turning to him for spiritual help.

Edwards' own account of what happened in his town during the Awakening suggests that he was a better man than his theology. Again and again he bent his views in shepherding his flock. Not until fourteen years later did he harden his position regarding the presence of unconverted persons at the Lord's Table, thereby sealing his own fate in Northampton. The very ones he had led to Christ ousted him from his pulpit and forbade him to preach in the town. Edwards, it seemed, had overlooked a cardinal Christian doctrine: "faith worketh by love" (Galatians 5:6).

Jonathan Edwards was born into a Connecticut minister's family, and was writing a tract on "the nature of the soul" by the time he was ten years old. He entered Yale College at age thirteen and graduated as valedictorian four years later. The call to Northampton's Congregational church came to him at age twenty-four, and shortly afterward he married Sarah Pierrepont, the seventeen-year-old daughter of one of *the founders of Yale. She was according to accounts an excellent woman, bearing him twelve children and presiding over a home known for its cheerfulness and hospitality.*

Northampton's church embraced one of the largest, wealthiest, and most cultured congregations in Massachusetts. Edwards brought to it not only a distinguished background of lineage and scholarship, but also a deepening of his own spiritual life which had taken place during his Yale years. Later he was to compose many famous treatises on Freedom of the Will, Original Sin, the Religious Affections, etc. His theological writings, however, lack the personal quality found in the "Faithful Narrative of the Surprising Works of God," which reflects somewhat the kind of man he really was.

Some of Edwards' best-known work was done after he left Northampton to minister to Indians and whites in the frontier town of Stockbridge. In 1757 he was elected president of the College of New Jersey, which is now Princeton University. He entered upon his duties in January 1758, but two months later succumbed to a smallpox inoculation. Writes Paul Elmer More: "In his service to a particular dogma, Edwards threw away the opportunity of making for himself one of the very great names in literature." Perhaps. But if it were a choice between revival and a great name, there is little doubt which Edwards would have chosen.

These excerpts from the "Faithful Narrative" are taken from the 1834 edition of The Works of Jonathan Edwards with a Memoir by Sereno E. Dwight, *Vol. 1, revised and corrected by Edward Hickman and published in Bungay, England.*

A Faithful Narrative of the Surprising Work of God in Northampton
by Jonathan Edwards

The people of the country [around Northampton], in general I suppose, are as sober, orderly and good sort of people as in any part of New England; and I believe they have been preserved the freest by far of any part of the country from error and variety of sects and opinions. Our being so far within the land, at a distance from seaports and in a corner of the country, has doubtless been one reason why we have not been so much corrupted with vice as most other parts. Being much separated from other parts of the province, we have always managed our ecclesiastical affairs within ourselves. But without question the religion and good order of the county, and purity in doctrine, has under God been very much owing to the great abilities and eminent piety of my venerable and honored grandfather Stoddard [minister of the Congregational church of Northampton].

The town of Northampton is of about eighty-two years' standing, and has now about two hundred families, which mostly dwell more compactly together than any town of such a size in these parts. Take the town in general, and so far as I can judge they are as rational and intelligent a people as most I have been acquainted with. Many of them have been noted for religion, and particularly for their distinct knowledge in things that relate to heart religion and Christian experience.

The Rev. Mr. Stoddard continued in the work of the ministry here near sixty years. He was blessed from the beginning with extraordinary success in his ministry in the conversion of many souls. I was settled with him in the ministry [as his assistant] about two years before his death in 1728, and I have reason to bless God for the great advantage I had by it. But there was nothing of any general awakening [in the community]. Just after my grandfather's death it seemed to be a time of extraordinary dullness in religion. Licentiousness for some years greatly prevailed among the youth of the town. They were many of them very much addicted to night-walking and frequenting the tavern, and lewd practices wherein some, by their example, exceedingly corrupted others.

It was their manner very frequently to get together in conventions of both sexes for mirth and jollity, which they called frolics; and they would often spend the greater part of the night in them, without regard to any order in the families they belonged to. Indeed, family government did too much fail in the town. It was becoming very customary with many of our young people to be indecent in their carriage at meeting. There had also long prevailed in the town a spirit of contention between two parties, into which they had for many years been divided, and were prepared to oppose one another in all public affairs.

But in two or three years after Mr. Stoddard's death there began to be a sensible amendment of these evils. At the latter end of 1733 there appeared a very unusual flexibleness and yielding to advice in our young people. It had been too long their manner to make the evening after the Sabbath, and after our public lecture, to be especially the times of their mirth and company-keeping. The young people declared themselves convinced by what they had heard from the pulpit, and were willing of themselves to comply with the counsel that had been given; and there was a thorough reformation of these disorders thenceforward, which has continued ever since.[1]

In the April following, *anno* 1734, there happened a very sudden and awful death of a young man in the bloom of his youth. Being violently seized with a pleurisy, and taken immediately very delirious, [he] died in about two days. This (together with what was preached publicly on that occasion) much affected many young people. This was followed with another death of a young married woman who had been considerably exercised in mind about the salvation of her soul before she was ill; but seemed to have satisfying evidences of God's saving mercy before her death. She died very full of comfort, in a most earnest and moving manner warning and counseling others. This seemed to contribute to render solemn the spirits of many young persons;

and there began evidently to appear more of a religious concern on people's minds.

In the fall of the year I proposed it to the young people that they should agree among themselves to spend the evenings after lectures in social religion, and to that end divide themselves into several companies to meet in various parts of the town. This was accordingly done, and those meetings have been since continued.

About this time began the great noise in this part of the country about Arminianism,[2] which seemed to appear with a very threatening aspect upon the interest of religion here. The friends of vital piety trembled for fear of the issue; but it seemed, contrary to their fear, strongly to be overruled for the promoting of religion. Many who looked on themselves as in a Christless condition seemed to be awakened by it.

And then it was, in the latter part of December, that the Spirit of God began extraordinarily to set in, and wonderfully to work amongst us. There were, very suddenly, one after another, five or six persons who were to all appearance savingly converted, and some of them wrought upon in a very remarkable manner. Particularly, I was surprised with the relation of a young woman who had been one of the greatest company-keepers in the whole town. When she came to me, I had never heard that she was become in any wise serious, but by the conversation I then had with her it appeared to me that what she gave an account of was a glorious work of God's infinite power and sovereign grace. God had given her a new heart, truly broken and sanctified. I could not then doubt of it, and have seen much in my acquaintance with her since to confirm it.

Though the work was glorious, yet I was filled with concern about the effect it might have upon others. I was ready to conclude (though too rashly) that some would be hardened by it. But the event was the reverse, to a wonderful degree. God made it, I suppose, the greatest occasion of awakening to others of anything that ever came to pass in the town. I have had abundant opportunity to know the effect it had, by my private conversation with many. The news of it seemed to be almost like a flash of lightning upon the hearts of young people all over the town, and upon many others. Those amongst us who used to be the farthest from seriousness, and that I most feared would make an ill improvement of it, seemed greatly to be awakened with it. Many went to talk with her concerning what she had met with; and

what appeared in her seemed to be to the satisfaction of all that
did so.

Presently upon this, a great and earnest concern about the
great things of religion and the eternal world became universal in
all parts of the town, and among persons of all degrees and all
ages. The noise amongst the dry bones waxed louder and louder.
All other talk but about spiritual and eternal things was soon
thrown by. All the conversation, in all companies and upon all
occasions, was upon these things only, unless so much as was
necessary for people carrying on their ordinary secular business.
The minds of people were wonderfully taken off from the world.
It was treated amongst us as a thing of very little consequence.
The temptation now seemed to lie on that hand, to neglect
worldly affairs too much, and to spend too much time in the
immediate exercise of religion. This was misrepresented by re-
ports that were spread in distant parts of the land, as though the
people here had wholly thrown by all worldly business, and
betook themselves entirely to reading and praying, and such-like
religious exercises.

But although people did not ordinarily neglect their worldly
business, yet religion was with all sorts the great concern, and the
world was a thing only by-the-bye. The only thing in their view
was to get the Kingdom of Heaven, and everyone appeared pressing into it. The engagedness of their hearts in this great concern
could not be hid; it appeared in their very countenances. It then
was a dreadful thing amongst us to lie out of Christ. What persons' minds were intent upon was to escape for their lives and to
fly from wrath to come. All would eagerly lay hold of opportunities for their souls, and were wont very often to meet together in
private houses for religious purposes; and such meetings when
appointed were greatly thronged.

There was scarcely a single person in the town, old or
young, left unconcerned about the great things of the eternal
world. Those who were wont to be the vainest and loosest, and
had been most disposed to think and speak slightly of vital and
experimental religion, were now generally subject to great awakenings. The work of conversion was carried on in a most astonishing manner, and increased more and more. Souls did as it
were come by flocks to Jesus Christ. From day to day, for many
months together, might be seen evident instances of sinners
brought out of darkness into marvelous light, with a new song of
praise to God in their mouths.

The work of God, as it was carried on, and the number of true saints multiplied, soon made a glorious alteration in the town, so that in the spring and summer following, *anno* 1735, the town seemed full of the presence of God; it never was so full of love, nor of joy, and yet so full of distress, as it was then. There were remarkable tokens of God's presence in almost every house. It was a time of joy in families on account of salvation being brought to them: parents rejoicing over their children as newborn, and husbands over their wives, and wives over their husbands.

The goings of God were seen in His sanctuary. God's day was a delight, and his tabernacles were amiable. Our public assemblies then were beautiful. The congregation was alive in God's service, everyone earnestly intent on the public worship, every hearer eager to drink in the words of the minister. The assembly were from time to time in tears while the Word was preached: some weeping with sorrow and distress, others with joy and love, others with pity and concern for the souls of their neighbors.

Our public praises were then greatly enlivened. Our congregation excelled all that ever I knew in the external part of the duty, before [the awakening], the men generally carrying three parts of music regularly and well, and the women a part of themselves. But now they were evidently wont to sing with unusual elevation of heart and voice, which made the duty pleasant indeed.

On whatever occasion persons met together, Christ was to be heard of and seen in the midst of them. Our young people, when they met, were wont to spend their time in talking of the excellency and dying love of Jesus Christ, the glory of the way of salvation, the wonderful, free, and sovereign grace of God, His glorious work in the conversion of a soul, the truth and certainty of the great things of God's Word. Even at weddings, which formerly were mere occasions of mirth and jollity, there was now no appearance of any but spiritual mirth. Many who before had labored under difficulties about their own state, had now their doubts removed by more satisfying experience, and more clear discoveries of God's love, [being] renewed with fresh and extra ordinary incomes of the Spirit of God; though some much more than others, according to the measure of the gift of Christ.

We have about 620 communicants, which include almost all our adult persons. The church was very large before, but persons never thronged into it as they did in the late extraordinary time. Our sacraments are eight weeks asunder [that is, Holy Communion was observed every eight weeks, at which time baptisms were performed], and I received into our communion about a hundred before one sacrament, fourscore of them at one time. [Their] appearance, when they presented themselves together to make an open, explicit profession of Christianity, was very affecting to the congregation. I took in near sixty before the next sacrament day; and I had very sufficient evidence of the conversion of their souls through divine grace, though it is not the custom here, as it is in many other churches in this country, to make a credible relation of their inward experiences the ground of admission to the Lord's Supper.[3]

I am far from pretending to be able to determine how many have lately been the subjects of such mercy; but if I may be allowed to declare anything that appears to me probable in a thing of this nature, I hope that more than three hundred souls were savingly brought home to Christ in this town, in the space of half a year, and about the same number of males as females. This has also appeared to be a very extraordinary dispensation, in that the Spirit of God has so much extended not only His awakening, but regenerating influences, both to elderly persons and also to those who are very young. It has been heretofore rarely heard of that any were converted past middle age; but now we have ground to think that many such have at this time been savingly changed, and that others have been so in more early years.

When this work first appeared and was so extraordinarily carried on amongst us in the winter, others round about us seemed not to know what to make of it. Many scoffed at and ridiculed it, and some compared what we called conversion to certain distempers. But it was very observable of many who occasionally came amongst us from abroad with disregardful hearts, that what they saw here cured them of such a temper of mind. Strangers were generally surprised to find things so much beyond what they had heard, and were wont to tell others that the state of the town could not be conceived of by those who had not seen it.

The notice that was taken of it by the people who came to town on occasion of the court that sat here in the beginning of March was very observable. And those who came from the neighborhood to our public lectures were for the most part remarkably affected. Many who came to town on one occasion or other had their consciences smitten, and awakened. They went home with wounded hearts, and with those impressions that never wore off till they had hopefully a saving issue. Those who before had serious thoughts had their awakenings and convictions greatly increased. There were many instances of persons who had not been here long, before to all appearance they were savingly wrought upon, and partook of that shower of divine blessing which God rained down here, and went home rejoicing. At length the same work began evidently to appear and prevail in several other towns in the county.

In the month of March the people in South Hadley[4] began to be seized with deep concern about the things of religion, which soon became universal. The work of God has been very wonderful there—not much, if anything, short of what it has been here, in proportion to the size of the place. About the same time it began to break forth in the west part of Suffield, where it also has been very great; and it soon spread into all parts of the town. It next appeared at Sunderland, and soon overspread the town, and was for a season, I believe, not less remarkable than it was here. About the same time it began to appear in a part of Deerfield called Green River, and afterwards filled the town, and there has been a glorious work there. It began also to be manifest in the south part of Hatfield, in a place called the Hill. In the second week in April the whole town seemed to be seized, as it were at once, with concern about the things of religion; and the work of God has been great there.

There has also been a very general awakening at West Springfield and Long Meadow; and at Enfield there was for a time a pretty general concern amongst some who before had been very loose persons. About the same time that this appeared at Enfield, the Rev. Mr. Bull, of Westfield, informed me that there had been a great alteration there, and that more had been done in one week than in seven years before. Something of this work likewise appeared in the first precinct in Springfield, principally in the north and south extremes of the parish. And in Hadley old town there gradually appeared so much of a work of God on souls, as at another time would have been thought worthy of much notice.

For a short time there was also a very great and general concern of the like nature at Northfield. And wherever this concern appeared, it seemed not to be in vain; but in every place God brought saving blessings with Him, and His Word, attended with His Spirit (as we have all reason to think), returned not void.

As what other towns in the county heard of and found in this was a means of awakening them, so our hearing of such a swift and extraordinary propagation and extent of this work did doubtless for a time serve to uphold the work amongst us. The continual news did greatly quicken and rejoice the hearts of God's people, and much awakened those who looked on themselves as still left behind, and made them the more earnest that they also might share in the great blessings that others had obtained.

This remarkable pouring out of the Spirit of God, which thus extended from one end to the other of this county, was not confined to it, but many places in Connecticut have [also] partaken in the same mercy. For instance, the first parish in Windsor, under the pastoral care of the Rev. Mr. Marsh, was thus blest about the same time as we in Northampton, while we had no knowledge of each other's circumstances. There has been a very great ingathering of souls to Christ in that place, and something considerable of the same work begun afterwards in East Windsor.

But this shower of divine blessing has been yet more extensive. There was no small degree of it in some part of the Jerseys, as I was informed when I was at New York by some people of the Jerseys whom I saw. Especially the Rev. William Tennent told me of a very great awakening of many in a place called The Mountains; and of a very considerable revival of religion in another place under the ministry of his brother, the Rev. Gilbert Tennent; and also at another place under the ministry of a very pious young gentleman, a Dutch minister whose name as I remember was Freelinghousa.[5]

This seems to have been a very extraordinary dispensation of Providence. God has in many respects gone out of and much beyond His usual and ordinary way. The work in this town, and some others about us, has been extraordinary on account of the universality of it, affecting all sorts, sober and vicious, high and low, rich and poor, wise and unwise. It reached the most considerable families and persons, to all appearance, as much as others. In former stirrings of this nature, the bulk of the young people have been greatly affected; but old men and little children have been so now. Many of the [latter] have, of their own accord, formed themselves into religious societies in different parts of the town. A loose, careless person could scarcely be found in the whole neighborhood; and if there was anyone that seemed to remain senseless or unconcerned, it would be spoken of as a strange thing. I hope that by far the greater part of persons in this town above sixteen years of age are such as have the saving knowledge of Jesus Christ. By what I have heard I suppose it is so in some other places, particularly at Sunderland and South Hadley.

This has also appeared to be a very extraordinary dispensation, in that the Spirit of God has so much extended not only His awakening, but regenerating influences, both to elderly persons and also to those who are very young. It has been heretofore rarely heard of, that any were converted past middle age; but now we have the same ground to think that many such have at this time been savingly changed, as that others have been so in more early years. I suppose there were upwards of fifty persons converted in this town above forty years of age; more than twenty of them above fifty, and ten of them above sixty; and two of them above seventy years of age.

It has heretofore been looked upon as a strange thing when any have seemed to be savingly wrought upon and remarkably changed in their childhood. But now, I suppose, near thirty were, to appearance, savingly wrought upon between ten and fourteen years of age; two between nine and ten, and one of about four years of age. The influences of God's Holy Spirit have also been very remarkable on children in some other places, particularly at Sunderland, South Hadley, and the west part of Suffield. There are several families in this town who are all hopefully pious.[6] Yea, there are several numerous families in which, I think, we have reason to hope that all the children are truly godly, and most of them lately become so. There are very few houses in the whole town, into which salvation has not lately come, in one or more instances. There are several Negroes who, from what was seen in them then, and what is discernible in them since, appear to have been truly born again in the late remarkable season.

God has also seemed to have gone out of His usual way in the quickness of His work, and the swift progress His Spirit has made in His operations on the hearts of many. It is wonderful that persons should be so suddenly and yet so greatly changed. Many have been taken from a loose and careless way of living, and seized with strong convictions of their guilt and misery, and in a very little time old things have passed away, and all things have become new with them.

This work seemed to be at its greatest height in this town in the former part of the spring, in March and April. At that time God's work in the conversion of souls was carried on amongst us in so wonderful a manner that, so far as I can judge, it appears to have been at the rate, at least, of four persons in a day, or near thirty in a week, take one with another, for five or six weeks together. When God in so remarkable a manner took the work into His own hands, there was as much done in a day or two as at ordinary times (with all endeavors that men can use, and with such a blessing as we commonly have) is done in a year.

I am very sensible how apt many would be, if they should see the account I have here given, presently to think within themselves that I am very fond of making a great many converts, and of magnifying the matter; and to [imagine] that for want of judgment, I take every religious pang and enthusiastic conceit for saving conversion. For this reason I have forborne to publish an account of this great work of God, though I have often been solicited. But having now a special call to give an account of it, upon mature consideration I thought it might not be beside my duty to declare this amazing work, as it appeared to me to be indeed divine, and to conceal no part of the glory of it; leaving it with God to take care of the credit of His own work.

These awakenings, when they have first seized on persons, have had two effects. One was, that they have brought them immediately to quit their sinful practices. The looser sort [of people] have been brought to forsake and dread their former vices and extravagances. When once the Spirit of God began to be so wonderfully poured out in a general way through the town, people had soon done with their old quarrels, backbitings, and intermeddling with other men's matters. The tavern was soon left empty, and persons kept very much at home. None went abroad unless on necessary business, or on some religious account, and every day seemed like a Sabbath-day.

The other effect was, that it put them on earnest application to the means of salvation, reading, prayer, meditation, the ordinances of God's house, and private conference. Their cry was, "What shall we do to be saved?" The minister's house was thronged far more than ever the tavern had been wont to be.

In this town there has always been a great deal of talk about conversion and spiritual experiences. People in general had formed a notion in their own minds what these things were. But when they come to be the *subjects* of them, they find themselves much confounded in their notions, and overthrown in many of their former conceits. And it has been very observable that persons of the greatest understanding, and who had studied most about things of this nature, have been more confounded than others. Some such persons declare that all their former wisdom is brought to nought, and that they appear to have been mere babes who knew nothing. It seems to have been with delight that they have seen themselves thus brought down, and become nothing, that free grace and divine power may be exalted in them.

It was very wonderful to see how persons' affections were sometimes moved—when God did as it were suddenly open their eyes, and let into their minds a sense of the greatness of His grace, the fullness of Christ, and His readiness to save—after having been broken with apprehensions of divine wrath, and sunk into an abyss, under a sense of guilt which they were ready to think was beyond the mercy of God. Their joyful surprise has caused their hearts as it were to leap, so that they have been ready to break forth into laughter, tears often at the same time issuing like a flood, and intermingling a loud weeping. Sometimes they have not been able to forbear crying out with a loud voice, expressing their great admiration.

I have been much blamed and censured by many, that I should make it my practice, when I have been satisfied concerning persons' good estate [in the sight of God], to signify it to them. This has been greatly misrepresented abroad; as innumerable other things concerning us, to prejudice the country against the whole affair. Let it be noted that what I have undertaken to judge of has rather been qualifications and declared experiences, rather than persons. Yet I should count it a great calamity to be deprived of the comfort of rejoicing with those of my flock who have been in great distress, whose circumstances I have been acquainted with, when there seems to be good evidence that those who were dead are alive, and that those who were lost are found.

There is no one thing that I know of which God has made such a means of promoting His work amongst us, as the news of others' conversion. This has been owned in awakening sinners, engaging them earnestly to seek the same blessing, and in quickening saints. Conversion is a great and glorious work of God's power, at once changing the heart, and infusing life into the dead soul, though the grace then implanted displays itself more gradually in some than in others. There are very many who do not know, even when they have it, that it is the grace of conversion, and sometimes do not think it to be so till a long time after. The manner of God's work on the soul is very mysterious.

Persons after their conversion often speak of religious things as seeming new to them; that preaching is a new thing; that it seems to them they never heard preaching before; that the Bible is a new book; they find there new chapters, new psalms, new histories, because they see them in a new light. Many have spoken much of their hearts being drawn out in love to God and Christ. I have seen some, and conversed with them, who have certainly been perfectly sober, and very remote from anything like enthusiastic wildness. And they have talked of the glory of God's perfections, the wonderfulness of His grace in Christ, and their own unworthiness, in such a manner as cannot be perfectly expressed after them.

Many, while their minds have been filled with spiritual delights, have as it were forgot their food. Their bodily appetite has failed, while their minds have been entertained with "meat to eat that others knew not of."[7] The light and comfort which some of them enjoy give a new relish to their common blessings, and cause all things about them to appear as it were beautiful, sweet, and pleasant. All things abroad, the sun, moon, and stars, the clouds and sky, the heavens and earth, appear as it were with a cast of divine glory and sweetness upon them.

Some speak much of the exquisite sweetness and rest of soul that is to be found in the exercise of resignation to God, and humble submission to His will. Many express earnest longings of soul to praise God, but at the same time complain that they cannot praise Him as they would, and they want to have others help them in praising Him. They want to have everyone praise God, and are ready to call upon everything to praise Him. They express a longing desire to live to God's glory, and to do something to His honor; but at the same time complain of their insufficiency and barrenness.

While God was so remarkably present amongst us by His Spirit, there was no book so delightful as the Bible; especially the Book of Psalms, the Prophecy of Isaiah, and the New Testament. Some, by reason of their love to God's Word, have been wonderfully delighted and affected at times at the sight of a Bible. Also, there was no time so prized as the Lord's Day, and no place in this world so desired as God's house. Our converts then remarkably appeared united in dear affection to one another, and many have expressed much of that spirit of love which they felt toward all mankind, and particularly to those who had been least friendly to them.

Never, I believe, was so much done in confessing injuries, and making up differences, as the last year. After their own conversion, persons have commonly expressed an exceeding great desire for the conversion of others. Some have thought that they should be willing to die for the conversion of any soul; and many have, indeed, been in great distress with desires and longings for it. This work of God had also a good effect to unite the people's affections much to their minister.

There is a vast difference, as observed, in the degree, and also in the particular manner, of persons' experiences, both at and after conversion. Some have grace working more sensibly in one way, others in another. But it seems evidently to be the same work, the same habitual change wrought in the heart. It all tends the same way and to the same end; and it is plainly the same Spirit that breathes and acts in various persons. There is an endless variety in the particular manner and circumstances in which persons are wrought on. God is further from confining Himself to a particular method in His work on souls, than some imagine.

I believe it has occasioned some good people amongst us, who were before too ready to make their own experience a rule to others, to be less censorious and more extended in their charity; and this is an excellent advantage indeed. The work of God has been glorious in its variety. It has the more displayed the manifold and unsearchable wisdom of God, and wrought more charity among His people.

It is easily perceived by the foregoing account, that it is very much the practice of the people here to converse freely with one another about their spiritual experiences—which many have been disgusted at. But however our people may have in some respects gone to extremes in it, it is doubtless a practice that the circumstances of this town and neighboring towns have naturally led them into. And it has been a practice which, in the general, has been attended with many good effects, and what God has greatly blessed amongst us. But it must be confessed that there may have been some ill consequences of it; which yet are rather to be laid to in indiscreet management of it, than to the practice itself.

In the former part of this great work of God amongst us, till it got to its height, we seemed to be wonderfully smiled upon and

blessed in all respects. Satan seemed to be unusually restrained.
Persons who before had been involved in melancholy, seemed to
be as it were waked up out of it; and those who had been
entangled with extraordinary temptations, seemed wonderfully
freed. And not only so, but it was the most remarkable time of
health that ever I knew since I have been in the town. We
ordinarily have several bills put up every Sabbath for sick persons; but now we had not so much as one for many Sabbaths
together. But after this it seemed to be otherwise.

In the latter part of May it began to be very sensible that the
Spirit of God was gradually withdrawing from us, and after this
time Satan seemed to be more let loose, and raged in a dreadful
manner. The first instance wherein it appeared, was a person
putting an end to his own life by cutting his throat. The news of
this extraordinarily affected the minds of people here, and struck
them as it were with astonishment. After this, multitudes in this
and other towns seemed to have it strongly suggested to them,
and pressed upon them, to do as this person had done. Many had
it urged upon them as if somebody had spoken to them, "Cut
your own throat, now is a good opportunity. Now! Now!" So that
they were obliged to fight with all their might to resist it, and yet
no reason suggested to them why they should do it.

About the same time there were two remarkable instances
of persons led away with strange enthusiastic delusions, one at
Suffield, and another at South Hadley. After these things, the
instances of conversion were rare here in comparison of what
they had before been. The Spirit of God appeared very sensibly
withdrawing from all parts of the country, though we have heard
of the work going on in some places of Connecticut, and that it
continues to be carried on even to this day.

But religion remained here, and I believe in some other
places, the main subject of conversation for several months after.
And there were some turns wherein God's work seemed to re-
vive; yet in the main, there was a gradual decline of that engaged,
lively spirit in religion which had been. Several things have
happened since, which have diverted people's minds, and turned
their conversation more to other affairs. Our people in this town
have been engaged in the building of a new meeting-house.

But as to those who have been thought converted at this
time, they generally seem to have had an abiding change
wrought on them. They generally appear to be persons who have
a new sense of things, new apprehensions and views of God, of

the divine attributes of Jesus Christ, and the great things of the gospel. They have a new sense of their truth, and they affect them in a new manner. Their hearts are often touched, and sometimes filled, with new sweetnesses and delights; there seems to express an inward ardor and burning of heart, like to which they never experienced before—sometimes, perhaps, occasioned only by the mention of Christ's name, or some one of the divine perfections. There are new appetites, and a new kind of breathings and pantings of heart, and groanings that cannot be uttered. There is a new kind of inward labor and struggle of soul towards Heaven and holiness.

Some who before were very rough in their temper and manners, seemed to be remarkably softened and sweetened. And some have had their souls exceedingly filled and overwhelmed with light, love, and comfort, long since the work of God has ceased to be so remarkably carried on in a general way; and some have had much greater experiences of this nature than they had before. There is still a great deal of religious conversation continued in the town amongst young and old. A religious disposition appears to be still maintained amongst our people by their holding frequent private religious meetings; and all sorts are generally worshiping God at such meetings on Sabbath-nights, and in the evening after our public lecture. Many children in the town still keep up such meetings among themselves. I know of no one young person in the town who has returned to former ways of looseness and extravagance in any respect; but we still remain a reformed people, and God has evidently made us a new people.

I cannot say that there has been no instance of any one person who has conducted himself unworthily; nor am I so vain as to imagine that we have not been mistaken in our good opinion concerning any; or that there are none who pass amongst us for sheep, that are indeed wolves in sheep's clothing; and who probably may, some time or other, discover [i.e., uncover] themselves by their fruits.

We are not so pure but that we have great cause to be humbled and ashamed that we are so impure; nor so religious, but that those who watch for our halting, may see things in us, whence they may take occasion to reproach us and religion. But in the main, there has been a great and marvelous work of conversion and sanctification among people here.

A great part of the country have not received the most favorable thoughts of this affair; and to this day many retain a jealousy concerning it, and prejudice against it. I have reason to think that the meanness and weakness of the instrument that has been made use of in this town, has prejudiced many against it; nor does it appear to me strange that it should be so.[8] But yet the circumstance of this great work of God is analogous to other circumstances of it. God has so ordered the manner of the work in many respects, as very signally and remarkably to show it to be His own peculiar and immediate work, and to secure the glory of it wholly to His own Almighty power and sovereign grace. And whatever the circumstances and means have been, and though we are so unworthy, yet so hath it pleased God to work! And we are evidently a people blessed of the Lord! For here, in this corner of the world, God dwells, and manifests His glory.

Northampton, November 6, 1736

NOTES

1. The time of writing, as Edwards indicates at the end of his narrative, was November 1736.
2. Arminian teaching contradicted the main doctrines of Calvinism, insisting that Christ died for all men, not just for the elect; and that it was possible for Christians to fall from grace and be lost, thus denying the tenet of divine predestination.
3. Edwards' insistence that only "visible" and converted Christians be admitted to the Lord's Supper was a later development in his thinking, and ultimately led to his dismissal from the Northampton pulpit in 1750.
4. South Hadley is located only a few miles from Northampton, on the east side of the Connecticut River in Massachusetts.
5. Edwards' memory served him fairly well. Theodore Jacobus Frelinghuysen (1691-1747) preached in the Raritan Valley area of New Jersey beginning in 1720, and was an instrument of revival in the Great Awakening, along with George Whitefield and Gilbert and William Tennent. Born in Holland, Frelinghuysen became a founder of the Dutch Reformed Church in America.
6. "Hopefully pious" is Calvinist argot for "converted to Christ."
7. Cf. John 4:32.
8. The "instrument" that Edwards refers to is himself.

David Brainerd

"And Melancholy mark'd him for her own."

Thomas Gray's line might well have been penned to describe David Brainerd (1718-1747), pioneer missionary to the American Indians. He begins his diary with the admission, "I was from my youth somewhat sober, and inclined rather to melancholy than the opposite extreme." And yet in just twenty-nine years of life and six years of ministry, this young man inspired millions of Christians to a deeper devotion to Jesus Christ, and sent hundreds of young people into the mission field. John Wesley was one of many who commended his writings.

When one adds to Brainerd's somber disposition a frail, sickly physique, the incredible hardships of travel beyond the frontier, the difficulties of communicating with primitive, unlettered tribes, and his continuing sense of failure and injustice resulting from his expulsion from Yale College, one can only marvel at the lasting effects of his lifework. Dr. Andrew Blackwood once said, "God can strike a powerful blow on a crooked stick." There is no doubt that God was at work in David Brainerd's life.

These excerpts, being taken both from his private diary and the public journal he wrote for his sponsors, are sufficient introduction to Brainerd's personality and missionary labors. They do indicate fully the mood swings that frequently plunged him into despondency even in the midst of success in his labors. (Jonathan Edwards, in whose house Brainerd died, perceptively discerned that his young colleague's "gloominess of mind" was "owing to the disease of melancholy" rather than to "spiritual desertion.") Nor do the excerpts convey adequately the loneliness Brainerd must have felt in his wilderness ministry, or the bodily discomforts that never left him, day or night.

But if Brainerd was melancholic, he was no misanthrope. The Indians to whom he ministered obviously loved him. At the time of his death he was engaged to marry one of President Edwards' daughters. Earlier he turned down calls to two fine churches which sought him as their pastor. The first was in Millington, Connecticut, and the second in East Hampton, Long Island, a prospering church in "the fairest, pleasantest town on the whole island." Brainerd sent his regrets in each case, knowing full well what a rugged life awaited him in his continuing work among the Indians. It's because he turned away from these comfortable parishes that we are now reading the story of his life.

A word should be said about the incident in his brief career that caused him the most grief: being expelled from Yale College. As Edwards tells it, the Awakening kindled by George Whitefield, Gilbert Tennent, and others in 1740 touched several in the Yale student body, including Brainerd. One day three or four young men were speaking together in the college hall, and Brainerd, a third-year student, was asked what he thought of a tutor who had just been praying with the students. The prayer, it seems, was on the ineffectual side, and Brainerd remarked, "He has no more grace than this chair." A freshman overheard him, repeated his remark to a woman in town, and she informed the rector of the college. Brainerd was ordered to make a public confession and humble himself before the whole college. Feeling himself ill-used, he refused. For this reason, and for attending a proscribed meeting, he was ordered to leave. Later efforts at reinstatement were turned down. It is to Brainerd's credit that he surmounted this blow and was eventually ordained to a remarkable gospel ministry.

These excerpts are taken from The Diary and Journal of David Brainerd, *two volumes, published for the Scottish Society for the Propagation of Christian Knowledge (Church of Scotland) by Andrew Melrose in London, 1902.*

From the
Diary of David Brainerd

I was, I think, from my youth, something sober, and inclined rather to melancholy than the contrary extreme; but do not remember anything of conviction of sin worthy of remark till I was, I believe, about seven or eight years of age. Then I became something concerned for my soul, and terrified at the thoughts of death. Alas! this religious concern was short-lived. I thus lived till I was above thirteen years of age. Sometime in the winter of 1732 I was roused out of carnal security by I scarce know what, but was much excited by the prevailing of a mortal sickness in Haddam. I was much melted in [religious] duties, and took great delight in the performance of them, and sometimes hoped that I was converted. I was also exceedingly distressed at the death of my mother in March.

In April 1733 I moved to East Haddam [Connecticut] where I spent four years. At nineteen years of age I moved to Durham and began to work on my farm and continued the year out, frequently longing after a liberal education. When I was about twenty I applied myself to study, and now engaged more than ever in the duties of religion. I became very strict and watchful over my thoughts, words and actions, and thought I must be sober indeed, because I designed to devote myself to the ministry. I read my Bible more than twice through in less than a year; I spent much time every day in secret prayer, and other secret duties; I gave great attention to the Word preached, and endeavored to my utmost to retain it. I agreed with some young persons to meet privately on Sabbath evenings for religious exercises, and had many thoughts of joining the church. In short, I had a very good outside, and rested entirely on my duties, though I was not sensible of it.

Sometime in the beginning of winter in 1738 it pleased God,

on one Sabbath-day morning, as I was walking out for some secret duties, to give me on a sudden such a sense of my danger, and the wrath of God, that I stood amazed. My former good frames [feelings] that I had pleased myself with all vanished. I was much dejected, and kept much alone, and sometimes begrudged the birds and beasts their happiness. The work of conversion appeared so great, I thought I should never be the subject of it. Though I hundreds of times renounced all pretenses of any worth in my [actions], yet still I had a secret latent hope of recommending myself to God by my religious duties.

At times the gate appeared so very strait that it looked next to impossible to enter; yet at other times I flattered myself that it was not so very difficult, and hoped that by diligence and watchfulness I should soon gain the point. Sometime in February I set apart a day for secret fasting and prayer, and spent the day in almost incessant cries to God for mercy. But still I trusted in all the duties I performed. Yet God was pleased to make my endeavors that day a means to show me in some measure my helplessness.

Sometimes I grew remiss and sluggish, without any great convictions of sin for a considerable time; but after such a season conviction sometimes seized me more violently. The many disappointments and great distresses and perplexity I met with, put me into a most horrible frame of contesting with the Almighty with virulence, finding fault with His ways of dealing with mankind. I found great fault with the imputation of Adam's sin to his posterity. My wicked heart often wished for some other way of salvation than by Jesus Christ. I had strange projections, full of atheism, contriving to disappoint God's designs and decrees concerning me.

While I was in this distressed, bewildered, and tumultuous state of mind, the corruption of my heart was especially irritated with the following:

First, the strictness of the divine law. I found it was impossible for me after my utmost pains to answer the demands of it.

Second, that faith alone was the condition of salvation. [I was annoyed] that God would not come down to lower terms, that He would not promise life and salvation upon my sincere and hearty prayers and endeavors. I could not bear that all I had done should stand for mere nothing, who had been very conscientious in duty and had been exceeding religious a great while, and had, as I thought, done much more than many others who had obtained mercy.

Third, I could not find out what faith was. I read the calls of Christ, and thought I would gladly come, if I knew how. I read Mr. Stoddard's "Guide to Christ," which I trust was, in the hand of God, the happy means of my conversion, but my heart rose against the author. For here he failed: he did not tell me anything I could do that would bring me to Christ. He left me as it were with a great gulf between me and Christ, without any direction to get through.

Fourth, I found a great inward opposition to the sovereignty of God. I dreaded more than ever to see myself in God's hands, and at His sovereign disposal. It was the sight of truth concerning myself, truth respecting my state as a creature fallen and alienated from God, and that consequently could make no demands on God for mercy, but must subscribe to the absolute sovereignty of the divine Being; the sight of the truth, I say, my soul shrank away from, and trembled to think of beholding.

One morning, while I was walking as usual in a solitary place, I at once saw that all my contrivances and projections to effect or procure deliverance and salvation for myself were utterly in vain. I was brought quite to a stand as finding myself totally lost. The tumult that had been before in my mind was now quieted, and I was something eased of that distress which I felt while struggling against a sight of myself and of the divine sovereignty. I had the greatest certainty that my state was forever miserable, for all that I could do. I wondered that I had never been sensible of it before.

In the time I remained in this state, my notions respecting my duties were quite different. Before this, the more I did in duty, the more I thought God was obliged to me. But now, the more I prayed, the more I saw I was indebted to God for allowing me to ask for mercy; for I saw it was self-interest that had led me to pray, and that I had never once prayed from any respect to the glory of God. I saw that I had been heaping up my devotions before God, fasting, praying, pretending; whereas I never once truly intended to aim at the glory of God, but only my own happiness. I saw that, as I had never done anything for God, I had no claim to lay to anything from Him.

I continued in this state of mind from Friday morning till the Sabbath evening following, July 12, 1739, when I was walking again in the same solitary place. In a mournful, melancholy state I was attempting to pray, but found no heart to engage in it. I thought the Spirit of God had quite left me, but still was not distressed; yet disconsolate as if there was nothing in Heaven or earth could make me happy. And thus I was, as I thought, very stupid and senseless, for nearly half an hour. I remember by this time the sun was about half an hour high.

Then, as I was walking in a dark thick grove, unspeakable glory seemed to open to the view and apprehension of my soul. I do not mean any external brightness, for I saw no such thing; nor do I intend any imagination of a body of light, somewhere away in the third heavens, or anything of that nature. But it was a new inward apprehension or view that I had of God, such as I never had before, nor anything which had the least resemblance of it. I stood still, and wondered, and admired. I knew that I never before had seen anything comparable to it for excellency and beauty. It was widely different from all the conceptions that ever I had of God or things divine.

I had no particular apprehension of any one Person in the Trinity, either the Father, the Son, or the Holy Spirit, but it appeared to be divine glory that I then beheld. My soul "rejoiced with joy unspeakable" to see such a God, such a glorious divine Being, and I was inwardly pleased and satisfied that He should be *God over all,* forever and ever. My soul was so captivated and delighted with the excellency, loveliness, greatness, and other perfections of God, that I was even swallowed up in Him, at least to the degree that I had no thought, as I remember at first, about my own salvation, and scarce reflected there was such a creature as myself.

Thus God, I trust, brought me to a hearty disposition to exalt Him and set Him on the throne, and principally and ultimately to aim at His honor and glory as King of the universe.

I continued in this state of inward joy and peace, yet astonishment, till near dark, without any sensible abatement, and then began to think and examine what I had seen; and felt sweetly composed in my mind all the evening following. I felt myself in a new world, and everything about me appeared with a different aspect from what it was wont to do.

At this time the way of salvation opened to me with such infinite wisdom, suitableness, and excellency, that I wondered I should ever think of any other way of salvation, and was amazed that I had not dropped my contrivances, and complied with this lovely, blessed, and excellent way before. If I could have been saved by my own duties, or any other way, my whole soul would now have refused. I wondered that all the world did not see and comply with this way of salvation, entirely by the righteousness of Christ.

In the beginning of September [1739] I went to [Yale] College, and entered there, but with some degree of reluctancy, fearing lest I should not be able to lead a life of strict religion in the midst of so many temptations. In the vacancy before I went to tarry at College, it pleased God to visit my soul with clearer manifestations of Himself and His grace. I was spending some time in prayer and self-examination, and the Lord by His grace so shined into my heart that I enjoyed full assurance of His favor for that time, and my soul was unspeakably refreshed with divine and heavenly enjoyments. At this time especially, sundry passages of God's Word opened to my soul with divine clearness, power, and sweetness, so as to appear exceeding precious, with clear and certain evidence of its being the Word of God. I enjoyed considerable sweetness in religion all the winter following.

* * *

Extracts from His Diary

Friday, April 1, 1742—I felt somewhat happy in secret prayer, much resigned, calm, and serene. What are all the storms of this lower world, if Jesus by His Spirit does but come walking on the seas! Some time past I had much pleasure in the prospect of the heathen being brought home to Christ, and desired that the Lord would employ me in that work; but now my soul more frequently desires to die, to be with Christ. In the evening I was refreshed in prayer, with the hopes of the advancement of Christ's kingdom in the world.

Monday, April 12—I was specially assisted to intercede and plead for poor souls, and for the enlargement of Christ's kingdom in the world, and for special grace for myself, to fit me for special services. It was no matter when, nor where, nor how Christ should send me, nor what trials He should still exercise me with, if I might but be prepared for His work and will.

Tuesday, April 20—This day I am twenty-four years of age. O how much mercy have I received the year past! How often has God caused His goodness to pass before me! I want to wear out my life in His service and for His glory.

Thursday, July 29—Was examined by the Association met at Danbury as to my learning, and also my experience in religion, and received a license from them to preach the gospel of Christ. Went to bed resolving to live devoted to God all my days.

Thursday, August 12—This morning I had in a great measure lost my hopes of God's sending me among the heathen afar off, and of seeing them flock home to Christ. It seemed as though I never could nor should preach any more; yet about nine or ten o'clock the people came over and I was forced to preach [at Southbury]. And blessed be God, He gave me His presence and Spirit in prayer and preaching, so that I was much assisted, and spoke with power from Job 14:14.[1] Some Indians cried out in great distress, and all appeared greatly concerned.

Friday, November 19—At New Haven. Received a letter from the Rev. Mr. Pemberton of New York, desiring me speedily to go down thither, and consult about the Indian affairs in those parts. I retired with two or three Christian friends and prayed.

Wednesday, November 24—Came to New York. Put up many earnest requests to God for help and direction; was confused with the noise and tumult of the city. Enjoyed but little time alone with God, but my soul longed after Him.

Thursday, November 25—Was examined by some gentlemen relative to my Christian experience, my acquaintance with divinity, and some other studies, in order to my improvement in that important affair of evangelizing the heathen.

Wednesday, February 2, 1743—Preached my farewell sermon last night. Having taken leave of friends, I set out in the morning on my journey toward the Indians. By the way I was to spend some time at East Hampton on Long Island, by leave of the commissioners who employed me in the Indian affair.

Wednesday, March 9—Rode sixteen miles to Montauk, and had some inward sweetness on the road, but something of flatness and deadness after I came there and saw the Indians. I withdrew and endeavored to pray, but found myself awfully deserted. However, I went and preached from Isaiah 53:10.[2] Had some assistance, and I trust something of the divine presence was among us. In the evening also I prayed and exhorted among them. May the God of all grace succeed my poor labors in this place.

Friday, April 1—I rode to Kaunaumeek, near twenty miles from Stockbridge [near Albany, New York], where the Indians live with whom I am concerned, and there lodged on a little heap of straw.

Lord's Day, April 10—Rose early in the morning and walked out; spent considerable time in the woods in prayer and meditation. Preached to the Indians, both forenoon and afternoon. They behaved soberly in general. Two or three in particular appeared under some religious concern, with whom I discoursed privately; and one told me her heart had cried ever since she heard me preach first.

Wednesday, May 18—My circumstances are such that I have no comfort of any kind but what I have in God. I live in the most lonesome wilderness; have but one single person to converse with that can speak English [his Indian interpreter, John Wauwaumpequunnaunt]. I live poorly with regard to the comforts of life. Most of my diet consists of boiled corn, hasty-pudding, etc. I lodge on a bundle of straw, and my labor is hard and extremely difficult. I have little appearance of success to comfort me. The Indians' affairs are very difficult, having no land to live on but what the Dutch people lay claim to and threaten to drive them off from. They [the Dutch] have no regard to the souls of the poor Indians, and by what I can learn, they hate me because I come to preach to them [the Indians].

Tuesday, May 1, 1744—Having received new orders to go to a number of Indians on Delaware River in Pennsylvania, and my people here being mostly removed, I took all my clothes and books this day and disposed of them. I then set out for Delaware River. Rode several hours in the rain through the howling wilderness, though in a state of feebleness and great affliction.

Lord's Day, May 13—Rose early; felt very poorly after my long journey, and after being wet and fatigued. There appeared to be no Sabbath. All circumstances seemed to conspire to render my affairs dark and discouraging. Was disappointed respecting an interpreter, and heard that the Indians were much scattered. Yet God was pleased to support my soul, so that I never entertained any thought of quitting my business among the poor Indians.

Monday, May 28—Set out from the Indians above the Forks of Delaware on a journey towards Newark in New Jersey, according to my orders.

Monday, June 11—This day the Presbytery met together at Newark, in order to consider my ordination. At three in the afternoon preached my probation sermon from Acts 26:17, 18,[3] being a text given me for that purpose. God carried me through comfortably. Afterwards passed an examination before the Presbytery.

Tuesday, June 12—Was this morning further examined respecting my experimental acquaintance with Christianity. At ten o'clock my ordination was attended to; the sermon preached by the Rev. Mr. Ebenezer Pemberton.[4]

Tuesday, June 26—Was busy most of the day in translating prayers into the language of the Delaware Indians. Met with great difficulty, seeing that my interpreter was altogether unacquainted with the business. Yet God supported me.

Thursday, June 28—Spent the morning in reading several parts of the Holy Scripture, and in fervent prayer for my Indians, that God would set up His kingdom among them, and bring them into His church. I could freely tell the Lord, He knew that the cause was not mine which I was engaged in; but it was His own cause, and it would be for His own glory to convert the poor Indians. Blessed be His Name, I felt no desire for their conversion that I might receive honor from the world as being the instrument of it. Had some freedom in speaking to the Indians.

Lord's Day, September 2—Was enabled to speak to my poor Indians with much concern and fervency. I perceived that some of them were afraid to hearken to and embrace Christianity, lest they should be enchanted and poisoned by some of the Powwows. But I was enabled to plead with them not to fear these; and I bid a challenge to all these powers of darkness to do their worst upon me first. I told my people I was a Christian, and asked them why the Powwows did not bewitch and poison me.

Tuesday, December 18—Went to the Indians, and discoursed to them near an hour, but without any power to come close to their hearts. At last I felt some fervency, and God helped me to speak with warmth. My interpreter also was amazingly assisted; and I doubt not but the Spirit of God was upon him, though I had no reason to think he had any true and saving grace, but was only under conviction of his lost state. Presently most of the grown persons were much affected, and the tears ran down their cheeks. Came home and spent most of the evening in prayer and thanksgiving, and found myself much enlarged and quickened.

Lord's Day, January 6, 1745—Preached to my poor Indians, but had little heart or life.

Lord's Day, February 24—My interpreter being absent, I knew not how to perform my work among the Indians. However, I rode to them, and got a Dutchman to interpret for me, though he was but poorly qualified for the business.

June 19—Having spent most of my time for more than a year

past amongst the Indians in the Forks of Delaware in Pennsylvania, and having in that time made two journeys to Susquehanna River, far back in that province, in order to treat with the Indians respecting Christianity, I was not having any considerable appearance of special success in either of those places. Upon hearing that there was a number of Indians in and about a place called by the Indians Crossweeksung, in New Jersey, near fourscore miles southeast from the Forks of Delaware, I determined to make them a visit, and see what might be done towards their conversion. I accordingly arrived among them this day. Found very few persons in the place I visited, and perceived the Indians in those parts were very much scattered. However, I preached to those few women and children I found, who appeared well-disposed, and not inclined to object and cavil, as the Indians had frequently done elsewhere.

June 22—Preached to the Indians again. Their number, which at first consisted of about seven or eight persons, was now increased to near thirty. Some considerable impressions, it was apparent, were made upon their minds by divine truth.

Lord's Day, June 23—Preached to the Indians and spent the day with them. Their number still increased, and all with one consent seemed to rejoice in my coming among them.

June 24—Preached to the Indians at their own desire. To see poor pagans desirous of hearing the gospel of Christ animated me. Some concern for their souls' salvation appeared among them.

June 27—Visited and preached to the Indians again. Their number now amounted to about forty persons. Their solemnity and attention still continued.

June 28—The Indians being now gathered, a considerable number of them from their several and distant habitations requested me to preach twice a day. I cheerfully complied.

July 1—Preached again twice. Between forty and fifty of them, old and young, were present. It was amazing to see how they received and retained the instructions given them, and what a measure of knowledge some of them had acquired in a few days.

July 2—Was obliged to leave these Indians at Crossweeksung, thinking it my duty again to visit those at the Forks of Delaware. When I came to take leave of them, they all earnestly enquired when I would come again, and expressed a great desire of being further instructed. I then promised them to return as speedily as my health and business would permit. It appeared that if God should now, after I passed through so considerable a series of almost fruitless labors and fatigues, and after my rising hopes had been so often frustrated among these poor pagans, give me any special success in my labors with them, that I could not believe, and scarcely dared to hope, that the event would be so happy. I never found myself more suspended between hope and fear than on this occasion.

August 3—Having [returned to Crossweeksung], I found [the Indians] serious, and a number of them under deep concern for an interest in Christ. I preached to them this day with some view to Revelation 22:17, "And whosoever will, let him take the water of life freely." The Lord enabled me, in a manner somewhat uncommon, to set before them the Lord Jesus Christ as a kind and compassionate Savior, inviting distressed and perishing sinners to accept everlasting mercy, and a surprising concern soon became apparent among them. There were about twenty adult persons altogether (many of the Indians at remote places not having had time to come since my return hither), and not above two that I could see with dry eyes.

Lord's Day, August 4—Being invited by a neighboring minister to assist in the administration of the Lord's Supper, I complied with his request, and took the Indians along with me. There were nearly fifty in all, old and young. Some of them that could understand English were much affected. Now a change in their manners began to appear. When they came to sup together, they would not taste a morsel till they had sent to me to come and ask a blessing on their food. At the time several of them wept, especially when I reminded them how they had in times past eaten their feasts in honor to devils.

August 5—After a sermon had been preached by another minister, I preached and concluded the solemnity from John 7:37.[5] In my discourse I addressed the Indians in particular, who stay by themselves in a part of the house. One or two of them were struck with deep concern, who had been little affected before. Others had their concern increased to a considerable degree. In the evening (the greater part of them being at the house where I lodged), I discoursed to them, and found them universally engaged about their souls' concern. They were inquiring what they should do to be saved. All their conversation among themselves turned upon religious matters, in which they were much assisted by my interpreter, who was with them day and night. A woman who had been much concerned for her soul ever since she first heard me preach in June last, obtained, I trust, some solid and well-grounded comfort. She seemed to be filled with love to Christ, and at the same time behaved humbly and tenderly, and appeared afraid of nothing so much as of grieving and offending him whom her soul loved.

August 6—In the morning I discoursed to the Indians at the house where we lodged. Many of them were tenderly affected. There were about fifty-five persons in all, about forty that were capable of attending divine service with understanding. I insisted upon 1 John 4:10, "Herein is love." Near the close of my discourse there were scarcely three in forty that could refrain from tears and bitter cries. It was surprising to see how their hearts seemed to be pierced with the tender and melting invitations of the gospel, when there was not a word of terror spoken to them.

August 8—In the afternoon I preached to the Indians; their number was now about sixty-five persons, men, women and children. I discoursed from Luke 14:16-23,[6] and was favored with uncommon freedom in my discourse. There was much visible concern among them while I was discoursing publicly; but afterwards when I spoke to one and another more particularly, whom I perceived under much concern, the power of God seemed to descend upon the assembly like a rushing mighty wind, and with an astonishing energy bore all before it.

I stood amazed at the influence which seized the audience almost universally. Almost all persons of all ages were bowed down with concern together. Old men and women, who had been drunken wretches for many years, and some little children, not more than six or seven years of age, appeared in distress about their souls, as well as persons of middle age. The most stubborn hearts were now obliged to bow. A principal man among the Indians, who with a great degree of confidence the day before told me he had been a Christian more than ten years, was now brought under solemn concern for his soul, and wept bitterly. Another man, considerable in years, who had been a murderer, a Powwow or conjurer, and a notorious drunkard, was likewise brought to cry for mercy with many tears.

Some of the white people, who came out of curiosity to "hear what this babbler would say" to the poor ignorant Indians, were also much awakened, and some appeared to be wounded with a view of their perishing state. Those who had lately obtained relief were filled with comfort; they appeared calm and composed, and seemed to rejoice in Christ Jesus. Some took their distressed friends by the hand, telling them of the goodness of Christ and the comfort that is to be enjoyed in Him, and invited them to come and give up their hearts to Him. A young Indian woman, who I believe never knew before she had a soul, hearing that there was something strange among the Indians, came to see what was the matter. Earlier she had laughed and mocked at me, but I had not proceeded far in my discourse before she felt effectually that she had a soul. She seemed like one pierced through with a dart, and cried out incessantly. After the service was over I hearkened to hear what she said, and perceived the burden of her prayer to be, *Guttummaukalumneh mechaumeh kmeleh Ndah,* "Have mercy on me, and help me to give Thee my heart." Thus she continued praying for many hours together.

This was indeed a surprising day of God's power, and seemed enough to convince an atheist of the truth, importance, and power of God's Word.

August 9—Spent almost the whole day with the Indians. In the afternoon, discoursed to them publicly. There were now present about seventy persons, old and young. I opened and applied the parable of the sower, Matthew 13. Was enabled to speak with much plainness, and found afterwards that this discourse was very instructive to them. It was very affecting to see the poor Indians, who the other day were hallooing and yelling in their idolatrous feasts and drunken frolics, now crying to God with such importunity for an interest in His dear Son.

Lord's Day, August 25—Preached in the forenoon from Luke 15:3-7.[7] There being a multitude of white people present, I made an address to them at the close of my discourse to the Indians, but could not so much as keep them orderly. Scores of them [the whites] kept walking and gazing about, and behaved more indecently than any Indians I ever addressed. In the afternoon I baptized twenty-five of the Indians, fifteen adults and ten children. After the crowd of spectators was gone I called the baptized persons together, at the same time inviting others to attend. I reminded them of the solemn obligations they were now under. This was a delightful season indeed. Their hearts were engaged and cheerful in duty. Love seemed to reign among them. They took each other by the hand with tenderness and affection as if their hearts were knit together. Several other Indians, seeing and hearing these things, were much affected and wept bitterly, longing to be partakers of the same joy and comfort.

August 26—Being fully convinced it was now my duty to take a journey far back to the Indians on Susquehanna River, I asked [my people] if they could not be willing to spend the remainder of the day in prayer for me. They cheerfully complied, and continued praying all night till nearly break of day. This day an old Indian, who had all his days been an obstinate idolater, was brought to give up his rattles (which they use for music in their idolatrous feasts and dances) to the other Indians, who quickly destroyed them. This was done without any attempt of mine in the affair. It seemed to be nothing but the power of God's Word. May the glory be ascribed to Him who is the sole Author of it!

God was pleased to give these truths such a powerful influence upon the minds of the people, their lives were quickly reformed without my insisting upon the precepts of morality in repeated harangues. My work was to lead them into a further view of their helplessness and the corruption of their hearts, and at the same time open to them the glorious and complete remedy provided in Christ for sinners, and offered freely to those who have no goodness of their own, no works of righteousness which they have done to recommend them to God. When these truths were felt at heart, there was now no vice unreformed, no external duty neglected. Drunkenness, the darling vice, was broken off, and scarcely an instance of it known among my hearers for months together. The abusive practice of husbands and wives in putting away each other and taking others in their stead was quickly reformed. Three or four couples have voluntarily dismissed those they had wrongfully taken, and now live together in love and peace. The same might be said of all other vicious practices, all springing from the internal influence of divine truth upon their hearts, and not from any external restraints. Family prayer was set up and maintained. The Lord's Day was observed. Some of them were brought to pray without ever being instructed in the duty of prayer.

I have found that solemn applications of divine truth to the conscience tend directly to strike death to the root of all vice, while smooth and plausible harangues upon moral virtues at best are likely to do no more than lop off the branches of corruption, while the root remains still untouched. I have now baptized seventy-seven persons; thirty-eight adults and thirty-nine children, all within the space of eleven months past. There are many others under solemn concern for their souls. Surely Christ's little flock here, so suddenly gathered from among pagans, may justly say, "The Lord hath done great things for us; whereof we are glad."[8] The attempts to raise a school among them have succeeded, and a kind Providence has sent them a schoolmaster. He has generally thirty or thirty-five children in his school who, he tells me, learn with surprising readiness.

Extracts from His Public Journal

I shall now attempt something with regard to the last particular required by the Honorable Society in their letter, namely, to give some account of the "difficulties I have already met with in my work, and the methods I make use of for surmounting the same." What I have to say upon the subject, I shall reduce to the following heads:

First, I have met with great difficulty in my work among the Indians from the rooted aversion to Christianity that generally prevails among them. This aversion arises partly from a view of the immorality and vicious behavior of many who are called Christians. They observe that horrid wickedness in nominal Christians which the light of nature condemns in themselves. They are ready to look upon all the white people alike, and to condemn them alike for the abominable practices of some. Hence, when I have attempted to treat with them about Christianity, they have frequently objected [to] the scandalous practices of Christians, and cast in my teeth all they could think of that was odious in the conduct of any of them.

They have observed to me that the white people lie, defraud, steal, and drink worse than the Indians; that they have taught the Indians these things. Before the coming of the English they knew of no such thing as strong drink; and the English have by these means made them quarrel and kill one another, and brought them to the practice of all those vices which now prevail among them. So that they are now more vicious and much more miserable than they were before the coming of the white people into the country.

I am forced to own that many nominal Christians are more abominably wicked than the Indians. But then I attempt to show them that there are some who feel the power of Christianity who are not so. The great difficulty is that the traders that go in the backcountry among them are generally of the most irreligious and vicious sort.

Another thing that serves to make them averse to Christianity is a fear of being enslaved. They are extremely averse to a state of servitude; hence they are always afraid of some design forming against them. If anything be proposed to them for their good, they are rather ready to suspect that there is at bottom some design. When I have attempted to recommend Christianity to their acceptance, they have sometimes objected that the white people have come among them, have cheated them out of their lands, driven them back to the mountains from the pleasant places they used to enjoy by the seaside; that therefore they have no reason to think the white people are now seeking their welfare. Rather, they have sent me out to draw them together under a pretense of kindness to them, that they [the whites] may have an opportunity to make slaves of them as they do of the poor Negroes, or else to ship them on board their vessels and make them fight with their enemies.

To give them assurance of the contrary is not an easy matter. I inform them that I am not sent out by those persons in these provinces, but by pious people at a great distance [Scotland] who never had an inch of their lands, nor ever thought of doing any hurt. But here will arise so many frivolous and impertinent questions that it would tire one's patience and wear out one's spirits to hear them. They would say, "But why did not these good people send you to teach us *before*, when we had our lands down by the seaside?"

Another spring of aversion to Christianity in the Indians is their strong attachment to their own religious notions, if they may be called religious. It is a notion pretty generally prevailing among them that it was not the same God made them who made us, but that they were made after the white people. They give much heed to dreams, and to the influence that their Powwows, conjurers or diviners, have upon them. To remove this difficulty, I have labored to show the Indians that these diviners have no power to recover the sick when the God whom Christians serve has determined them for death. And when I have apprehended them afraid of embracing Christianity, lest they should be enchanted and poisoned, I have endeavored to relieve their minds by asking them why their Powwows did not enchant and poison me, seeing they had much reason to hate me for preaching to them and desiring them to become Christians.

Another great difficulty I have met with in my attempts to Christianize the Indians has been to convey divine truths to their understanding, and to gain their assent to them. It was sometimes extremely discouraging when I could not make my interpreter understand what I designed to communicate, and when he addressed the Indians in a lifeless, indifferent manner, without any heart or fervency. The method God was pleased to take for the removal of the difficulty [was the conversion of the interpreter].

Another thing that rendered it difficult to convey divine truth to the understanding of the Indians was the defectiveness of their language, the want of terms to express and convey ideas of spiritual things. There are no words in the Indian language to answer our English words, *Lord, Savior, salvation, sinner, justice, faith, repentance, grace, glory, Heaven,* etc.

The last difficulty I mention is what has proceeded from the attempts that some ill-minded persons have designedly made to hinder the propagation of the gospel and a work of divine grace among the Indians. The Indians in New Jersey have been sued for debt and threatened with imprisonment more since I came among them, as they inform me, than in seven years before. The reason of this I suppose was, they left frequenting those tippling houses where they used to consume most of what they gained by hunting and other means. These persons seeing that the hope of future gain was lost, were resolved to make sure of what they could.

This has been very distressing to me. In order to remove this difficulty I pressed the Indians with all possible speed to pay their debts, exhorting those of them that had skins or money, and were themselves in a good measure free from debt, to help others that were oppressed. Frequently upon such occasions I have paid money out of my own pocket.

Thus I have endeavored to answer the demands of the Honorable Society in relation to the particulars mentioned in their letter. If what I have written may be in any measure agreeable and satisfactory, and serve to excite in them or any of God's people a spirit of prayer and supplication for the furtherance of a work of grace among the Indians here, and the propagation of it to their distant tribes, I shall have abundant reason to rejoice and bless God in this as well as in other respects.

D.B., June 20, 1746

NOTES

1. "If a man die, shall he live again?"
2. "Yet it pleased the Lord to bruise Him; He hath put Him to grief: when thou shalt make His soul an offering for sin, He shall see His seed, He shall prolong his days, and the pleasure of the Lord shall prosper in His hand."
3. "Delivering thee from the people, and from the Gentiles, unto whom now I send thee, to open their eyes, and to turn them from darkness to light, and from the power of Satan unto God, that they may receive forgiveness of sins, and inheritance among them which are sanctified by faith that is in Me."
4. See page 38.
5. "In the last day, that great day of the feast, Jesus stood and cried, saying, If any man thirst, let him come unto Me, and drink."
6. The parable of the great supper ("and they all with one consent began to make excuse").
7. The parable of the lost sheep (and the ninety and nine).
8. Psalm 126:3.

Timothy Dwight

Timothy Dwight (1752-1817) was not born great, but came close to it. His mother, Mary, was the third daughter of Jonathan and Sarah Edwards, and he was born at Northampton, Massachusetts, scene of the famous revival of 1735. He graduated with honors at age seventeen from Yale College and taught in a New Haven grammar school until appointed a tutor at Yale from 1771 to 1777. After being licensed to preach, he served as chaplain in a Revolutionary Army regiment for one year. Not only did he inspire the troops by his sermons, he wrote a number of popular war songs, including "Columbia" with its refrain,

Columbia, Columbia, to glory arise,
The queen of the world and the child of the skies.

From 1778 to 1783 Dwight farmed, preached, and dabbled in politics at Northampton until he was called to pastor the Congregational church at Greenfield, Connecticut. There he opened an academy which acquired a high reputation. In 1795 he was chosen president of Yale College, and served as both president and professor of divinity until his death. His preaching in the Yale chapel brought about a student revival. Where there was only one church member among the graduates in 1800, two years later a third of the students had been converted to faith in Christ.

Timothy Dwight has been called "the last of the Puritans" and "the first of our great college presidents." He proved an able administrator; he reformed the college's curriculum and tripled its enrollment. He was known for his force of character and his remarkable ability as a teacher. His moderate Calvinistic convictions determined his world view and caused him to abhor the teachings of Rousseau, Paine, Jefferson, and their sympathizers.

During the last two decades of the eighteenth century, Dwight and a group of younger writers formed a literary center in Connecticut. All were associated with Yale College, and became known as the "Hartford wits." They were extremely popular. Dwight himself wrote a great deal of poetry, which today is considered labored, ponderous, and dull, but in his day ranked with the reading public as genius. One poem consisted of ten thousand lines of heroic couplets.

Lyman Beecher, who says he was converted at Yale under Dwight's teaching, writes, "He was of noble form, with a noble head and body, and had one of the sweetest smiles that ever you saw." His voice was enriched by a remarkable memory. He delivered his sermons with vigor, free of mannerisms.

Dr. Ralph W. Turnbull writes, "Dwight appealed especially to the well-educated, attacking the infidelity and skepticism prevalent in intellectual circles. The transcendentalism of the new era had denied the deity of the Christ, disbelieved the total veracity of the Bible, discounted miracle and prayer. In this context came the preaching of the president of Yale. Dwight thundered against the naturalism of the day, and the Second Great Awakening moved in to change the atmosphere."

This sermon was one of a series published posthumously in 1818. It was originally delivered in the Yale chapel, perhaps about 1799. It is taken from The World's Great Sermons, *Grenville Kleiser, compiler, Volume 3, published in 1908 by Funk & Wagnalls, New York.*

EIGHT

The Sovereignty of God
by Timothy Dwight

"O Lord, I know that the way of man is not in
himself: it is not in man that walketh to direct his steps."
(Jeremiah 10:23)

In this passage of Scripture the prophet exhibits the progress of
life as a way. In this way all men are considered as traveling. We
commence the journey at our birth, pass on through the several
stages of childhood, youth, manhood, and old age, and finish it
when we enter eternity. The accommodations and the fare are
greatly varied among the various travelers. The enterprise is not
contrived by ourselves. We are placed in it, and necessitated to
accomplish it, by a superior and irresistible hand.

It cannot but seem strange that in such a journey we should
originally be prevented from the ability to direct ourselves; yet
such is unquestionably the fact. Nor is the explanation so difficult. God intended that all His creatures should be dependent on
Him for aid, guidance, and protection. The sovereignty of God
has ever been questioned, and very often denied, by mankind.
But God never acts arbitrarily. To say that He wills a thing
because He wills it is to speak without meaning. All His pleasure,
all His determinations, are perfectly wise and good, founded on
the best of reasons, and directed to the best of all purposes. Were
He to act in any other manner His Providence would be less
wise, and less desirable.

Few in this audience will probably deny the truth of a direct
Scriptural quotation. With as little reason can it be denied that
most of them apparently live in the very manner in which they
would live if the doctrine were false; or that they rely, chiefly at
least, on their own sagacity, contrivance, and efforts for success in
this life and that which is to come. As little can it be questioned
that such self-confidence is a guide eminently dangerous and

deceitful. Safe as we may feel under its direction, our safety is imaginary. The folly of others in trusting to themselves we discern irresistibly. The same folly they perceive, with equal evidence, in us. Our true wisdom lies in willingly feeling, and cheerfully acknowledging, our dependence on God; and in committing ourselves with humble reliance to His care and direction.

With these observations I will now proceed to illustrate the truth of the doctrine. The mode which I shall pursue will probably be thought singular. I hope it will be useful. Metaphysical arguments, which are customarily employed for the purpose of establishing this and several other doctrines of theology are, if I mistake not, less satisfactory to the minds of men at large than the authors of them appear to believe. Facts, wherever they can be fairly adduced to this end, are attended with a superior power of conviction, and commonly leave little doubt behind them. On these, therefore, I shall at the present time rely for the accomplishment of my design.

In the first place, the doctrine of the text is evident from the great fact that the birth and education of all men depend not on themselves. The succeeding events of life are derived, in a great measure at least, from our birth. By this event it is in a prime degree determined whether men shall be princes or peasants, opulent or poor, learned or ignorant, honorable or despised; whether they shall be civilized or savage, freemen or slaves, Christians or heathen, Mohammedans or Jews.

A child is born of Indian parents in the western wilderness. By his birth he is of course a savage. His friends, his mode of life, his habits, his knowledge, his opinions, his conduct all grow out of this single event. His first thoughts, his first instructions, and all the first objects with which he is conversant, the persons whom he loves, the life to which he assumes are all savage. He is an Indian from the cradle to the grave. To say that he could not be otherwise, we are not warranted; but that he is not is certain.

Another child is born of a Bedouin Arab. Before he can walk or speak, he is carried through pathless wastes in search of food. He roams in the arms of his mother or on the back of a camel from spring to spring, and pasture to pasture. He begins his conflict with hunger and thirst, is scorched by a vertical sun, shriveled by the burning sand beneath, and poisoned by the breath of the simoom.[1] Hardened thus through his infancy and childhood both in body and mind, he becomes, under the exhortations and example of his father, a robber from his youth; attacks every stranger whom he is able to overcome; and plunders every valuable thing on which he can lay his hand.

A third receives his birth in the palace of a British nobleman. He is welcomed to the world as the heir apparent of an ancient, honorable, and splendid family. As soon as he opens his eyes to the light, he is surrounded by all the enjoyments which opulence can furnish, ingenuity contrive, or fondness bestow. He is dandled on the knee of indulgence; encircled by attendants who watch and prevent alike his necessities and wishes; cradled on down, and charmed to sleep by the voice of tenderness and care. From the dangers and evils of life he is guarded with anxious solicitude. To its pleasures he is conducted by the ever-ready hand of maternal affection.

His person is shaped and improved by a succession of masters; his mind is opened, invigorated, and refined by the assiduous superintendence of learning and wisdom. While a child, he is served by a host of menials and flattered by successive trains of visitors. When a youth, he is regarded by a band of tenants with reverence and awe. His equals in age bow to his rank, and multitudes of superior years acknowledge his distinction by continual testimonies of marked respect. When a man, he engages the regard of his sovereign, commands the esteem of the senate, and earns the love and applause of his country.

A fourth child, in the same kingdom, is begotten by a beggar and born under a hedge. From his birth he is trained to suffering and hardihood. He is nursed, if he can be said to be nursed at all, on a coarse, scanty, and precarious pittance; holds life only as a tenant at will; combats from the first dawnings of intellect with insolence, cold, and nakedness; is originally taught to beg and steal; is driven from the doors of men by the porter or the house dog; and is regarded as an alien from the family of Adam. Like his kindred worms, he creeps through life in the dust; dies under the hedge where he is born; and is then, perhaps, cast into a ditch and covered with earth by some stranger who remembers that, although a beggar, he was still a man.

A child enters the world in China and unites, as a thing of course, with his countrymen in the stupid worship of the idol Fo. Another prostrates himself before the Lama in consequence of having received his being in Tibet, and of seeing the Lama worshiped by all around him.

A third, who begins his existence in Turkey, is carried early to the mosque and taught to lisp with profound reverence the name of Mohammed. He is habituated to repeat the prayers and sentences of the Koran as the means of eternal life, and induced, in a manner irresistible, to complete his title to Paradise by a pilgrimage to Mecca.

The Hindu infant grows into a religious veneration for the cow, and perhaps never doubts that if he adds to this solemn devotion to Juggernaut [Jagannath], the gurus, and the dewtahs [devatas], and performs carefully his ablutions in the Ganges, he shall wash away all his sins and obtain, by the favor of Brahma, a seat among the blest.

In our own favored country, one child is born of parents devoted solely to this world. From his earliest moments of understanding he hears and sees nothing but what is commended by hunting, horse-racing, visiting, dancing, dressing, riding, parties, gaming, acquiring money with eagerness and skill, and spending it in gaiety, pleasure, and luxury. These things, he is taught by conversation and example, constitute all the good of man. His taste is formed, his habits are riveted, and the whole character of his soul is turned to them before he is fairly sensible that there is any other good. The question whether virtue and piety are either duties or blessings he probably never asks. In the dawn of life he sees them neglected and despised by those whom he most reverences; and learns only to neglect and despise them also. Of Jehovah he thinks as little, and for the same reason, as a Chinese or a Hindu. They pay their devotions to Fo and to Juggernaut: he his to money and pleasure. Thus he lives and dies a mere animal; a stranger to intelligence and morality, to his duty and his God.

Another child comes into existence in the mansion of knowledge and virtue. From his infancy his mind is fashioned to wisdom and piety. In his infancy he is taught and allured to remember his Creator, and to unite, first in form and then in affection, in the household devotions of the morning and evening.

God he knows almost as soon as he can know anything. The presence of that glorious Being he is taught to realize almost from the cradle; and from the dawn of intelligence to understand the perfections and government of his Creator. His own accountableness, as soon as he can comprehend it, he begins to feel habitually and always. The way of life through the Redeemer is explained to him early and regularly by the voice of parental love, and enforced and endeavored in the house of God. As soon as possible he is enabled to read and persuaded to "search the Scriptures."[2] Of the approach, the danger, and the mischiefs of temptations he is tenderly warned. At the commencement of sin he is kindly checked in his dangerous career. To God he was solemnly given in baptism. To God he was daily commended in fervent prayer. Under this happy cultivation he grows up "like an olive tree in the courts of the Lord"[3] and, green, beautiful, and flourishing, he blossoms, bears fruit, and is prepared to be transplanted by the divine hand to a kinder soil in the regions above.

How many, and how great, are the differences in these several children! How plainly do they all, in ordinary circumstances, arise out of their birth! From their birth is derived, of course, the education which I have ascribed to them; and from this education spring in a great measure both character and their destiny. The place, the persons, the circumstances, are here evidently the great things which, in the ordinary course of Providence, appear chiefly to determine what the respective men shall be, and what shall be those allotments which regularly follow their respective characters. As then they are not at all concerned in contriving or accomplishing either their birth or their education, it is certain that, in these most important particulars, *the way of a man is not in himself.* God only can determine what child shall spring from parents, wise or foolish, virtuous or sinful, rich or poor, honorable or infamous, civilized or savage, Christian or heathen.

I wish it to be distinctly understood, and carefully remembered, that "in the moral conduct of all these individuals no physical necessity operates." Every one of them is absolutely a free agent, as free as any created agent can be. Whatever he does is the result of choice, absolutely unconstrained. Let me add that not one of them is placed in a situation in which, if he learns and performs his duty to the utmost of his power, he will fail of being finally accepted.

Secondly, the doctrine is strikingly evident from this great fact also, that the course of life which men usually pursue is very different from that which they have intended. Human life is ordinarily little else than a collection of disappointments. Rarely is the life of man such as he designs it shall be. Often do we fail of pursuing at all the business originally in our view. The intentional farmer becomes a mechanic, a seaman, a merchant, a lawyer, a physician, or a divine. The very place of settlement and of residence through life is often different and distant from that which was originally contemplated. Still more different is the success which follows our efforts.

All men intend to be rich and honorable; to enjoy ease and to pursue pleasure. But how small is the number of those who compass these objects! In this country the great body of mankind are, indeed, possessed of competence, a safer and happier lot than that to which they aspire. Yet few, very few, are rich. Here, also, the great body of mankind possess a character generally reputable. But very limited is the number of those who arrive at the honor which they so ardently desire, and of which they feel assured. Almost all stop at the moderate level where human efforts appear to have their boundary established in the determination of God. Nay, far below this level creep multitudes of such as began life with full confidence in the attainment of distinction and splendor.

The lawyer, emulating the eloquence, business, and fame of Murray or Dunning,[4] and secretly resolved not to slacken his efforts until all his rivals in the race for glory are outstripped, is often astonished, as well as broken-hearted, to find business and fame pass by his door, and stop at the more favored mansion of some competitor, in his view less able and less discerning than himself.

The physician, devoted to medical science and possessed of distinguished powers of discerning and removing diseases, is obliged to walk, while a more fortunate empiric [quack], ignorant and worthless, rolls through the streets in his coach.

The legislator beholds with anguish and amazement the suffrages of his countrymen given eagerly to a rival candidate devoid of knowledge and integrity, but skilled in flattering the base passions of men, and deterred by no hesitations of conscience and no fears of infamy from saying and doing anything which may secure his election.

The merchant often beholds with a despairing eye his own ships sunk in the ocean. His debtors fail, his goods are unsold, his business is cramped, and himself, his family, and his hopes are ruined; while a less skillful but more successful neighbor sees wealth blown to him by every wind, and floated on every wave.

The crops of the farmer are stunted, his cattle die, his markets are bad, and the purchaser of his commodities proves to be a cheat who deceives his confidence and runs away with his property.

Thus the darling schemes and fondest hopes of man are daily frustrated by time. While sagacity contrives, patience matures, and labor industriously executes, disappointment laughs at the curious fabric, formed by so many efforts and gay with so many brilliant colors, and while the artists imagine the work arrived at the moment of completion, brushes away the beautiful web and leaves nothing behind.

The designs of man, however, are in many respects not infrequently successful. The lawyer and physician acquire business and fame; the statesman, votes; and the farmer, wealth. But their real success even in this case is often substantially the same with that already recited. In all plans and all labors the supreme object is to become happy. Yet when men have actually acquired riches and honor, or secured to themselves popular favor, they still find the happiness which they expected eluding their grasp. Neither wealth, fame, office, nor sensual pleasure can yield such good as we need. As these coveted objects are accumulated, the wishes of man always grow faster than his gratifications. Hence whatever he acquires, he is usually as little satisfied as before, and often less.

A principal design of the mind in laboring for these things is to become superior to others. But almost all rich men are obliged to see, and usually with no small anguish, others richer than themselves; honorable men, others more honorable; voluptuous men, others who enjoy more pleasure. The great end of the strife is therefore unobtained; and the happiness expected never found. Even the successful competitor in the race utterly misses his aim. The real enjoyment existed, although it was unperceived by him, in the mere strife for superiority. When he has outstripped all his rivals the contest is at an end, and his spirits, which were invigorated only by contending, languish for want of a competitor.

Besides, the happiness in view was only the indulgence of pride, or mere animal pleasure. Neither of these can satisfy or endure. A rational mind may be and often is so narrow and groveling as not to aim at any higher good, to understand its nature or to believe its existence. Still, in its original constitution, it was formed with a capacity for intellectual and moral good, and was destined to find in this good its only satisfaction. Hence no inferior good will fill its capacity or its desires. Nor can this bent of its nature ever be altered. Whatever other enjoyment it may attain it will, without this, still crave and still be unhappy.

No view of the ever-varying character and success of mankind in their expectations of happiness, and their efforts to obtain it, can illustrate this doctrine more satisfactorily than that of the progress and end of a class of students in this seminary.[5] At their first appearance here they are all exactly on the same level. Their character, their hopes, and their destination are the same. They are enrolled on one list, and enter upon a collegiate life with the same promise of success. At this moment they are plants, appearing just above the ground, all equally fair and flourishing. Within a short time, however, some begin to rise above the others. They indicate by a more rapid growth a structure of superior vigor, and promise both more early and more abundant fruit.

Some are studious, steadfast, patient of toil, resolved on distinction, in love with science, and determined with unbroken ambition never to be left behind by their companions. Of these a part are amiable, uniform in their morals, excellent in their dispositions, and honorable by their piety. Another part, although less amiable, are still decent and reputable in their character.

Others are thoughtless, volatile, fluttering from object to object, particularly from one scene of pleasure to another, alighting only for a moment, never settling, regardless of everything except the present gratification, and most regardless of their time, their talents, their duty, and their souls. Others still are openly vicious, idle, disorderly; gamblers, profane, apparently infidels; enemies to themselves, undutiful to their parents, corrupters of their companions, and disturbers of the collegiate peace.

When the class which these individuals originally constituted leaves this seat of science, a number of them will always be missing. Some have been sent away by the mandate of law; some have voluntarily deserted their education; some have gone to the grave. Of those who remain, the character and the prospects have usually become widely different. The original level is broken, and broken forever. How different from all this were their parents' expectations and their own!

Still, when they enter the world, they all intend to be rich, honorable, and happy. Could they look into futurity, how changed would be their apprehensions! One, almost at his entrance into life, knowing but inexperienced, discerning but not wise, urged by strong passions and secure in self-confidence, pushes boldly forward to affluence and distinction; but, marked as the prey of cunning and the victim of temptation, is seduced from prudence and worth to folly, vice, and ruin. His property is lost by bold speculation, his character by licentiousness, and the man himself by the disappointment of his hopes and the breaking of his heart.

Another, timid, humble, reluctant to begin, and easily discouraged from pursuing, insensible to the charms of distinction, and a stranger to the inspiration of hope, without friends to sustain and without prospects to animate, begins to flag. When he commences his connection with the world, he creeps through life because he dares not attempt to climb, and lives and dies, scarcely known beyond the limits of his native village.

A third yields himself up a prey to sloth, and shrinks into insignificance for want of exertion.

A fourth, possessed of moderate wishes, and preferring safety to grandeur, steers between poverty and riches, obscurity and distinction, walks through life without envying those who ride, and finds, perhaps, in quiet and safety, and in the pleasure of being beloved rather than admired, the happiness which his more restless companions seek from opulence, power, and splendor in vain.

A fifth, cheerful, fraught with hope, and assured by the gaiety and bustle which he sees around him that the world is filled with good, moves onward to acquire it. He is at once astonished to find that men who look pleasantly on him are not his friends; that a smile of approbation is no evidence of goodwill; and that professions and promises convey to him no assurance of aid or comfort. To be dependent, he soon learns, is to be friendless, and to need assistance a sufficient reason for having it refused. Business flies from him; the countenance on which he reposed is withdrawn. Alone, forgotten, unprepared for struggles, he is overset by the suddenness and violence of the shock, and either falls into listlessness and stupor, or dies of a broken heart.

A sixth, from imbecility of constitution or the malignant power of accident, sickens and expires when he has scarcely begun to live.

A seventh, with vigorous industry, effort, and perseverance, goes steadily forward to wealth and distinction. Yet even he finds the void of his mind unsupplied by real good. He is rich and great, but not happy. That enchanting object, happiness, wrought into such elegance of form and adorned with such brilliant colors, has ever fascinated his mind. Gazing with an eager and bewildered eye, he never considered that in this world the rainbow with all its splendor was only painted on a cloud.

Were I to ask the youths who are before me what are their designs and expectations concerning their future life, and write down their several answers, what a vast difference would ultimately be found between those answers and the events which would actually befall them! To how great a part of that difference would facts, over which they could have no control, give birth! How many of them will in all probability be less prosperous, rich, and honorable than they now intend? How many will be devoted to employments of which at present they do not even dream, in circumstances of which they never entertained even a thought, behind those whom they expected to outrun, poor, sick, in sorrow, or in the grave.

Thirdly, the doctrine is further evident from the fact that life does not depend upon man. Where now are multitudes of those who a little while since lived and studied and worshiped here, with fond views of future eminence and prosperity, and with as fair a promise as can be found of future success, usefulness, and honor? How many asterisks appear with a melancholy aspect even in the younger classes of the triennial catalogue, marking solemnly the termination of parental hopes and the vanity of youthful designs!

As we are unable to assure ourselves even of a single day, much more of a long life, it is plain that our eternal state lies beyond our control. I have not called up this doctrine at the present time for the purpose of entering into any metaphysical disquisitions, but to give it its proper place, and to derive from it several practical observations which, there is reason to hope, may by the blessing of God be useful to those who hear me, especially to those who are students in this seminary.

You see here, my young friends, first, the most solid reasons for gratitude to your Creator. Only God directed that you should be born in this land, in the midst of peace, plenty, civilization, freedom, learning, and religion; and that your existence should not commence in a Tartarian forest or an African waste. God alone ordered that you should be born of parents who knew and worshiped Him, the glorious and eternal Jehovah, and not of parents who bowed before the Lama or the ox, an image of brass or the stock of a tree.

In the book of His counsels your names, so far as we are

able to judge, were written in the fair lines of mercy. It is of His overflowing goodness that you are now here, surrounded with privileges, beset with blessings, educated to knowledge, usefulness, and piety, and prepared to begin an endless course of happiness and glory. All these delightful things have been poured into your lap and have come, unbidden, to solicit your acceptance. If these blessings awaken not your gratitude, it cannot be awakened by the blessings in the present world. If they are not thankfully felt by you, it is because you know not how to be thankful. Think what you are, and where you are; and what and where you just as easily might have been. Remember that instead of cherishing tender affections, imbibing refined sentiments, exploring the field of science, and assuming the name and character of the sons of God, you might as easily have been dozing in the smoke of a wigwam, brandishing a tomahawk, or dancing around an emboweled captive; or that you might yourself have been emboweled by the hand of superstition and burned on the altars of Moloch. If you remember these things, you cannot but call to mind also, who made you to differ from the miserable beings who have thus lived and died.

This doctrine forcibly demands of you, secondly, to moderate desire and expectations. There are two modes in which men seek happiness in the enjoyments of the present world. Most people, it is said, freely indulge their wishes, and intend to find objects sufficient in number and value to satisfy them. A few aim at satisfaction by proportioning their desires to the number and measure of their probable gratifications. By the doctrine of the text, the latter method is stamped with the name of wisdom, and on the former is inscribed the name of folly.

Desires indulged grow faster and farther than gratifications extend. Ungratified desire is misery. Expectations eagerly indulged and terminated by disappointment are often exquisite misery. But how frequently are expectations raised only to be disappointed, and desires let loose only to terminate in distress! The child pines for a toy; the moment he possesses it, he throws it by and cries for another. When they are piled up in heaps around him, he looks at them without pleasure, and leaves them without regret. He knew not that all the good which they could yield lay in expectation; nor that his wishes for more would increase faster than toys could be multiplied, and is unhappy at last for the same reason as at first: his wishes are ungratified. Still indulging them, and still believing that the gratification of them will furnish the enjoyment for which he pines, he goes on, only to be unhappy.

Men are merely taller children. Honor, wealth, and splendor are the toys for which grown children pine; but which, however accumulated, leave them still disappointed and unhappy. God never designed that intelligent beings should be satisfied with these enjoyments. By His wisdom and goodness they were formed to derive their happiness and virtue from Him alone.

Moderated desires constitute a character fitted to acquire all the good which this world can yield. He who is prepared, in whatever situation he is, therewith to be content,[6] has learned effectually the science of being happy, and possesses the alchemic stone which will change every metal into gold. Such a man will smile upon a stool, while Alexander the Great at his side sits weeping on the throne of the world.

The doctrine of the text teaches you irresistibly that, since you cannot command gratifications, you should command your desires; and that, as the events of life do not accord with your wishes, your wishes should accord with them. Multiplied enjoyments fall to but few men, and are no more rationally expected than the highest prize in a lottery. But a well-regulated mind, a dignified independence of the world, and a wise preparation to possess one's soul in patience, whatever circumstances may exist, is in the power of every man, and is greater wealth than that of both Indies, and greater honor than Caesar ever required.

As your course and your success through life are not under your control, you are strongly urged, thirdly, to commit yourselves to God, who can control both.

That you cannot direct your course through the world, that your best concerted plans will often fail, that your sanguine expectations will be disappointed, and that your fondest worldly wishes will terminate in mortification, cannot admit of a momentary doubt. That God can direct you, that He actually controls all your concerns, and that, if you commit yourselves to His care, He will direct you kindly and safely, can be doubted only of choice. Why, then, do you hesitate to yield yourselves and your interests to the guidance of your Maker?

There are two reasons which appear especially to govern mankind in this important concern; they do not and will not realize the agency of God in their affairs, and they do not choose to have them directed as they imagine He will direct them. The former is the result of stupidity; the latter, of impiety. Both are foolish in the extreme, and not less sinful than foolish.

The infinitely wise, great, and glorious Benefactor of the universe has offered to take men by the hand, lead them through the journey of life, and conduct them to His own house in the heavens. The proof of His sincerity in making this offer has already been produced. He has given His own Son to live, and die, and rise, and reign, and intercede for our race. "Herein is love," if ever there was love, "not that we have loved Him, but that He has loved us."[7] That He, who has done this, should not be sincere is impossible. St. Paul therefore triumphantly asks what none can answer: "He that spared not His own Son, but delivered Him up for us all, how shall He not with Him also freely give us all things?"[8]

Trust then, His word with undoubting confidence; take His hand with humble gratitude, and with all your heart obey His voice, which you will ever hear, saying, "This is the way, walk therein."[9] In sickness and in health, by night and by day, at home and in crowds, He will watch over you with tenderness inexpressible. He will make you lie down in green pastures, lead you beside the still waters, and guide you in paths of righteousness for His Name's sake. He will prepare a table before you in the presence of your enemies, and cause your cup to run over with blessings. When you pass through the waters of affliction He will be with you, and through the rivers they shall not overflow you. When you walk through the fire you shall not be burned, neither shall the flame kindle on you. From their native heavens He will commission those charming twin sisters, goodness and mercy, to descend and "follow you all your days."

But if you wish God to be your guide and your friend, you must conform to His pleasure. Certainly you cannot wonder that the infinitely Wise One should prefer His own wisdom to yours, and that He should choose for His children their allotments, rather than leave them to choose for themselves. That part of His pleasure which you are to obey is all summed up in the single word *duty,* and it is perfectly disclosed in the Scriptures. The whole scheme is so formed as to be plain, easy, profitable, and delightful—profitable in hand, delightful in the possession. Every part and precept of the whole is calculated for this end, and will make you only wise, good, and happy.

Life has often been styled an ocean, and our progress through it a voyage. The ocean is tempestuous and billowy, overspread by a cloudy sky, and fraught beneath with shelves and quicksands. The voyage is eventful beyond comprehension, and at the same time full of uncertainty and replete with danger. Every adventurer needs to be well prepared for whatever may befall him, and well secured against the manifold hazards of losing his course, sinking in the abyss, or of being wrecked against the shore.

These evils have all existed at all times. The present, and that part of the past which is known to you by experience, has seen them multiplied beyond example. It has seen the ancient and acknowledged standards of thinking violently thrown down. Religion, morals, government, and the estimate formed by man of crimes and virtues, and of all the means of usefulness and enjoyment, have been questioned, attacked, and in various places, and with respect to millions of the human race, finally overthrown.[10] A licentiousness of opinion and conduct, daring, outrageous, and rending asunder every bond formed by God or man, has taken the place of former good sense and sound morals, and has long threatened the destruction of human good.

Industry, cunning, and fraud have toiled with unrivaled exertions to convert man into a savage and the world into a desert. A wretched and hypocritical philanthropy, also, not less mischievous, has stalked forth as the companion of these ravages: a philanthropy born in a dream, bred in a hovel, and living only in professions. This guardian genius of human interests, this friend of human rights, this redresser of human wrongs, is yet without a heart to feel, and without a hand to bless; but she is well furnished with lungs, with eyes and a tongue. She can talk, sigh, and weep at pleasure, but can neither pity nor give. The objects of her attachment are either knaves and villains at home, or unknown sufferers beyond her reach abroad. To the former, she ministers the sword and the dagger, that they may fight their way into place and power and profit. At the latter she only looks through a telescope of fancy, as an astronomer searches for stars invisible to the eye. To every real object of charity within her reach she complacently says, "Be thou warmed, and be thou filled; depart in peace."[11]

By the daring spirit, the vigorous efforts, and the ingenious cunning so industriously exerted on the one hand, and the smooth and gentle benevolence so softly professed on the other, multitudes have been, and you easily may be, destroyed. The mischief has indeed been met, resisted, and overcome; but it has the heads and the lives of the Hydra, and its wounds, which at times have seemed deadly, are much more readily healed than any good man could wish, than any sober man could expect.

Hope not to escape the assaults of this enemy. To feel that you are in danger will ever be a preparation for your safety. But it will be only such a preparation; your deliverance must ultimately flow from your Maker. Resolve, then, to commit yourselves to Him with a cordial reliance on His wisdom, power, and protection. Consider how much you have at stake; that you are bound to eternity, that your existence will be immortal, and that you will either rise to endless glory or be lost in absolute perdition.

Heaven is your proper home. The path which I have recommended to you will conduct you safely and certainly to that happy world. Fill up life, therefore, with obedience to God: with faith in the Lord Jesus Christ and repentance unto life (the obedience to the two great commands of the gospel), and supreme love to God and universal goodwill to men (the obedience to the two great commands of the law). On all your sincere endeavors to honor Him and befriend your fellowmen, He will smile; every virtuous attempt He will bless; every act of obedience He will reward.

Life in this manner will be pleasant amid all its sorrows, and beams of hope will continually shine through the gloom, by which it is so often overcast. Virtue, the seed that cannot die, planted from Heaven, and cultivated by the divine hand, will grow up in your hearts with increasing vigor, and blossom in your lives with supernal beauty. Your path will be that of the just, and will gloriously resemble the dawning light, "which shines brighter and brighter to the perfect day."[12] Peace will take you by the hand and offer herself as the constant and delightful companion of your progress. Hope will walk before you and with an unerring finger point out your course; and joy, at the end of the journey, will open her arms to receive you. You will wait on the Lord, and renew your strength; will mount up with wings as eagles; will run, and not be weary; will walk, and not faint.[13]

NOTES

1. A hot wind of the Arabian desert.
2. John 5:39.
3. Cf. Psalm 52:8.
4. William Murray, first Earl of Mansfield (1705-1793), British lord chief justice and speaker of the House of Lords; John Dunning, first Baron Ashburton (1731-1783), noted English lawyer and member of Parliament.

5. Dwight became president of Yale College (here called "seminary") in 1795.
6. Cf. Philippians 4:11.
7. 1 John 4:10.
8. Romans 8:32.
9. Cf. Isaiah 30:21.
10. The entire passage reflects Dwight's attitude toward the French Revolution (beginning in 1789) and its leaders.
11. Cf. James 2:16.
12. Cf. Proverbs 4:18.
13. Cf. Isaiah 40:31.

John Newton

John Newton's inspiring life story (1723-1795) was tailor-made for telling and retelling. Here is swashbuckling sailing-ship adventure on the high seas with a Christian climax. From slave trader in the West Indies to priest of the Church of England! From a derelict trapped as a slave himself in Africa, to the author of "Amazing Grace"! What nobler proof could be found of God working in the soul of an incorrigible sinner? Surely this is the pure gold of evangelism.

And yet there are strange twists to the story, when the truth is known. For seven years after his conversion to Christ in 1748, Newton continued to engage in his trade as captain of a slave ship, carrying cargo after cargo of African Negroes to the West Indies. Furthermore, his journal reveals how personally he was involved; that he himself bargained for bodies on Africa's west coast, buying this one, rejecting that one, as if they were pork instead of human flesh. The groans of the captives in his fetid hold seldom pricked the Bible-reading master in his cabin. He was not above applying torture, as he admits, to would-be escapees from his ship. And at no time did he ever think of his profession as anything but honorable in the sight of God and men.

Newton's spiritual blindness was, of course, a common affliction in the mid-eighteenth century. Piety and slavery were amiable bedfellows. Wilberforce had not yet begun to prick the conscience of the British Parliament. But Newton did finally make a turn; his conscience awakened, he became an active participant in Wilberforce's political campaign to end the slave trade. Newton's inside knowledge proved a powerful factor in swaying the mind of the British public.

John Newton was born in London, the son of a shipmaster in the Mediterranean trade. He lost his mother early, and at age twelve went to sea with his father. After five years he was seized by a press gang in London and forced to sail on a British man-of-war, the HMS Harwich. *He tried to desert the Royal Navy in Plymouth, was recaptured, degraded, tortured, and finally, as a confirmed troublemaker (he wrote rhymes ridiculing the ship's officers, and had the crew singing them) was exchanged at sea and put aboard an African trader. Again he jumped ship and was arrested, and eventually became virtually the slave of a white slavetrader's black wife off the African coast. For two years she kept him humiliated, hungry, and destitute. Through his father's influence he was rescued, and during a storm en route home to England, John Newton turned to God.*

Now married to his cousin, Mary Catlett, Newton again put out to sea as captain of a slave ship, and made several voyages. In 1755, at age thirty-two, he finally left the sea and became tide surveyor at Liverpool. He studied Greek, Latin, Hebrew, and Syriac, and became an active churchman and a devotee of George Whitefield, the evangelist. He applied to the Archbishop of York for ordination, but was turned down. Six years later he was ordained by the Bishop of Lincoln and offered the curacy at Olney. There he became friends with the poet William Cowper, and together they produced the famous Olney Hymns. In 1779 he was appointed rector of St. Mary Woolnoth church in the heart of London, and became a force in the Evangelical Revival. Says Edward Dargan, "His earnest devotion to his duties, rather than shining gifts in the pulpit, gave him his strength and influence as a preacher." Newton's hymns, remarkable for their directness and simplicity, are still sung today. Among the more popular, besides "Amazing Grace," are "Glorious Things of Thee Are Spoken," and "How Sweet the Name of Jesus Sounds."

Thoughts Upon the African Slave Trade *was first published in 1788. This excerpt is taken from that edition, published in London by J. Buckland and J. Johnson.*

NINE

Thoughts Upon the African Slave Trade
by John Newton

The nature and effects of that unhappy and disgraceful branch of commerce which has long been maintained on the coast of Africa, with the sole and professed design of purchasing our fellow creatures, in order to supply our West India islands and the American colonies, when they were ours, with slaves, is now generally understood. I hope it will always be a subject of humiliating reflection to me, that I was once an active instrument in a business at which my heart now shudders. My headstrong passions and follies plunged me, in early life, into a succession of difficulties and hardships which, at length, reduced me to seek a refuge among the natives of Africa. There, for about the space of eighteen months, I was in effect a captive and slave myself, and was depressed to the lowest degree of human wretchedness.

Possibly I should not have been so completely miserable, had I lived among the natives only, but it was my lot to reside with white men. At that time several persons of my own color and language were settled upon that part of the Windward coast [of Africa] which lies between Sierra Leone and Cape Mount,[1] for the purpose of purchasing and collecting slaves, to sell to the vessels that arrived from Europe.

This is a bourne [realm] from which few travelers return, who have once determined to venture upon a temporary residence there, but the good providence of God, without my expectation and almost against my will, delivered me from those scenes of wickedness and woe. I arrived at Liverpool in May 1748.

Soon I revisited the place of my captivity as mate of a ship and, in the year 1750, I was appointed commander [*i.e.*, ship's captain], in which capacity I made three voyages to the Windward coast for slaves. I first saw the coast of Guinea in the year

1745, and took my last leave of it in 1754. It was not intentionally a farewell, but, through the mercy of God, it proved so. I fitted out for a fourth voyage, and was upon the point of sailing, when I was arrested by a sudden illness, and I resigned the ship to another captain.

Thus I was unexpectedly freed from this disagreeable service. Disagreeable I had long found it; but I think I should have quitted it sooner had I considered it, as I now do, to be unlawful and wrong. But I never had a scruple upon this head at the time, nor was such a thought once suggested to me by any friend. What I did, I did ignorantly, considering it as the line of life which Divine Providence had allotted me. I had no concern, in point of conscience, but to treat the slaves, while under my care, with as much humanity as a regard to my own safety would admit.[2]

The experience and observation of nine years would qualify me for being a competent witness upon this subject, could I safely trust to the report of memory after an interval of more than thirty-three years. But in the course of so long a period, the ideas of past scenes and transactions grow indistinct. I am aware that what I have seen, and what I have only heard related, may by this time have become so insensibly blended together that, in some cases, it may be difficult, if not impossible for me, to distinguish them with absolute certainty. It is, however, my earnest desire that I may offer nothing in writing, as from my own knowledge, which I could not cheerfully, if requisite, confirm upon oath.

I am not qualified, and if I were, I should think it rather unsuitable to consider the African slave trade merely in a political light, in my present character as a minister of the gospel. This disquisition more properly belongs to persons in a civil life. Only thus far my character as a minister will allow. It requires me to observe that the best human policy is that which is connected with a reverential regard to Almighty God, the supreme governor of the earth. Every plan which aims at the welfare of a nation, in defiance of His authority and laws, however apparently wise, will prove to be essentially defective, and if persisted in, ruinous. The righteous Lord loveth righteousness, and He has engaged to plead the cause and vindicate the wrongs of the oppressed. It is righteousness that exalteth a nation. Wickedness is the present reproach, and will sooner or later, unless repentance intervene, prove the ruin of any people.

Though I were even sure that a principal branch of the [British] public revenue depended upon the African trade (which

I apprehend is far from being the case), if I had access and influence, I should think myself bound to say to Government, to Parliament, and to the nation, "It is not lawful to put it into the treasury, because it is the price of blood."[3]

I account an intelligent farmer to be a good politician in this sense: that if he has a large heap of good corn [wheat], he will not put a small quantity that is damaged to the rest, for the sake of increasing the heap. He knows that such an addition would spoil the whole. God forbid that any supposed profit we derive from the groans, agonies, and blood of the poor Africans should draw down His heavy curse upon all that we might otherwise honorably and comfortably possess.

For the sake of method I wish to consider the African trade, first, with regard to the effect it has upon our own people; secondly, as it concerns the blacks, or as they are more contemptuously styled, the Negro slaves, whom we purchase upon the coast. But these two topics are so interwoven together that it will not be easy to keep them exactly separate.

1. The first point I shall mention is surely of political importance, if the lives of our fellow-subjects be so, and if a rapid loss of seamen deserves the attention of a maritime people. This loss, in the African trade, is truly alarming. Many of them are cut off in their first voyage and consequently before they can properly rank as seamen, though they would have been seamen had they lived. But the neighborhood of our seaports is continually drained of men and boys to supply the places of those who die abroad; and if they are not all seamen, they are all our brethren and countrymen, subjects of the British government.

The people who remain on shipboard upon the open coast [of West Africa], if not accustomed to the climate, are liable to the attack of an inflammatory fever which is not often fatal, unless the occurrence of unfavorable circumstances makes it so. When this danger is over, the sailors must be exposed to the weather, especially on the Windward coast. There a great part of the [human] cargo is procured by boats which are often sent to the distance of thirty or forty leagues,[4] and are sometimes a month before they return.

Many vessels arrive upon the coast before the rainy season, which continues from about May to October, is over. Ships which arrive in the dry season often remain till the rains return before they can complete their purchase. A proper shelter from the weather in an open boat, when the rain is incessant, night and day, for weeks and months, is impracticable. I have myself, in such a boat, been five or six days together without a dry thread about me, sleeping or waking. The boats seldom return without bringing some of the people ill of dangerous fevers, occasioned either by the weather or by unwholesome diet, such as the crude fruits and palm wine.

The article of women, likewise, contributes largely to the loss of our seamen. When they are on shore they often involve themselves in quarrels with the natives, and if not killed upon the spot, are frequently poisoned. In some ships, perhaps in the most, the license allowed in this particular was almost unlimited. Moral turpitude was seldom considered. These excesses, if they do not induce fevers, at least render the constitution less able to support them; and lewdness, too frequently, terminates in death.

The risk of insurrections is to be added. They are seldom suppressed without considerable loss; and sometimes they succeed, to the destruction of a whole ship's company at once. Seldom a year passes, but we hear of one or more such catastrophes; and we likewise hear sometimes of whites and blacks involved in one moment in one common ruin, by the gunpowder taking fire and blowing up the ship.

The fact is sure that a great number of our seamen perish in the slave trade. I believe I shall state the matter sufficiently low if I suppose that at least one-fifth of those who go from England to the coast of Africa, in ships that trade for slaves, never return from thence.

2. There is a second [point] which is, or ought to be, deemed of importance, considered in a political light: I mean, the dreadful effects of this trade upon the minds of those who are engaged in it. In general I know of no method of getting money, not even highway robbery, which has so direct a tendency to efface the moral sense and rob the heart of every gentle and humane disposition.

Usually about two-thirds of a cargo of slaves are males. When a hundred and fifty or two hundred stout men, torn from their native land, many of whom never saw the sea, much less a ship; who have probably the same natural prejudice against a white man as we have against a black; and who often bring with them an apprehension they are bought to be eaten: I say, when thus circumstanced, it is not to be expected that they will tamely resign themselves to their situation. It is always taken for granted that they will attempt to gain their liberty if possible. Accordingly as we dare not trust them, we receive them on board from the first as enemies, and they are all put in irons.

One unguarded hour, or minute, is sufficient to give the slaves the opportunity they are always waiting for. An attempt to rise upon the ship's company brings on instantaneous and horrid war; for when they are once in motion, they are desperate. Sometimes when the slaves are ripe for an insurrection, one of them will impeach the affair. The traitor to the cause of liberty is [then] caressed, rewarded, and deemed an honest fellow. The patriots, who formed and animated the plan, if they can be found out, must be treated as villains and punished to intimidate the rest.

I have seen them sentenced to unmerciful whippings, continued till the poor creatures have not had power to groan under their misery, and hardly a sign of life has remained. I have seen them agonizing for hours, I believe for days together, under the torture of the thumbscrews.[5] There have been instances in which cruelty has proceeded still further.

A mate of a ship purchased a young woman with a fine child of about a year old in her arms. In the night, in the longboat, the child cried much and disturbed his sleep. He rose up in great anger and swore that if the child did not cease making such a noise, he would presently silence it. The child continued to cry. At length he rose up a second time, tore the child from the mother, and threw it into the sea. But it was not so easy to pacify the woman; she was too valuable to be thrown overboard, and he was obliged to bear the sound of her lamentations till he could put her on board his ship. But why do I speak of one child when we have heard and read a melancholy story, too notoriously true to admit of contradiction, of more than a hundred grown slaves thrown into the sea at one time from on board a ship, when fresh water was scarce. [This fixed] the loss upon the underwriters, which otherwise, had they died on board, must have fallen upon the owners of the vessel.

These instances are specimens of the spirit produced by the African trade in men who once were no more destitute of the milk of human kindness than ourselves.

Hitherto I have considered the condition of the men slaves only. From the women there is no danger of insurrection, and they are carefully kept from the men; I mean from the black men. I speak not of what is universally, but of what is too commonly and, I am afraid, too generally prevalent. When the women and girls are taken on board a ship, naked, trembling, terrified, perhaps almost exhausted with cold, fatigue, and hunger, they are often exposed to the wanton rudeness of white savages. The poor creatures cannot understand the language they hear, but the looks and manner of the speakers are sufficiently intelligible. But I forbear.

Perhaps some hard-hearted pleader may suggest that such treatment would indeed be cruel in Europe, but the African women are Negroes, savages, who have no idea of the nicer sensations which obtain among civilized people. I dare contradict them in the strongest terms. I have lived long and conversed much amongst these supposed savages. I have often slept in their towns, in a house filled with goods for trade, with no person in the house but myself, and with no other door than a mat. [I slept] in that security which no man in his senses would expect in this civilized nation, especially in this metropolis [London], without the precaution of having strong doors locked and bolted.

With regard to the women, in Sherbro,[6] where I was most acquainted, I have seen many instances of modesty, and even delicacy, which would not disgrace an English woman. Yet such is the treatment which I have known permitted, if not encouraged, in many of our ships, they have been abandoned without restraint to the lawless will of the first comer.

The conduct of many of our people to the natives with whom they trade, as far as circumstances admit, is very similar. They are considered as a people to be robbed and spoiled with impunity. Every art is employed to deceive and wrong them. Not an article that is capable of diminution or adulteration is delivered genuine or entire. The spirits are lowered by water. False heads are put into the kegs that contain gunpowder. The linen and cotton cloths are opened and two or three yards, according to the length of piece, cut off—not from the end, but out of the middle where it is not so readily noticed.

The natives are cheated in the number, weight, measure, or quality of what they purchase in every possible way; and by habit and emulation, a marvelous dexterity is acquired in these practices. And thus the natives in their turn, in proportion to their commerce with the Europeans, and (I am sorry to add) particularly the English, become jealous, insidious, and revengeful. They know with whom they deal, and are accordingly prepared. With a few exceptions, the English and the Africans reciprocally consider each other as consummate villains, who are always watching opportunities to do mischief. In short, we have, I fear, too deservedly a very unfavorable character upon the [African] coast. When I have charged a black with unfairness and dishonesty, he has answered, if able to clear himself, with an air of disdain: "What! Do you think I am a white man?"

Such is the nature, and such are the concomitants of the slave trade; and such is the school in which many thousands of our seamen are brought up. Can we then wonder at that impatience of subordination, and that disposition to mutiny amongst them—which has been of late so loudly complained of and so severely felt? Will not sound policy suggest the necessity of some expedient here? Or can sound policy suggest any effectual expedient but the total suppression of a trade which, like a poisonous root, diffuses its malignity into every branch?

I believe many of the slaves purchased in Sherbro, and probably upon the whole Windward coast, are convicts who have forfeited their liberty by breaking the laws of their country. But I apprehend that the neighborhood of our ships, and the desire of our goods, are motives which often push the rigor of the [Africans'] laws to an extreme which would not be exacted if they were left to themselves.

Slaves are the staple article of the traffic; and though a considerable number may have been born near the sea, I believe the bulk of them are brought from far. I have reason to think that some travel more than a thousand miles before they reach the seacoast. Whether there may be convicts amongst these likewise, or what proportion they may bear to those who are taken prisoners in war, it is impossible to know.

I judge [that] the principal source of the slave trade is the wars that prevail among the natives. The English and other Europeans have been charged with fomenting them. Human nature is much the same in every place, and few people will be willing to allow that the Negroes in Africa are better than themselves. Supposing therefore [that] they wish for European goods, may they not wish to purchase them from a ship just arrived? Of course they must wish for slaves to go to market with; and if they have not slaves, and think themselves strong enough to invade their neighbors, they will probably wish for war. And if once they wish for it, how easy it is to find, or to make, pretexts for breaking an inconvenient peace, or (after the example of greater heroes of Christian name) to make depredations without condescending to assign any reasons.

I verily believe that the far greater part of the wars in Africa would cease if the Europeans would cease to tempt them, by offering goods for slaves. And though they do not bring legions into the field, their wars are bloody. I believe the captives reserved for sale are fewer than the slain.

I have not sufficient data to warrant calculation, but I suppose not less than one hundred thousand slaves are exported annually from all parts of Africa, and that more than one half of these are exported in English bottoms. If but an equal number are killed in war, and if many of these wars are kindled by the incentive of selling their prisoners, what an annual accumulation of blood there must be, crying against the nations of Europe concerned in this trade, and particularly against our own!

I have often been gravely told as a proof that the Africans, however hardly treated, deserve but little compassion, that they are a people so destitute of natural affection that it is common among them for parents to sell their children, and children their parents. I never heard of one instance of either, while I used the Coast. To steal a free man or woman and to sell them on board a ship would, I think, be a more difficult and more dangerous attempt in Sherbro than in London.

I have, to the best of my knowledge, pointed out the principal sources of that immense supply of slaves which furnishes so large an exportation every year. If all that are taken on board the ships were to survive the voyage, and be landed in good order, possibly the English, French, and Dutch islands and colonies would soon be overstocked, and fewer ships would sail to the coast. But a large abatement must be made for mortality. After what I have already said of their treatment, I shall, now that I am again to consider them on board the ships, confine myself to this point.

In the Portuguese ships, which trade from Brazil to the Gold Coast[7] and Angola, I believe, a heavy mortality is not frequent. The slaves have room, they are not put in irons (I speak from information only), and are humanely treated. With our ships, the great object is to be full. When the ship is there, it is thought desirable she should take as many as possible.

The cargo of a vessel of a hundred tons, or little more, is calculated to purchase from 220 to 250 slaves. Their lodging-rooms below the deck, which are three (for the men, the boys, and the women), besides a place for the sick, are sometimes more than five feet high, and sometimes less. This height is divided toward the middle, for the slaves lie in two rows, one above the other, on each side of the ship, close to each other, like books upon a shelf. I have known them so close that the shelf would not, easily, contain one more. And I have known a white man sent down among the men, to lay them in these rows to the greatest advantage, so that as little space as possible might be lost.

Let it be observed that the poor creatures, thus cramped for want of room, are likewise in irons, for the most part both hands and feet, and two together. This makes it difficult for them to turn or move, to attempt either to rise or to lie down, without hurting themselves or each other. Nor is the motion of the ship, especially her heeling, or stoop on one side when under sail, to be omitted. As they lie athwart, or across the ship, this adds to the uncomfortableness of their lodging, especially to those who lie on the leeward or leaning side of the vessel.

Dire is the tossing, deep the groans.

The heat and smell of these rooms, when the weather will not admit of the slaves being brought upon deck, and of having their rooms cleaned every day, would be almost insupportable to a person not accustomed to them. If the slaves and their rooms can be constantly aired, and they are not detained too long on board, perhaps there are not many [who] die; but the contrary is often their lot.

They are kept down by the weather to breathe a hot and corrupted air, sometimes for a week. This, added to the galling of their irons, and the despondency which seizes their spirits when thus confined, soon becomes fatal. And every morning, perhaps, more instances than one are found of the living and the dead, like the captives of Mezentius,[8] fastened together.

Epidemical fevers and fluxes, which fill the ship with noisome and noxious effluvia, often break out and infect the seamen likewise, and thus the oppressors and the oppressed fall by the same stroke. I believe nearly one-half of the slaves on board have sometimes died, and that the loss of a third part in these circumstances is not unusual. The ship in which I was mate left the [African] coast with 218 slaves on board. Though we were not much affected by epidemical disorders, I find by my journal of that voyage (now before me) that we buried sixty-two on our passage to South Carolina, exclusive of those which died before we left the coast, of which I have no account.

I believe upon an average between the more healthy and

the more sickly voyages, and including all contingencies, one-fourth of the whole purchase may be allotted to the article of mortality. [Thus] if the English ships purchase sixty thousand slaves annually, upon the whole extent of the [African] coast, the annual loss of lives cannot be much less than fifteen thousand.

I am now to speak of the survivors. When the ships make the land (usually the West India islands), and have their port in view, after having been four, five, six weeks, or a longer time, at sea, then, and not before, they venture to release the men slaves from their irons. And then the sight of the land, and their freedom from long and painful confinement, usually excite in them a degree of alacrity and a transient feeling of joy.

The prisoner leaps to loose his chains.[9]

But this joy is short-lived indeed. The condition of the unhappy slaves is in a continual progress from bad to worse. Their case is truly pitiable, from the moment they are in a state of slavery in their own country; but it may be deemed a state of ease and liberty compared with their situation on board our ships.

Yet perhaps they would wish to spend the remainder of their days on shipboard, could they know beforehand the nature of the servitude which awaits them on shore. The dreadful hardships and sufferings they have already endured would, to the most of them, only terminate in excessive toil, hunger, and the excruciating tortures of the cart-whip, inflicted at the caprice of an unfeeling overseer, proud of the power allowed him of punishing whom, and when, and how he pleases.

I hope the slaves in our islands are better treated now than they were at the time when I was in the trade. Even then, I know, there were slaves who, under the care and protection of humane masters, were comparatively happy. But I saw and heard enough to satisfy me that their condition, in general, was wretched to the extreme. However, my stay in Antigua and St. Christopher's [now St. Kitts] (the only islands I visited) was too short to qualify me for saying much from my own certain knowledge upon this painful subject. Nor is it needful; enough has been offered by several respectable writers who have had opportunity of collecting surer and fuller information.

One thing I cannot omit, which was told me by the gentleman to whom my ship was consigned at Antigua in the year

1751, and who was himself a planter. He said that calculations had been made, with all possible exactness, to determine which was the preferable, that is, the more saving method of managing slaves:

"Whether to appoint them moderate work, plenty of provision, and such treatment as might enable them to protract their lives to old age?"—or

"By rigorously straining their strength to the utmost, with little relaxation, hard fare, and hard usage, to wear them out before they became useless and unable to do service; and then to buy new ones to fill up their places?"

He further said that these skillful calculators had determined *in favor of the latter mode, as much the cheaper;* and that he could mention several estates in the island of Antigua, on which it was seldom known that a slave had lived above nine years. *Ex pede Herculem!*[10]

When the slaves are landed for sale (for in the Leeward Islands they are usually sold on shore), it may happen that after a long separation in different parts of the ship, when they are brought together in one place, some who are nearly related may recognize each other. If pleasure should be felt upon such a meeting, it can be but momentary. The sale disperses them wide, to different parts of the island, or to different islands. Husbands and wives, parents and children, brothers and sisters, must suddenly part again, probably to meet no more.

After a careful perusal of what I have written, weighing every paragraph distinctly, I can find nothing to retract. As it is not easy to write altogether with coolness upon this business, and especially not easy to me, who have formerly been so deeply engaged in it, I have been jealous lest the warmth of imagination might have insensibly seduced me. I might thereby have aggravated and overcharged some of the horrid features of the African trade which I have attempted to delineate. But on a strict review, I am satisfied.

I have apprised the reader that I write from memory, after an interval of more than thirty years. But at the same time I believe many things which I saw, heard, and felt, upon the coast of Africa are so deeply engraven in my memory that I can hardly forget, or greatly mistake them, while I am capable of remembering anything. I am certainly not guilty of willful misrepresentation.

Upon the whole, I dare appeal to the Great Searcher of hearts, in Whose presence I write, and before Whom I and my readers must all shortly appear, that (with the restrictions and exceptions I have made) I have advanced nothing but what, to the best of my judgment and conscience, is true.

I have likewise written without solicitation, and simply from the motive I have already assigned: a conviction that the share I have formerly had in the trade binds me, in conscience, to throw what light I am able upon the subject, now it is likely to become a point of Parliamentary investigation.[11] No one can have less interest in it than I have at present, further than as I am interested by the feelings of humanity, and a regard for the honor and welfare of my country.

Though unwilling to give offense to a single person, in such a cause I ought not to be afraid of offending many by declaring the truth. If, indeed, there can be many whom even interest can prevail upon to contradict the common sense of mankind, by pleading for a commerce so iniquitous, so cruel, so oppressive, so destructive, as the African Slave Trade!

AMAZING GRACE

Amazing grace! how sweet the sound
  that saved a wretch like me!
I once was lost, but now am found,
  was blind, but now I see.

'Twas grace that taught my heart to fear,
  and grace my fears relieved;
How precious did that grace appear
  the hour I first believed!

Through many dangers, toils, and snares,
  I have already come;
'Tis grace hath brought me safe thus far,
  and grace will lead me home.

The Lord has promised good to me,
  His Word my hope secures;
He will my shield and portion be
  as long as life endures.

—John Newton, 1779

GLORIOUS THINGS OF THEE ARE SPOKEN

Glorious things of thee are spoken,
    Zion, city of our God;
He whose word cannot be broken
    Formed thee for His own abode.
On the Rock of Ages founded,
    What can shake thy sure repose?
With salvation's walls surrounded,
    Thou may'st smile at all thy foes.

See! the streams of living waters,
    Springing from eternal love,
Well supply thy sons and daughters,
    And all fear of want remove.
Who can faint while such a river
    Ever flows their thirst t'assuage—
Grace, which like the Lord the Giver
    Never fails from age to age?

Round each habitation hov'ring
    See! The cloud and fire appear,
For a glory and a cov'ring
    Showing that the Lord is near.
Blest inhabitants of Zion,
    Washed in the Redeemer's blood,
Jesus, whom their souls rely on,
    Makes them kings and priests to God.

Savior, if of Zion's city
    I, through grace, a member am,
Let the world deride or pity,
    I will glory in Thy Name.
Fading is the worldling's pleasure,
    All his boasted pomp and show;
Solid joys and lasting treasure
    None but Zion's children know.

—John Newton, 1779

NOTES

1. Newton writes, "That part of the African shore which lies between the river Sierra Leone and Cape Palmas [that is, between Sierra Leone and a point on the border of present-day Liberia and Ivory Coast] is usually known by the name of Windward or Grain Coast." The "grain" was a kind of pepper known to traders as "grains of paradise." Cape Mount is a promontory on the southeast coast of Liberia.

2. In his *Authentic Narrative*, published in 1764, Newton elaborates on this point, as well as on his "sudden illness": "My stay at home was intended to be but short and by the beginning of November [1754] I was again ready for the sea [in a ship named the *Bee*], but the Lord saw fit to overrule my design. During the time I was engaged in the slave trade, I never had the least scruple as to its lawfulness. I was upon the whole satisfied with it, as the appointment Providence had worked out for me; yet it was, in many respects, far from eligible. It is indeed accounted a genteel employment and is usually very profitable, though to me it did not prove so, the Lord seeing that a large increase of wealth would not be good for me. However, I considered myself a sort of gaoler or turnkey, and I was sometimes shocked with an employment that was perpetually conversant with chains, bolts, and shackles. In this view I had often petitioned in my prayers that the Lord (in His own time) would be pleased to fix me in a more humane calling, and (if it might be) place me where I might have more frequent converse with His people and ordinances and be freed from those long separations from home which very often were hard to bear. My prayers were now answered, though in a way I little expected. I was within two days of sailing [from Liverpool] and to all appearance in good health as usual; but in the afternoon, as I was sitting with Mrs. N------, drinking tea and talking over past events, I was in a moment seized with a fit, which deprived me of sense and motion and left no other sign of life than that of breathing. I suppose it was of the apoplectic kind. It lasted about an hour, and when I recovered, it left a pain and dizziness in my head which continued with such symptoms as induced the physicians to judge it would not be safe or prudent for me to proceed on the voyage. I resigned the command the day before she sailed. . . . The future consequences of that voyage proved extremely calamitous. The person who went in my room [that is, the new captain], most of the officers and many of the crew died, and the vessel was brought home with great difficulty."

3. Cf. Matthew 27:6.

4. An English league is roughly the equivalent of three miles.

5. Newton himself, when master of a slave-carrying vessel, used the thumbscrew to punish blacks who threatened insurrection, according to his *Journal*.

6. Sherbro is located on an estuary on the southwest coast of Sierra Leone, opposite Sherbro Island.

7. Ghana was formerly known as the Gold Coast. Before becoming independent in 1960 it was occupied by the Dutch, Portuguese, and British.

8. In Roman mythology, Mezentius was a cruel Etruscan king who fought against Aeneas. He bound living persons face to face with dead ones, leaving them to starve.

9. From Isaac Watts' hymn, "Jesus Shall Reign Where'er the Sun," *circa* 1719.

10. "Hercules from his foot"—i.e., one can judge the whole from the part.

11. Newton himself gave evidence to the Privy Council in the year 1789 on his experience as a slave trader, one year after this document was published.

Jean Baptiste Massillon

The closing years of the seventeenth century and the beginning years of the eighteenth were remarkable for producing in France some of the finest preachers in the history of the Roman Catholic church. Three names in particular—Bossuet, Bourdaloue, and Massillon—could be said to rank with the greatest pulpiteers in Christian history.

Jean Baptiste Massillon (1663-1742) was born in Hières, Provence, on the French Riviera east of Marseilles. Though a gifted orator from childhood, he was reluctant to become a preacher. But he was trained in the college of the Oratorian order, became a priest in 1691, and five years later was appointed to head the Seminary of St. Magloire in Paris. Soon he was preaching before King Louis XIV, who paid him a striking compliment: "Father, I have heard in this chapel many great orators, and have been much pleased with them; but whenever I have heard you, I have been displeased with myself."

Crowds flocked to hear Massillon wherever he preached, and when Louis XIV died in 1715, he was called to preach the funeral sermon before a vast congregation in Notre Dame Cathedral. Two years later he was made bishop of Clermont and was elected to the French Academy. He retired from the Parisian scene and spent his remaining years living and laboring in his diocese.

Edwin Dargan, professor of homiletics at Southern Baptist Seminary in Louisville, Kentucky, from 1892 to 1907, wrote in his History of Preaching, "Bossuet and Fénelon gained distinction in other fields, including literature; but Massillon's sermons are literature. It is said that Voltaire kept a volume of them on his table that by frequent reading he might improve his own style. But exquisite as it is, the style of these sermons is not their chief merit. In Massillon as much as in any orator is found the exemplification of Matthew Arnold's famous requirement of sweetness and light. But the light keeps the sweetness from cloying upon the taste. Massillon's was clear and trained intelligence. His breadth of culture and sobriety of judgment are apparent in his work, and his knowledge of human nature in general and of his own age in particular is amply in evidence. Someone asked him once how it *was that, being a priest, he knew so much of the sinfulness of mankind. His answer was at once honest and correct: 'From my own heart.'"*

Two of his sermons may be said to have withstood the erosion of time. One is the message you are about to read, which was originally called, "The Fewness of the Elect," or "The Small Number of the Saved," and was preached in 1704. It is taken by permission from Volume 3 of The World's Great Sermons, *compiled by Grenville Kleiser and published in 1908 by Funk & Wagnalls, New York and London. The other was Massillon's oration at the funeral of Louis XIV, "the Great," which he began by reading from Ecclesiastes 1:16, "I spoke in my heart, saying, Behold, I have become great." He paused to let the text sink into the minds of his elegant audience, gathered in all the pageantry of the cathedral. Then he broke the silence by saying, "Dieu seul est grand. God alone is great, my brethren."*

The Small Number
of the Saved
by Jean Baptiste Massillon

"And many lepers were in Israel in the time of
Elisha the prophet; and none of them was cleansed except
Naaman the Syrian."

(Luke 4:27)

Every day, my brethren, you continue to ask us whether the
road to Heaven is really so difficult, and the number of the saved
really so small as we represent. To a question so often proposed,
our Savior answers you here. [He tells us] that there were many
widows in Israel suffering from famine, but the widow of Sarepta
alone was found worthy of help by the prophet Elijah; and that
the number of lepers was great in Israel in the time of the
prophet Elisha, but that only Naaman was cured by the man of
God.[1]

Were I here, brothers and sisters, for the purpose of alarming rather than instructing you, I would need only to recapitulate
what we find in the holy writings with regard to this great truth.
The family of Noah alone was saved at the time of the flood.
Abraham was chosen from among men to be the sole depository
of the covenant with God. Joshua and Caleb were the only two of
six hundred thousand Hebrews who saw the land of promise. Job
was the only upright man in the land of Uz, and similarly Lot in
Sodom.[2]

In the book of Isaiah you would see [God's] elect as rare as
the grapes that are found after the vintage, that have escaped the
search of the gleaner; as rare as the blades in the field that escape
the scythe of the mower.[3] I might have spoken to you of two
roads,[4] one of which is narrow, rugged, and the path of a very
small number; the other broad, open, and strewn with flowers,
and almost the general path of men. I might have told you that
everywhere in the holy writings the multitude is always spoken of

as forming the party of the reprobate, while the saved, compared with the rest of mankind, form only a small flock. I would have left you in fears with regard to your salvation, which would have been cruel to those who have not renounced faith and hope. But what would it serve to limit the fruits of this instruction to the single point of setting forth how few persons will be saved? It would make the danger known without instructing you how to avoid it. It would allow you the sword of the wrath of God suspended over your heads without assisting you to escape the threatened blow. It would alarm but not instruct the sinner.

My intention is therefore to search for the cause of this small number in our morals and manner of life. As everyone flatters himself he will not be excluded, it is of importance to examine if his confidence be well-founded. I wish not to make you generally conclude that few will be saved, but to bring you to ask yourselves if, living as you live, *you* can hope to be saved.

Who am I? What am I doing for Heaven? And what can be my hopes in eternity? I propose no other order in a matter of such importance. What are the causes which render salvation so rare? I mean to point out three principal causes, which is the only arrangement of this discourse. Art, and far-sought reasonings, would be ill-timed here. No subject can be more worthy of your attention, since it goes to inform you what may be the hopes of your eternal destiny.

I.

Among the saved we can only comprehend two descriptions of persons: those who have been so happy as to preserve their innocence pure and undefiled, and those who, after having lost it, have regained it by repentance. Heaven is open only to the innocent or to the penitent. Now, of which party are you? Are you innocent? Are you penitent?

Nothing unclean shall enter the Kingdom of God. We carry there either an innocence unsullied, or an innocence regained. Now, to die innocent is a grace to which few souls can aspire; and to live penitently is a mercy which the relaxed state of our morals renders equally rare. Who, indeed, will pretend to salvation by the claim of innocence? Where are the pure souls in whom sin has never dwelt, and who have preserved to the end the sacred treasure of grace confided to them by baptism?

In those happy days when the whole church was still an

assembly of saints, it was uncommon to find an instance of a believer who, after having acknowledged Jesus Christ and received the gifts of the Holy Spirit, fell back to his former irregularities of life. Ananias and Sapphira were the only prevaricators [we know of] in the church of Jerusalem; in Corinth [we know of] only one incestuous sinner.⁵ Repentance was then a remedy almost unknown. But since that time the number of the upright diminishes in proportion as that of believers increases. It would appear that the world, pretending now to have become almost generally Christian, has brought with it into the church its corruptions and its maxims.

Almost from the breast of our mothers we all go astray. Our first desires are passions. Our reason increases and expands on the wrecks of our innocence. The earth, says a prophet, is infected by the corruption of those who inhabit it.⁶ All have violated the laws, changed the ordinances, and broken the alliance which should have endured forever. All commit sin, and scarcely is there one to be found who does the work of the Lord. Injustice, calumny, lying, treachery, adultery, and the blackest crimes have deluged the earth. A brother lays snares for his brother; the father is divided from his children, the husband from his wife; there is no tie which a vile interest does not sever. Good faith and probity are no longer virtues except among the simple people. Animosities are endless. Reconciliations are feints, and never is a former enemy regarded as a brother. They tear, they devour each other. Assemblies are no longer but for the purpose of public and general censure. The purest virtue is no longer a protection from the malignity of tongues. Gaming has become either a trade, a fraud, or a fury. Repasts—those innocent ties of society—degenerate into excesses of which we dare not speak. Our age witnesses horrors with which our forefathers were unacquainted.

Behold, then, already one path of salvation shut to the generality of men. All have erred. Whoever are listening to me now, the time has been when sin reigned over you. Age may perhaps have calmed your passions, but what was your youth? Long and habitual infirmities may perhaps have disgusted you with the world, but what use did you formerly make of the vigor of health? A sudden inspiration of grace may have turned your heart, but do you not most fervently beseech that every moment prior to that inspiration might be effaced from the remembrance of the Lord?

But with what am I taking up time? We are all sinners, O

my God, and You know our hearts! What we know of our errors is perhaps the most pardonable in Your sight; and we all allow that by innocence we have no claim to salvation. There remains therefore only one resource, which is repentance. After our shipwreck, say the saints, it is the timely plank which alone can convey us into port. There is no other means of salvation for us. Whoever you are, prince or subject, high or low, repentance alone can save you. Now permit me to ask: Where are the penitent? You will find more, says a holy father, who have never fallen, than those who after their fall, have raised themselves by true repentance. This is a terrible saying, but let us not carry things too far. The truth is sufficiently dreadful without adding new terrors to it by vain declamation.

Let us only examine whether the majority of us have a right, through penitence, to salvation. Who is a penitent? According to Tertullian, a penitent is a believer who feels every moment his former unhappiness in forsaking and losing his God. One who has his guilt incessantly before his eyes; who finds everywhere the traces and remembrance of it.

A penitent is a man entrusted by God with judgment against himself. He refuses himself innocent pleasures because he had formerly indulged in those the most criminal. In the loss of riches or health he sees only a withdrawal of favors that he had formerly abused; in the humiliations that happen to him, only the pains of his guilt; in the agonies with which he is racked, only the commencement of those punishments he has justly merited. Such is a penitent.

But I again ask you, where among us are penitents of this description? Look around you. I don't tell you to judge your brethren, but just examine the manners and morals of those who surround you. I am not speaking of those open and avowed sinners who have thrown off even the appearance of virtue. I'm speaking of those who, like yourselves, live as most live, and whose actions present nothing particularly shameful or depraved to the public view. The others are sinners and admit it; you are not innocent and you confess it. Now, are they penitent? Or are you?

Age, avocation, more serious employments, may perhaps have checked the sallies of youth. Even the bitterness which the Almighty has made attendant on our passions—the deceits, the treacheries of the world, an injured fortune, with ruined constitution—may have cooled the ardor and confined the irregular desires of your hearts. Crimes may have disgusted you even with sin itself—for passions gradually extinguish themselves. Time, and the natural inconstancy of the heart, will bring these about.

Nevertheless, though detached from sin by incapability, you are no nearer your God. According to the world you are become more prudent, more regular, to a greater extent what it calls men of probity, more exact in fulfilling your public or private duties. But you are not repentant. You have ceased from your disorders, but you have not expiated them. You are not converted. This great stroke, this grand operation on the heart which regenerates man, has not yet been felt by you. But this situation, so truly dangerous, does not alarm you. Sins which have never been washed away by sincere repentance, and consequently never obliterated from the book of life, appear in your eyes as no longer existing. You will tranquilly leave this world in a state of impenitence, so much the more dangerous as you will die without being sensible of your danger.

What I say here is not merely a rash expression or an emotion of zeal. Nothing is more real or more exactly true. It is the situation of almost all men, even the wisest and most esteemed of the world. The morality of the younger stages of life is always lax, if not licentious. Age, disgust, and establishment for life, fix the heart and withdraw it from debauchery; but where are those who are converted? Where are those who expiate their crimes by tears of sorrow and true repentance? Where are those who, having begun as sinners, end as penitents?

Show me, in your manner of living, the smallest trace of penitence! Are your graspings at wealth and power, your anxieties to attain the favor of the great (and by these means an increase of employments and influence)—are these proofs of it? Would you wish to reckon even your crimes as virtues? Or that the results of your ambition, pride, and avarice should discharge you from an obligation which they themselves have imposed? You are penitent to the world, but are you so to Jesus Christ? The infirmities with which God afflicts you, the enemies He raises up against you, the disgraces and losses with which He tries you—do you receive them all as you ought, with humble submission to His will? Or rather, far from finding in them occasions of repentance, do you not turn them into the objects of new crimes?

It is the duty of an innocent soul to receive with submission the chastisements of the Almighty; to discharge, with courage, the painful duties of the station allotted to him, and to be faithful to the laws of the gospel. But do sinners owe nothing beyond this? And yet they pretend to salvation. Upon what claim? To say that you are innocent before God, your own consciences will witness against you. To endeavor to persuade yourselves that you are penitent, you dare not, and you would condemn yourselves by your own mouths. Upon *what*, then do you depend, O man, who continue to live so tranquil?

And what renders it still more dreadful is that, acting in this manner, you only follow the current. Your morals are the morals of well-nigh all men. You may, perhaps, be acquainted with someone still more guilty, for I suppose you too have still remaining some sentiments of religion and regard for your salvation. But do you know any real penitents? I am afraid we must search the deserts and solitudes for them. You possibly may mention, among persons of rank and worldly custom, a small number whose morals and mode of life, more austere and guarded than the generality, attract the attention (and very likely the censure) of the public. But all the rest walk in the uniform path. I see clearly that everyone comforts himself by the example of his neighbor. In that point, children succeed to the false security of their fathers. None live innocent, and none die penitent. I see it, and I cry, "O God! If You have not deceived us; if all You have told us with regard to the road to eternal life shall be strictly fulfilled; if the number of those who must perish shall not influence You to abate from the severity of Your laws, what will become of that immense multitude of creatures which every hour disappears from the face of the earth? Where are our friends, our relations who have gone before us? And what is their lot in the eternal regions of the dead? What shall we ourselves become?"

When a prophet complained to the Lord that all Israel had forsaken His protection, he was told that seven thousand still remained who had not bowed the knee to Baal.[7] Behold the number of pure and faithful souls which a whole kingdom then contained! But could You still, O my God, comfort the anguish of Your servants today in the same assurance? I know that Your eye still discerns some upright among us; that the priesthood still has its Phineases, the magistracy its Samuels, the sword its Joshuas, the court its Daniels, its Esthers, and its Davids. But those happy remnants of the children of Israel who shall inherit salvation—what are they, compared to the grains of sand in the sea—that is, to that number of sinners who fight for their own destruction?

And after this do you come, my brothers, to inquire if it be true that few shall be saved? You have said it, O my God! And therefore it is a truth which shall endure forever.

But even admitting that the Almighty had not spoken thus, I would wish to review for an instant what passes among men: the laws by which they are governed; the maxims by which the multitude is regulated. This is the force of habit and custom.

II.

The maxims most universally received in all countries, and upon which depend in general the morals of the multitude, are incompatible with salvation. The rules laid down, approved, and authorized by the world with regard to the application of wealth, the love of glory, Christian moderation, and the duties of offices and conditions, are directly opposed to those of the evangelists,[8] and consequently can lead only to death. I shall not at present enter into a detail too extended and too little serious, perhaps, for Christians.

I need not tell you that it is an established custom in the world to allow the liberty of proportioning expenses to rank and wealth. Provided it is a patrimony we inherit from our ancestors, we may distinguish ourselves by the use of it without restraint to our luxury, or without regard to anything but our pride and caprice.

But Christian moderation has its rules. We are not the absolute masters of our riches, nor are we entitled to abuse what the Almighty has bestowed upon us for better purposes. Above all, while thousands of unfortunate wretches languish in poverty, whatever we make use of beyond the wants and necessary expenses of our station is an inhumanity and a theft from the poor. "But these are refinements of devotion," they say, "and in matters of expense and profusion, nothing is excessive or blameable according to the world, but what may tend to devalue the fortune."

I need not tell you that it is an approved custom to decide out lots in life, and to regulate our choice of professions or situations, by the order of our birth or the interests of fortune. But O my God! Does the ministry of Your gospel derive its source from the worldly considerations of a carnal birth? "We cannot fix everything," says the world, "and it would be melancholy to see persons of rank and birth in avocations unworthy of their dignity. If you are born to a name distinguished in the world, you must get forward by dint of intrigue, meanness, and expense. Make fortune your idol. However much that ambition is condemned by the laws of the gospel, that sentiment is worthy of your name and birth. You are of a sex and rank which introduce you to the gaieties of the world. You cannot but do as others do. You must frequent all the public places where those of your age and rank assemble. You must enter into the same pleasures, pass your days in the same frivolities, and expose yourself to the same dangers. These are the received maxims, and you were not made to reform them." Such is the doctrine of the world!

Now permit me to ask you here, who confirms you in these ways? By what rule are they justified to your mind? Who authorizes you in this dissipation which is neither agreeable to the title you have received by baptism, nor perhaps to those you hold from your ancestors? Who authorizes those public pleasures which you only think innocent because your soul, already too familiarized with sin, feels no longer the dangerous impressions or tendency of them? Who authorizes you to lead an effeminate and sensual life, without virtue, sufferance, or any religious exercise? To live like a stranger in the midst of your own family, disdaining to inform yourself with regard to the morals of those dependent upon you? To be ignorant whether they believe in the same God, or whether they fulfil the duties of the religion you profess?

Who authorizes you in maxims so little Christian? Is it the gospel of Jesus Christ? Is it the doctrine of the apostles and saints? For surely some rule is necessary to assure us that we are in safety. What is yours? *"Custom!"* That is the only reply you can make! "We see none around us but those who conduct themselves in the same way and by the same rule. Entering into the world, we find the manners already established. Our fathers lived thus, and from them we copy our customs. An individual cannot be wiser than the whole world, and must not pretend to make himself singular by acting contrary to the general voice. All the wisest people conform to custom."

Such, my brethren, are your only comforters against all the terrors of religion! None act up to the law. The public example is the only guarantee of our morals. We never reflect that, as the Holy Spirit says, the laws of the people are vain; that our Savior has left us rules in which neither times, ages, nor customs can ever authorize the smallest change; that the heavens and the earth shall pass away, that customs and manners shall change, but that the divine laws will everlastingly be the same.

We content ourselves with looking around us. We do not reflect that what at present we call custom would in former times, before the morals of Christians became degenerated, have been regarded as monstrous singularities; and if corruption has gained since that period, these vices, though they have lost their singularity, have not lost their guilt. We do not reflect that we shall be judged by the gospel, and not by custom; by the examples of the holy, and not by men's opinions; that the habits which are only established among believers by the relaxation of faith are abuses we are to lament, not examples we are to follow. In changing the manners, they have not changed our duties. The common and general example which authorizes them only proves that virtue is rare, but not that profligacy is permitted. In a word, piety and a real Christian life are too repulsive to our depraved nature to be practiced by the majority of men.

Come now and say that you only do as others do. It is exactly by that you condemn yourselves. What? The only motive for your confidence, according to the Scriptures, is the road that conducts to death. Is it not that which the majority pursue? Which is the party of the reprobate? Is it not the multitude? You do nothing but what others do, you say. But thus, in the time of Noah, all perished who were buried under the waters of the deluge. All who, in the time of Nebuchadnezzar, prostrated themselves before the golden calf. All who, in the time of Elijah, bowed the knee to Baal. All who, in the time of Eleazar, abandoned the law of their father.[9] You only do what others do? But that is precisely what the Scriptures forbid. They tell us, "Do not conform yourselves to this corrupted age."[10]

Now, the corrupted age means not the small number of the just whom you endeavor not to imitate. It means the multitude whom you follow. You only do what others do? You will consequently experience the same lot. "Misery to you," cried St. Augustine, "fatal torrent of human customs. Will you never suspend your course? Will you, to the end, draw the children of Adam into your immense and terrible abyss?"

In the church of Christ are two roads, one broad and open, by which almost the whole world passes, and which leads to death, and the other narrow, where few indeed enter, and which conducts to life eternal. In which of these am I? Are my morals those which are common to persons of my rank, age, and situation in life? Am I with the great number? Then I am not in the right path. I am losing myself. The great number in every station is not the party saved.

In place of saying to ourselves, "What are my hopes?" we reason to ourselves, "I am not in a worse state than others! Those of my rank and age live as I do. Why should I not live like them?" *Why,* my dear hearers? For that very reason! The general mode of living cannot be that of a Christian life. In all ages the holy have been remarkable and singular men. Their manners were always different from those of the world, and they have only been saints because their lives had no similarity to those of the rest of mankind. In the time of Ezra, in spite of the defense, the custom prevailed of intermarrying with strange women.[11] This abuse became general. The priests and the people no longer made any scruple of it. But what did this holy restorer of the law? Did he [Ezra] follow the example of his brethren? Did he believe that guilt, in becoming general, became more legitimate? No. He recalled the people to a sense of the abuse. He took the book of the law in his hand and explained it to the affrighted people. He corrected the custom by the truth.

Follow the history of the just from age to age, and see if Lot conformed himself to the habits of Sodom, or if nothing distinguished him from the other inhabitants; if Abraham lived like the rest of his age; if Job resembled the other princes of his nation; if Esther conducted herself in the court of Ahasuerus like the other women of that prince;[12] if many widows in Israel resembled Judith; if among the children of the [Assyrian] captivity it is not said of Tobias alone that he copied not the conduct of his brethren, and that he even fled from the danger of their commerce and society.[13] See if in those happy days, when Christians were all saints, they did not shine like stars in the midst of the corrupted nations; and if they did not serve as a spectacle to angels and men by the singularity of their lives and manners. See if the pagans did not reproach them for their retirement, and their shunning of all public theaters, places, and pleasures. See if they did not complain that the Christians affected to distinguish themselves in everything from their fellow-citizens, by forming a separate people in the midst of the people, and having their particular laws and customs. If a man from the [pagan] side embraced the party of the Christians, see if they [the pagans] did not consider him as forever lost to their pleasures, assemblies, and customs. In a word, see if in all ages the saints whose lives and actions have been transmitted down to us have resembled the rest of mankind.

You will perhaps tell us that all these are singularities and exceptions, rather than rules which the world is obliged to follow. They are exceptions it is true, but the reason is that the general rule is to reject salvation. A religious and pious soul in the midst of the world is always a singularity approaching to a miracle. You say the whole world is not obliged to follow these examples. But is not piety alike the duty of all? To be saved, must we not be holy? Must Heaven be gained by some with difficulty and sufferance, and by others with ease? Have you any other gospel to follow? Any other duties to fulfill? Any other promises to hope for than those of the Holy Bible?

III.

After this will you console yourselves with the multitude, as if the greatness of the number could render the guilt unpunished, and the Almighty dare not condemn all those who live like you? What are all creatures in the sight of God? Did the multitude of the guilty prevent Him from destroying all flesh at the deluge? From making fire from Heaven descend upon the five iniquitous cities? From burying Pharaoh and all his army in the waters of the Red Sea? From striking with death all who murmured in the desert?[14] All the kings of the earth may reckon upon the number of the guilty, because the punishment becomes impossible, or at least difficult, when the fault is become general. But God, who as Job says, wipes the impious from the race of the earth,[15] as one wipes the dust from off a garment—God, in whose sight all people are as if they were not—numbers not the guilty. He has regard only to the crimes; and all that the weak and miserable sinner can expect from his unhappy accomplices is to have them as companions in his misery.

At your baptism you renounced the world. It is a promise you made to God before the holy altar. The Church has been the guaranty and depository of it. You are therefore required, by the most sacred of all vows, to hate the world; that is to say, not to conform yourselves to it. Now, what is this world which you ought to hate? I have only to answer that it is the one you love. It is a society of sinners whose desires, fears, hopes, cares, projects, joys, and chagrins turn upon the successes or misfortunes of this life. This world is an assemblage of people who look upon the earth as their country, the life to come as an exile, the promises of faith as a dream, and death as the greatest of all misfortunes. This world is a temporal kingdom where our Savior is unknown; where those acquainted with His Name hate His maxims, despise His followers, and neglect or insult Him in His sacraments and worship. It is the vast multitude. Behold the world which you ought to shun, hate, and war against by your example!

Now, is this your situation in regard to the world? Are its pleasures a fatigue to you? Do its excesses afflict you? On the contrary, are not its laws your laws, its maxims your maxims? Where are those who sincerely renounce the pleasures, habits, maxims, and hopes of this world? We find many who complain of it, and accuse it of injustice, ingratitude, and caprice; who speak warmly of its abuses and errors. But in decrying, they continue to love and follow it; they cannot bring themselves to do without it.

You have also renounced the flesh at your baptism; that is to say, you are engaged not to live according to the sensual appetites. This is not an acquired perfection; it is a vow. In a word, you have anathematized Satan and all his works. And what are his works? That which composes almost the thread and end of your life: pomp, pleasure, luxury, and dissipation; lying, of which he is the father; pride, of which he is the model; jealousy, of which he is the artisan. You continually demand of us if theaters and other public places of amusement be innocent recreations for Christians. Tertullian says if they are not the works of Jesus Christ they must be the works of Satan. Every Christian therefore ought to abstain from them. However innocent he may flatter himself to be in bringing from these places an untainted heart, it is sullied by being there.

Who shall be saved? Those who work out their salvation with fear and trembling; who live in the world without indulging in its vices. Who shall be saved? That Christian woman who, shut up in the circle of her domestic duties, rears up her children in faith and piety; divides her heart between her Savior and her husband; is adorned with delicacy and modesty; sits not down in the assemblies of vanity; makes not a law of the ridiculous customs of the world, but regulates these customs by the law of God, and makes virtue appear more amiable by her rank and her example.

Who shall be saved? That believer who, in the relaxation of modern times, imitates the manners of the first Christians: whose hands are clean and his heart pure; who is watchful; who has not lifted up his soul to vanity, but continually applies himself to purify it; who swears not deceitfully against his neighbor, nor is indebted to fraudulent ways; who with benefits repays the enemy who sought his ruin; who sacrifices not the truth to a vile interest; who makes his house and interest the refuge of his fellow-creatures, and himself the consolation of the afflicted; who regards his wealth as the property of the poor. Just, generous, sincere, charitable, humble in affliction, a Christian under injuries and penitent even in prosperity—who will merit salvation? You, my dear hearer, if you follow these examples, for such are the souls to be saved. Now these assuredly do not form the greatest number. While you continue, therefore, to live like the multitude, it is a striking proof that you disregard your salvation.

IV.

These, my brethren, are truths which should make us tremble! Nor are they those vague ones which are told to all men, and which none apply to themselves. The multitude tremble not. There is only a small number of the just who work out severally their salvation with fear and trembling. All the rest are tranquil. After having lived with the multitude, they flatter themselves that they shall be particularized at death. Everyone augurs favorably for himself, and vainly imagines that he shall be an exception.

On this account, my brethren, I confine myself to you who are gathered here. I speak no longer to the rest of mankind. I look at you as if you were the only ones on earth, and here is the thought that seizes me and terrifies me. I make the supposition that this is your last hour, and the end of the world; that the heavens are about to open above your heads, that Jesus Christ is to appear in His glory in the midst of this sanctuary, and that you are gathered here only to wait for Him, as trembling criminals on whom is to be pronounced either a sentence of grace or a decree of eternal death.

For it is vain for you to flatter yourselves. You will die in such character as you are today. All those impulses toward change with which you amuse yourselves, will continue to amuse you down to the bed of death. Such is the experience of all generations. The only thing new you will then find in yourselves will be, perhaps, a reckoning against you a trifle larger than that which you would have to answer for now. According to what you would be if you were at this moment to be judged, you may almost determine what will befall you at the termination of your life.

Now I ask you—and I ask it smitten with dread, not separating my own lot from yours in this matter, and putting myself into the same frame of mind in which I desire you to come—I ask you, if Jesus Christ were to appear in this sanctuary, in the midst of this assembly, the most illustrious in the world, to pass judgment on us, to make the awful line of separation between the goats and the sheep, do you believe that the majority of all of us who are here would be set on His right hand? Do you believe that things would even be equal? Or do you believe that there would be even ten upright and faithful servants of the Lord, when formerly five cities could not furnish that number?[16] I ask you, but you know not. I know not myself. You alone, O my God, You alone know who belong to You.

But if we don't know those who belong to Him, at least we know that sinners don't belong to Him. Now, of what classes of persons do the professing Christians in this assembly consist? Titles and dignities avail nothing here; you are stripped of all these before Jesus Christ. Who make up this assembly? Sinners in great number, who do not wish to be converted. In still greater number, sinners who would like to be saved, but who always put it off. Many others who have been converted only in appearance, and have fallen back into their former ways. Finally, a multitude who flatter themselves that they have no need of conversion.

You have now made up the company of the reprobate. Cut off these four classes of sinners from this sacred assembly, for they will be cut off from it at the great day! Stand forth now, you righteous! Where are you? Remnant of Israel, pass to the right hand! True wheat of Jesus Christ, disengage yourselves from this chaff, doomed to the fire! O God! Where are Your elect? And what remains there for Your portion?

But this danger affects you not, my dear hearer. You persuade yourself that in this great number who shall perish, you will be the happy individual. You, who have less reason perhaps than any other to believe it! Great God! How little are the terrors of Your law known to the world! But what are we to conclude? That all must despair of salvation? God forbid! The unbeliever alone, to quiet his own feelings in his debaucheries, tries to persuade himself that all men will perish as well as he. This idea ought not to be the fruit of the present discourse. It is intended to undeceive you with regard to the popular error of believing that we can do what everybody else is doing. It is also intended to convince you that in order to merit salvation you must distinguish yourself from the rest; that in the midst of the world you are to live for God's glory and not follow the multitude.

When the Jews were led in captivity from Judea to Babylon, the prophet Jeremiah spoke thus to them: "Children of Israel, when you arrive at Babylon you will behold the inhabitants of that country who carry upon their shoulders gods of silver and gold. But you are to say to yourselves in secret, " 'It is You, O Lord, whom we ought to adore.' "[17] At your departure from this temple you go to enter into another Babylon. You go to see the idols of gold and silver before which all men prostrate themselves. Then, my dear hearer, if you wish to be of the small number of true Israelites, say in the secrecy of your heart, "It is You alone, O my God, whom we ought to adore. You will be my God in the midst of this Babylon, as You will one day be in Jerusalem above!"[18]

Behold then the fruit which you ought to reap from this discourse. Live apart. Think, without ceasing, that the great number work their own destruction. Regard as nothing all customs of the earth, unless authorized by the law of God, and remember that holy men in all ages have been looked upon as a peculiar people. It is thus that, after distinguishing yourselves from the sinful ones on earth, you will be gloriously distinguished from them in eternity.

NOTES

1. Luke 4:26, 27; cf. 1 Kings 17:9; 2 Kings 5:1ff.
2. Genesis 6-9, 12:1 ff.; Numbers 14:6, 7; Job 1:1; Genesis 19.
3. Isaiah 17:6, 24:13.
4. Matthew 7:13, 14.
5. Acts 5:1ff., 1 Corinthians 5:1.
6. Genesis 6:11; Exodus 32:7.
7. Elijah (1 Kings 19:18).
8. *I.e.*, Matthew, Mark, Luke, and John.
9. Daniel 3:1ff; 1 Kings 18; Numbers 20:25, 26.
10. Acts 2:40; Romans 12:2.
11. Ezra 9:1ff.
12. Genesis 18:16-19:29, 19; Job, *passim;* Esther 4:16.
13. The character of Judith is described in the apocryphal Book of Judith (8ff.). Massillon seems to be referring to Tobias' departure from Nineveh, as related by his father, Tobit, in the apocryphal Book of Tobit (14:4-12). But Massillon may have been influenced by something Tobit wrote about himself: "And when I was carried into Nineveh, all my brothers and relatives ate the food of the heathen,

but I kept myself from eating it, because I remembered God in my heart" (Tobit
1:10-12).
14. Genesis 6-9, 19:24, 25, 28, 29; Exodus 14:21-28; Numbers 16:49.
15. Job 27:13-23.
16. See Genesis 18:23-32, 19:24, 25, 28, 29; also Jude 7.
17. Jeremiah 29:1-13.
18. Revelation 21:2.

William Penn

Not many Christians have carried the banner of Jesus Christ into the world of Caesar and, without sacrificing principle, achieved success and renown. William Penn (1644-1718) was such an exception, but he paid a heavy price. For years he lived under the stern displeasure of his father, a distinguished admiral who captured Jamaica for Britain. Four times Penn was thrown into prison for his nonconformist views and for debt. The proprietary colony of Pennsylvania, which was given to him and which he founded, rejected his authority. His own steward swindled him out of thousands of pounds and then sued him. And his son William "became the ringleader of all the dissolute characters in Philadelphia." As he himself wrote, "No cross, no crown."

Yet in spite of all his setbacks, the fickleness of political fortunes, and his own mistakes of judgment, William Penn the Quaker was a happy man. He was a loving husband and a conscientious believer, and he did enormous good. The excerpts that follow, taken from his writings, tell better than any biographer could what manner of man he was. To mention two achievements: he laid out the city of Philadelphia, and secured the release of hundreds of English Quakers from prison. Today, one of the fifty American states bears his name and holds him in high esteem as its founder. His benefactions to humanity were many, and his memory is unsullied.

William Penn was the only child of William and Margaret Penn. He was born at London's Tower Hill (where he was later confined), and at the age of sixteen entered Christ Church, Oxford, as a gentleman commoner. A year later he was expelled for refusing to attend chapel or otherwise conform to the rigors of Restoration Anglicanism. (Penn had earlier come under the influence of Thomas Loe, the Quaker.) The elder Penn, who had no quarrel with the Stuart royalists, was so angry about his son's banishment that when William returned home he was "whipped, beaten, and turned out of doors." Reconciliation with his father was followed by travel and study in France and Italy.

In 1665 Penn joined the Society of Friends and engaged in literary controversy, contending for toleration and religious freedom. Not only *his writings, but his street preaching, his refusal to take off his hat in court and his refusal to take the oath of allegiance caused him to be jailed again and again. Upon his father's death he inherited a large claim against the crown. To settle it, King Charles II gave Penn in 1680, at his request, charter to a huge grant of land in what was then New Jersey, as a "proprietary colony." For Penn the Quaker it was a "holy experiment." At royal insistence it was named not "Sylvania," as Penn desired, but "Pennsylvania" in honor of its father.*

The New World charter gave Penn almost unlimited power. He drew up a frame of government in which absolute religious freedom was decreed. Penn's faith in the people led him to delegate more privileges and powers than settlers possessed in any other colony, while his treaties with the Indians were so just and fair that he won their undying friendship.

Penn was able to spend only a few brief years in his new American colony; the end of the Stuart regime in 1688 brought him into fresh conflict with authority. He returned to London to find himself deprived of the governorship of Pennsylvania, and in his enforced retirement he began writing Some Fruits of Solitude, *publishing it in 1693. In 1702 he issued a second volume. Illness struck in 1712, and his second wife became his executrix until his death.*

The Fruits of Solitude *are considered "the most devotional and charming of all his works." The 858 maxims have been reprinted scores of times. This selection has been made from Volume I of the Harvard Classics Five Foot Shelf of Books, edited by Charles W. Eliot, published in 1909 by P. F. Collier and Son, New York.*

ELEVEN

Some Fruits of Solitude *in* Reflections and Maxims
by William Penn

Preface

This enchiridion [handbook] I present you with is the fruit of solitude, a school few care to learn in, though none instructs us better. Some parts of it are the result of serious reflection, others the flashings of lucid intervals, writ for private satisfaction and now published for a help to human conduct.

The author blesses God for his retirement, and kisses that gentle hand which led him into it, for though it should prove barren to the world, it can never do so to him. He has now had some time to call his own, a property he was never so much master of before, in which he has taken a view of himself and the world, and observed wherein he has hit and missed the mark. And this is the rather said, that it might quicken you, reader, to lose none of the time that is yet yours.

There is nothing of which we are apt to be so lavish as of time, and about which we ought to be more solicitous, since without it we can do nothing in this world. Time is what we want most, but what, alas, we use worst, and for which God will certainly most strictly reckon with us when time shall be no more.

To come but once into the world and trifle away our true enjoyment of it and of ourselves in it is lamentable indeed. This one reflection would yield a thinking person great instruction. And since nothing below man can so think, man in being thoughtless must fall below himself. And that, to be sure, such do as are unconcerned in the use of their most precious time.

We understand little of the works of God, either in nature or grace. We pursue false knowledge and mistake education extremely. We are violent in our affections, confused and unmethodical in our whole life, making that a burden which was given for a blessing, and so of little comfort to ourselves or others, misapprehending the true notion of happiness, and so missing the right use of life and [the] way of happy living. And till we are persuaded to stop and step a little aside, out of the noisy crowd and encumbering hurry of the world, and calmly take a prospect of things, it will be impossible [to] make a right judgment of ourselves or know our own misery. But after we have made the just reckonings which retirement will help us to, we shall begin to think the world in great measure mad, and that we have been in a sort of bedlam all this while.

Reader, whether young or old, think it not too soon or too late to turn over the leaves of your past life. The author does not pretend to deliver you an exact piece, his business being not ostentation but love. It is miscellaneous in the matter of it and by no means artful in the composition. But it contains hints that may serve you for texts upon which to preach to yourself, and which comprehend much of the course of human life. Whether you are parent or child, prince or subject, master or servant, single or married, public or private, mean or honorable, rich or poor, prosperous or unprosperous, in peace or controversy, in business or solitude, whatever be your inclination or aversion, practice or duty, you will find something not unsuitably said for your direction and advantage.

Accept and improve what deserves your notice; the rest excuse, and place to account of goodwill to you and the whole creation of God.

Pride

We are very apt to be full of our selves, instead of Him that made what we so much value; and but for whom we can have no reason to value our selves. For we have nothing that we can call our own; no, not our selves, for we are all but tenants, and at [the] will of the great Lord of our selves, and the rest of this great farm, the world that we live upon.

But methinks we cannot answer it to our selves as well as [to] our Maker, that we should live and die ignorant of our selves, and thereby of Him and the obligations we are under to Him for our selves. If the worth of a gift sets the obligations, and directs the return [determines the response] of the party that receives it, he that is ignorant of it will be at a loss to value it, and the Giver for it.

Here is man in his ignorance of himself. He knows not how to estimate his Creator, because he knows not how to value His creation. If we consider his make and lovely composition: the several stories of his lovely structure, his divers members, their order, function, and dependency; the instruments of food, the vessels of digestion, and how nourishment is carried and diffused through the whole body; how the animal spirit is thereby refreshed with an unspeakable dexterity; and last of all, how the rational soul is seated in the animal; I say if this rare fabric alone were but considered by us, surely man would have a more reverent sense of the power, wisdom, and goodness of God, and of the duty he owes to Him for it.

But man is become a strange contradiction to himself, not by constitution, but by corruption. He would have others obey him, but he will not obey God, who is so much above him, and who made him. He will lose none of his authority. He is humorous [capricious] to his wife, he beats his children, [is] strict with his neighbors, revenges all affronts to extremity; but alas, forgets all the while that he is a man, and is more in arrears to God, who is so very patient with him, than they are to him with whom he is so strict and impatient.

He is curious [particular] to wash and dress his body, but careless of his soul. The one shall have many hours, the other not so many minutes. If he is to receive or see a great man, how nice and anxious is he that all things be in order! And with what respect and address does he approach and make his court! But to God, how dry and formal and constrained in his devotion. In his prayers he says, "Thy will be done," but means his own; at least acts so.

Inconsideration

The want of due consideration is the cause of all the unhappiness man brings upon himself.

Disappointment and Resignation

Disappointments that come not by our own folly are the trials or corrections of Heaven, and it is our own fault if they prove not [to] our advantage. To repine at them does not mend the matter, it is only to grumble at our Creator. But to see the hand of God in them, with a humble submission to His will, is the way to turn our water into wine, and engage the greatest love and mercy on our side.

We cannot fall below the arms of God, how low soever it be we fall. For though our Savior's passion is over, His compassion is not. That never fails His humble, sincere disciples. In Him they find more than all they lose in the world.

Right Marriage

Never marry but for love; but see that you love what is lovely. If love be not your chiefest motive, you will soon grow weary of a married state and stray from your promise, to search out your pleasures in forbidden places. Let not enjoyment lessen, but augment affection. The difference betwixt lust and love is that one is volatile, the other fixed. Love grows, lust wastes by enjoyment. One is inward and deep, the other superficial; one permanent, the other transient.

Those who marry for money cannot have the true satisfaction of marriage, the requisite means being wanting. O, how sordid is man grown! Man, the noblest creature in the world, as a god on earth, and the image of Him that made it, thus to mistake earth for Heaven; and worship gold for God! Men are generally more careful of the breed of their horses and dogs than of their children.

Avarice

Covetousness is the greatest of monsters, as well as the root of all evil.[1] I have once seen the man that died to save charges. "What? Give ten shillings to a doctor, and have an apothecary's bill besides, that may come to I know not what!" No, not he, valuing life [as he does, at] less than twenty shillings.

But in marriage be wise: prefer the person before money, virtue before beauty, the mind before the body. Then you have a wife, a friend, a companion, a second self: one who bears an equal share with you in all your toils and troubles. Choose one that measures her satisfaction, safety, and danger by yours; a friend as well as a wife, which indeed a wife implies. For she is but half a wife that is not, or is not capable of being, such a friend.

Between a man and his wife nothing ought to rule but love.

As love ought to bring them together, so it is the best way to keep them well together.

Rules of Conversation

Avoid company where it is not profitable or necessary, and in those occasions speak little, and last. Silence is wisdom, where speaking is folly, and always safe. If you think twice before you speak once, you will speak twice the better for it. Better say nothing than not to the purpose. And to speak pertinently, consider both what is fit, and when it is fit to speak.

In all debates let truth be your aim, not victory or an unjust interest; and endeavor to gain, rather than to expose your antagonist. Give no advantage in argument, nor lose any that is offered. To inform, or to be informed, ought to be the end of all conferences. Men are too apt to be concerned for their credit more than for the cause.

Eloquence

There is a truth and beauty in rhetoric, but it oftener serves ill turns than good ones.

Wit

Wit is a happy and striking way of expressing a thought. Less judgment than wit is more sail than ballast; yet it must be confessed that wit gives an edge to sense and recommends it extremely. Where judgment has wit to express it, there's the best orator.

Temporal Happiness

Do good with what you have, or it will do you no good. The generality [of people] are the worse for their plenty. The voluptuous consumes it, the miser hides it. It's the good man who uses it, and to good purposes; but such are hardly found among the prosperous.

Moderation

Not to be provoked is best; but if moved, never correct till the fume is spent; for every stroke our fury strikes is sure to hit our selves at last. If we but observed the allowances our reason makes upon reflection, when our passion is over, we could not want a rule how to behave our selves again in the like occasions.

They that censure should practice; or else let them have the first stone, and the last too.

Tricks

Nothing needs a trick but a trick; sincerity loathes one.

Qualifications

Five things are requisite to a good officer: ability, clean hands, dispatch, patience, and impartiality.

A Private Life

Private life is to be preferred; the honor and gain of public posts [bears] no proportion with the comfort of it. The one is free and quiet, the other servile and noisy. It was a great answer of the Shunammite woman, "I dwell among my own people."[2]

Ostentation

The humble, in the parable of the Day of Judgment, forgot their good works: "Lord, when did we do so and so?"[3]

Religion

Religion is the fear of God, and its demonstration in good works, and faith is the root of both; for without faith we cannot please God, nor can we fear what we do not believe. The devils also believe and know abundance, but in this is the difference: their faith works not by love, nor their knowledge by obedience, and therefore they are never the better for them. And if ours be such, we shall be of their church, not of Christ's; for as the Head is, so must the body be.

He was holy, humble, harmless, meek, merciful, etc., when among us, to teach us what we should be when He was gone. And yet He is among us still, and in us too, a living and perpetual preacher of the same grace, by His Spirit in our consciences.

A minister of the gospel ought to be one of Christ's making, if he would pass for one of Christ's ministers. That minister whose life is not the model of his doctrine is a babbler rather than a preacher; a quack rather than a physician of value. The humble and true teacher meets with more than he expects. He accounts contentment with godliness great gain,[4] and therefore seeks not to make a gain of godliness.

As the ministers of Christ are made by Him, and are like Him, so they beget people into the same likeness. To be like Christ, then, is to be a Christian. And regeneration is the only way to the Kingdom of God, which we pray for. Let us today, therefore, hear His voice, and not harden our hearts, who speaks to us many ways, in the Scriptures, in our hearts, by His servants and His providences. And the sum of all is *holiness* and *charity.*

Amuse yourself not therefore with the numerous opinions of the world, nor value yourself upon verbal orthodoxy, philosophy, or your skill in tongues, or knowledge of the [Church] Fathers—(too much the business and vanity of the world). But rejoice in this, that you know God, who is the Lord, who exercises lovingkindness and judgment and righteousness in the earth.

Public worship is very commendable, if well performed. We owe it to God and good example. But we must know that God is not tied to time or place, who is everywhere at the same time. And this we shall know, as far as we are capable, if wherever we are, our desires are to be with Him. Serving God, people generally confine [themselves] to the acts of public and private worship, which the more zealous do oftener repeat, in hopes of acceptance. But if we consider that God is an Infinite Spirit, and as such, everywhere; and that our Savior has taught us that He will be worshiped in Spirit and in truth,[5] we shall see the shortness of such a notion.

Serving God concerns the frame of our spirits in the whole course of our lives, in every occasion we have in which we may show our love to His law. For as men in battle are continually in the way of shot, so we in this world are ever within the reach of temptation. And herein do we serve God, if we avoid what we are forbidden, as well as do what He commands.

God is better served in resisting a temptation to evil than in many formal prayers. This [latter] is but twice or thrice a day, but *that* [is] every hour and moment of the day. So much more is our continual watch than our evening and morning devotion.

Would you then serve God? Do not that [while] alone, which you would not that another should see you do. Don't take God's Name in vain, or disobey your parents, or wrong your neighbor, or commit adultery even in your heart. Neither be vain, lascivious, proud, drunken, revengeful, or angry; nor lie, detract, backbite, overreach, oppress, deceive, or betray. But watch vigorously against all temptations to these things, as knowing that God is present, the Overseer of all your ways and most inward thoughts, and the Avenger of His own law upon the disobedient. [This do,] and you will acceptably serve God.

Is it not reasonable, if we expect the acknowledgements of those to whom we are bountiful, that we should reverently pay ours to God, our most magnificent and constant benefactor? The world represents a rare and sumptuous palace, mankind the great family in it, and God the mighty Lord and Master of it. We are all sensible what a stately seat it is: the heavens adorned with so many glorious luminaries, and the earth with groves, plains, valleys, hills, fountains, ponds, lakes, and rivers; and variety of fruits, and creatures for food, pleasure, and profit. In short, how noble a house He keeps, and the plenty and variety and excellence of His table; His orders, seasons, and suitableness of every time and thing.

But though God has replenished this world with abundance of good things for man's life and comfort, yet they are all but imperfect goods. He only is the Perfect Good to whom they point. But alas! Men cannot see Him for them, though they should always see Him *in* them.

I have often wondered at the unaccountableness of man in this: that though he loves changes so well, he should care so little to hear or think of his last, great, and best change too. The truest end of life is to know the Life that never ends. He that makes this his care, will find it his crown at last. And he that lives to live ever, never fears dying. For death is no more than a turning of us over from time to eternity. Death, then, being the way and condition of life, we cannot love to live if we cannot bear to die.

Men may tire themselves in a labyrinth of search and talk of God; but if we would know Him indeed, it must be from the impressions we receive of Him; and the softer our hearts are, the deeper and livelier those will be upon us. If He has made us sensible of His justice by His reproof; of His patience by His forbearance; of His mercy by His forgiveness; of His holiness by the sanctification of our hearts through His Spirit, we have a grounded knowledge of God. This is experience, that [other is] speculation; this [is] enjoyment, that report [*i.e.,* hearsay]. In short, *this* is undeniable evidence [of] the realities of religion, and will stand all winds and weathers.

As our faith, so our devotion should be lively. Cold meat won't serve at those repasts. It's a coal from God's altar must kindle our fire; and without fire, true fire, no acceptable sacrifice. "Open Thou my lips, and then," said the Royal Prophet, "my mouth shall praise God."[6] But not till then.

The preparation of the heart, as well as [the] answer of the tongue, is of the Lord. And to have it, our prayers must be powerful, and our worship grateful. Let us choose, therefore, to commune where there is the warmest sense of religion; where devotion exceeds formality, and practice most corresponds with profession; and where there is at least as much charity as zeal. For where this society is to be found, there shall we find the church of God.

As good, so ill men are all of a church, and everybody knows who must be head of it. The humble, meek, merciful, just, pious, and devout souls are everywhere of one religion, and when death has taken off the mask, they will know one another, though the divers liveries they wear here make them strangers.

It is a sad reflection that many men hardly have any religion at all, and most men have none of their own. For that which is the religion of their education, and not of their judgment, is the religion of another, and not theirs. To have religion upon authority and not upon conviction, is like a finger watch, to be set forward or backward as he pleases that has it in keeping.

That religion cannot be right that a man is the worse for having. No religion is better than an unnatural one. To be unnatural in defense of grace is a contradiction. Hardly anything looks worse than to defend religion by ways that show it has no credit with us.   .

To be furious in religion is to be irreligiously religious. If he that is without bowels [that is, of compassion] is not a man, how then can he be a Christian? A good end cannot sanctify evil means, nor must we ever do evil that good may come of it. Some folks think they may scold, rail, hate, rob, and kill too, so it be but for God's sake. But nothing in us unlike Him can please Him.

We are too ready to retaliate rather than forgive, or gain by love and information. And yet we could hurt no man that we believe loves us. Let us then try what love will do; for if men did once see we love them, we should soon find they would not harm us. Force may subdue, but love gains, and he that forgives first, wins the laurel.

If I am even with my enemy, the debt is paid; but if I forgive it, I oblige him forever. Love is the hardest lesson in Christianity; but for that reason it should be most our care to learn it. It is a severe rebuke upon us, that God makes us so many allowances, and we make so few to our neighbor, as if love had nothing to do with faith, that ought to work by it.

He that lives in love lives in God, says the beloved disciple,[7] and to be sure a man can live nowhere better. Love is indeed Heaven upon earth, since Heaven above would not be Heaven without it. For where there is not love, there is fear; but perfect love casts out fear.[8] And yet we naturally fear most to offend what we most love.

What we love, we'll hear; what we love, we'll trust; and what we love, we'll serve; aye, and suffer for, too. If you love Me (says our Blessed Redeemer), keep My commandments. Why? Why, then He'll love us; then we shall be His friends; then He'll send us the Comforter; then whatsoever we ask, we shall receive; and then, where He is, we shall be also, and that forever.

Behold the fruits of love, the power, virtue, benefit, and beauty of love! Love is above all, and when it prevails in us all, we shall all be lovely, and in love with God and one with another.

The Moral Man

A right moralist is a great and good man, but for that reason he is rarely to be found. There are a sort of people who are fond of character, but who in my opinion have but little title to it. They think it enough not to defraud a man of his pay or betray his friend. But certainly he that covets can no more be a moral man than he that steals, since he does so in his mind. Nor can he be one that robs his neighbor of his credit, or that craftily undermines him of his trade or office.

If a man pays his tailor but debauches his wife, is he a current moralist? And what shall we say of the man that rebels against his father, is an ill husband or an abusive neighbor; one that's lavish of his time, of his health, and of his estate, in which his family is so nearly concerned? Must he go for a right moralist because he pays his rent well?

I would ask some of those men of morals whether he that robs God and himself too, though he should not defraud his neighbor, be the moral man? Do I owe myself nothing? And do I not owe all to God? And if paying what we owe makes the moral man, is it not fit we should begin to render our dues where we owe our very beginning; aye, our all?

The complete moralist begins with God. He gives Him His due—his heart, his love, his service. He that lives without a sense of this dependency and obligation cannot be a moral man, because he does not make his returns of love and obedience, as becomes an honest and a sensible creature—which very term implies he is not his own. As judgments are paid before bonds, and bonds before bills or book-debts, so the moralist considers his obligations according to their several dignities. In the first place, Him to whom he owes himself. Next, himself, in his health and livelihood. Lastly, his other obligations, whether rational or pecuniary—doing to others, to the extent of his ability, as he would have them do unto him.

In short, the moral man is he that loves God above all, and his neighbor as himself, which fulfils both tables [of the law] at once.

The World's Able Man

This is the present world's wise man and politician. At best he may be a cunning man, a sort of lurker in politics. He is for every cause that brings him gain, but implacable if disappointed of success. He sails with all winds, and is never out of his way where anything is to be had. True to nothing but himself, and false to all persons and parties, [he is] a privateer indeed, and everywhere a very bird of prey.

Such [men] as give themselves the latitude of saying what they do not mean, come to be errant jockeys at more things than one; but in religion and politics it's most pernicious. To hear two men talk the reverse of their own sentiments, with all the good breeding and appearance of friendship imaginable, on purpose to cozen or pump each other, is to a man of virtue and honor one of the melancholiest, as well as most nauseous things in the world.

I remember a passage in one of Queen Elizabeth's great men, as advice to his friend: "The advantage," says he, "I had upon others at court, was that I always spoke as I thought, which being not believed by them, I both preserved a good conscience and suffered no damage from that freedom"—which, as it shows the vice to be older than our times, [proves] that gallant man's integrity to be the best way of avoiding it.

It is as reasonable to think a whore makes the best wife, as [to think] a knave makes the best [public] officer. Are you a magistrate? Prefer such as have clean characters where they live, and that are under no temptation to strain points for a fortune. Are you a private man? Contract your acquaintance in a narrow compass, and choose those for the subjects of it that are men of principles—such as will make full stops where honor will not lead them on [to] a base compliance.

The Wise Man

The wise man governs himself by the reason of his case. He proposes just ends, and employs the fairest and probablest means and methods to attain them. He scorns to serve himself by indirect means. The wise man is cautious, but not cunning; judicious, but not crafty; making virtue the measure of using his excellent understanding in the conduct of his life.

To do evil that good may come of it is for bunglers in politics as well as morals. Like those surgeons that will cut off an arm they can't cure, to hide their ignorance and save their credit.

The wise man is never captious nor critical. He is always for some solid good, civil or moral; as, to make his country more virtuous, preserve her peace and liberty, employ her poor, improve land, advance trade, suppress vice, encourage industry and all mechanical knowledge. To conclude: he is just, and fears God, hates covetousness, and eschews evil, and loves his neighbor as himself.

On the Government of Thoughts

Man being made a reasonable, and so a thinking creature, there is nothing more worthy of his being than the right direction and employment of his thoughts, since upon this depends both his usefulness to the public and his own present and future benefit.

The consideration of this has often obliged me to lament the unhappiness of mankind, that through too great a mixture and confusion of thoughts, has been hardly able to make a right or mature judgment of things. To this is owing the various uncertainty and confusion we see in the world, and the intemperate zeal that occasions them. To this also is to be attributed the imperfect knowledge we have of things and the slow progress we make in attaining to a better. [We are] like the children of Israel, who were forty years upon their journey from Egypt to Canaan, which might have been performed in less than one.

Clear your head, therefore, and rally and manage your thoughts rightly, and you will save time, and see and do your business well; for your judgment will be distinct, your mind free, and your faculties strong and regular. Always remember to bind your thoughts to the present occasion.

If it be your religious duty, suffer nothing else to share in it. If any civil or temporal affair, observe the same caution, and you will be a whole man to everything, and do twice the business in the same time. If any point overlabors your mind, divert and relieve it by some other subject of a more sensible or manual nature. If it fall out that you have more affairs than one upon your hand, be sure to prefer that which is of most moment, and will least wait your leisure. Those who are least divided in their care always give the best account of their business.

Make not more business necessary than is so, but rather lessen than augment work for yourself. Don't be overeager in pursuit of anything, for the mercurial too often happen to leave judgment behind them. Upon the whole matter, employ your thoughts as your business requires, and let [each matter] have a place according to merit and urgency, giving everything a review and due digestion, and you will prevent many errors and vexations, as well as save much time to yourself in the course of your life.

Of Envy

Just and noble minds rejoice in other men's success, and help to augment their praise. They are not without a love to virtue, who take a satisfaction in seeing her rewarded.

Of Man's Life

Why is man less durable than the works of his hands, [unless it is] because this is not the place of his rest? Were it not more his wisdom to be concerned about those works that will go with him, and erect a mansion for him where time has power neither over him nor it?

Of Ambition

They that soar too high often fall hard; which makes a low and level dwelling preferable. The tallest trees are most in the power of the winds, and ambitious men of the blasts of fortune.

Of Praise or Applause

We are too apt to love praise, but not to deserve it. We cannot be too circumspect how we receive praise. For if we contemplate our selves in a false glass, we are sure to be mistaken about our due; and because we are too apt to believe what is pleasing, rather than what is true, we may be too easily swelled beyond our just proportion by the windy compliments of men.

Make allowances therefore for what is said; for an overvalue of our selves gives us but a dangerous security. We expect more than belongs to us, take all that's given us [even] though never meant [for us], and fall out with those who are not as full of us as we are of our selves. In short, it's a passion that abuses our judgment and makes us both unsafe and ridiculous. Be not fond therefore of praise, but seek virtue that leads to it.

And yet [you should] no more lessen or dissemble your merit than overrate it. For though humility be a virtue, an affected [show of it] is none.

Of Conduct in Speech

Inquire often, but judge rarely, and you will not often be mistaken. It is safer to learn than teach; and [he] who conceals his opinion has nothing to answer for.

Speak properly and in as few words as you can, but always plainly, for the end of speech is not ostentation, but to be understood. It too often happens in some conversations, as in apothecary shops, that those pots that are empty, or have things of small value in them, are as gaudily dressed and flourished as those that are full of precious drugs. This laboring of slight matter with flourished terms of expression is fulsome, and worse than the modern imitations of tapestry and East India goods in stuffs and linens. In short, it is but tawdry talk, and next to very trash.

Union of Friends

They that love beyond the world cannot be separated by it. Death cannot kill what never dies. This is the comfort of friends, that though they may be said to die, yet their friendship and society are, in the best sense, ever present because immortal.

Of Man's Inconsiderateness and Partiality

It's very observable [that] if our civil rights are invaded or encroached upon, we are mightily touched, and fill every place with our resentment and complaint; while we suffer our better and nobler selves to be the property and vassals of sin, the worst of invaders.

In vain do we expect to be delivered from such troubles till we are delivered from the cause of them, our disobedience to God. When He has His dues from us, it will be time enough for Him to give us ours out of one another.

On the Rule of Judging

In all things reason should prevail. It's quite another thing to be stiff [rather] than steady in an opinion. This [latter] may be reasonable, but that is ever willful. In such cases it always happens that the clearer the argument, the greater the obstinacy, where the design is not to be convinced.

Beasts act by sense, man should by reason, else he is a greater beast than God ever made; and the proverb is verified [that] the corruption of the best things is the worst and most offensive.

If like Theophilus and Timothy[9] we have been brought up in the knowledge of the best things, it is to our advantage. But neither they nor we lose by trying [testing] their truth; for so we learn its intrinsic worth. Truth never lost ground by inquiry, because she is most of all reasonable. Reason, like the sun, is common to all.

Of the Mean Notion We Have of God

Nothing shows more the low condition man is fallen into then the unsuitable notion we must have of God, by the ways we take to please Him. Of what benefit is it to say our prayers regularly, go to church, receive the sacraments, and maybe go to confession too; aye, feast the priest, and give alms to the poor, and yet lie, swear, curse, be drunk, covetous, unclean, proud, revengeful, vain, and idle at the same time? Can one excuse or balance the other? Or will God think Himself well served where

His law is violated? Or well used where there is so much more show than substance? Our blessed Savior most rightly and clearly distinguished and determined this case when He told the Jews that they were His mother, His brethren and sisters, who did the will of His Father.[10]

Of Jealousy

The jealous are troublesome to others, but a torment to themselves. Jealousy is a kind of civil war in the soul, where judgment and imagination are at perpetual jars. It violates contracts, dissolves society, breaks wedlock, betrays friends and neighbors. It has a venom that more or less rankles wherever it bites. Its rise is guilt or ill nature, and by reflection thinks its own faults to be other men's, [just] as he that's overrun with the jaundice takes others to be yellow. A jealous man only sees his own spectrum, when he looks upon other men, and gives his character in theirs.

The Vain Man

The vain man is so full of himself that he has no room for anything else, be it never so good or deserving. It's "I" at every turn that does this, or can do that. And as he abounds in his comparisons, so he is sure to give himself the better of everybody else; according to the proverb, all his geese are swans.

A humble able man is a jewel worth a kingdom. It is often saved by him, as Solomon's poor wise man did the city.[11]

Of Charity

Charity has various senses [meanings], but is excellent in all of them. It imports first, the commiseration of the poor and unhappy of mankind, and extends a helping hand to mend their condition. Next, charity makes the best construction of things and persons. It excuses weakness, extenuates miscarriages, and makes the best of everything. It moderates extremes, is always for expediences, labors to accommodate differences, and had rather suffer than revenge. It acts freely [and] zealously too, but it's always to do good, for it hurts nobody. It is a universal remedy against discord and a holy cement for mankind.

Lastly, [charity] is love to God and the brethren, which raises the soul above all worldly considerations, and gives a taste of Heaven upon earth. A man can never be a true and good Christian without charity. It seems it was [the Apostle Paul's] *unum necessarium,* or the one thing needful.[12] Would God this divine virtue were more implanted and diffused among mankind, [to] the pretenders to Christianity especially, and we should certainly [then] mind piety more than controversy, and exercise love and compassion instead of censuring and persecuting one another in any manner whatsoever.

NOTES

1. Cf. 1 Timothy 6:10.
2. 2 Kings 4:13.
3. Matthew 25:37.
4. 1 Timothy 6:6.
5. John 4:23, 24.
6. King David in Psalm 51:15.
7. 1 John 4:16.
8. 1 John 4:18.
9. Cf. Luke 1:3, 4; 2 Timothy 1:5, 6.
10. Mark 3:35.
11. Ecclesiastes 9:15.
12. A reference to Paul's First Letter to the Corinthians, chapter 13. See Wesley's sermon in Chapter 1 for a discussion of "charity."

William Law

In some ways William Law (1686-1761) seems more like a caricature than a real Englishman. Dignified, austere, celibate, strict in his habits, plain in his dress, terribly strong in his opinions, he began each day with devotions at 5 A.M. He fasted often, and, while forbidden to preach, made a point of never missing a single service, weekday or Sunday, in his own parish church. Yet this strange man is reported to have been affable with his neighbors, and after he retired he became the soul of generosity. He founded schools and alms-houses, and loved to be with little children. And Lord Lyttleton expressed himself as "not a little astonished that one of the finest books that ever was written had been penned by a crack-brained enthusiast."

Law was a nonjuror—which means that he never reconciled himself to the overthrow of the Stuart dynasty, and paid for his convictions. The son of a grocer, he grew up at King's Cliffe in Northamptonshire, and attended Cambridge University. In 1711 he was elected a fellow of Emmanuel College and ordained a priest of the Church of England. Three years later Queen Anne died and the sovereignty passed to the Hanoverians of Germany. Law, along with other clergy, was ordered to take the oath of allegiance to the new king, George I. He refused, lost his fellowship, and was denied the right to officiate at services.

For ten years, Law served as domestic tutor to the Gibbon family in Putney. His pupil, Edward, later became father to the famed historian and skeptic Edward Gibbon, who wrote The Decline and Fall of the Roman Empire. Despite his lack of sympathy for Law's views, young Edward, who as a boy knew the old gentleman well, spoke warmly of his integrity and ability, calling him "a nonjuror, a saint, and a wit."

Law's brilliance as a writer and controversialist became evident as early as 1717. It was after he moved to Cambridge with his pupil in 1727 that he published the Serious Call, a work which permanently established his reputation and was to have a worldwide influence in English second only to Bunyan's Pilgrim's Progress.

One frequently hears the comment in the late twentieth century that the rise of evangelical fervor has been accompanied by an alarming drop in morals. The situation in Law's day was not far different. Going to church was fashionable; freethinkers were unpopular; Christianity had powerful advocates in the pulpit. Yet in their personal lives, Christians were behaving as though church made no difference whatever. Immorality was "in." Even Gibbon spoke of the "strange contradiction which exists between the faith and practice of the Christian world."

To this easygoing community William Law issued his "serious call." He was not defending the faith; the faith had plenty of defenders. He was telling people to live up to the faith they had. Self-denial, humility, self-control, and above all love for each other: these qualities he sought to cultivate in churchgoers. As Professor Bromiley points out, the work is extremely well written, and it is sustained by the inner integrity of the author. Like the poor parson of Chaucer, "Cristes lore, and his apostles twelve, / He taughte, but first he folwed it him-selve." But here is more than moral counsel; Law calls for a deep personal relationship with God, and for what (as Dr. Bromiley says) might now be described as an act of commitment.

These excerpts from A Serious Call to a Devout and Holy Life, Adapted to the State and Condition of All Orders of Christians are taken from the 1898 edition published by Macmillan in London, and reprinted in 1966 by Eerdmans Publishing Co. of Grand Rapids, Michigan. They are used by permission.

TWELVE

A Serious Call to a Devout and Holy Life
by William Law

Devotion is neither private nor public prayer, but prayers whether private or public are particular parts or instances of devotion. Devotion signifies a life given or devoted to God. He therefore is the devout man, who lives no longer to his own will, or the way and spirit of the world, but to the sole will of God, who considers God in everything, who serves God in everything, who makes all the parts of his common life, parts of piety, by doing everything in the name of God, and under such rules as are conformable to His glory.

We readily acknowledge that God alone is to be the rule and measure of our prayers; that in them we are to look wholly unto Him, and act wholly for Him; that we are only to pray in such a manner, for such things and such ends as are suitable to His glory.

Now let anyone but find out the reason, why he is to be thus strictly pious in his prayers, and he will find the same as strong a reason to be as strictly pious in all the other parts of his life. For there is not the least shadow of a reason why we should make God the rule and measure of our prayers; why we should then look wholly unto Him, and pray according to His will; but what equally proves it necessary for us to look wholly unto God, and make Him the rule and measure of all the other actions of our life.

As sure, therefore, as there is any wisdom in praying for the Spirit of God, so sure is it, that we are to make that Spirit the rule of all our actions; as sure as it is our duty to look wholly unto God in our prayers, so sure is it, that it is our duty to live wholly unto God in our lives. But we can no more be said to live unto God, unless we live unto Him in all the ordinary actions of our life, unless He be the rule and measure of all our ways, than we can be said to pray unto God, unless our prayers look wholly unto Him. So that unreasonable and absurd ways of life, whether in labor or diversion, whether they consume our time or our money, are like unreasonable and absurd prayers, and are as truly an offense unto God.

'Tis for want of knowing, or at least considering this, that we see such a mixture of ridicule in the lives of many people. You see them strict as to some times and places of devotion, but when the service of the church is over, they are but like those who seldom or never come there. In their way of life, their manner of spending their time and money, in their cares and fears, in their pleasures and indulgences, in their labor and diversions, they are like the rest of the world. This makes the loose part of the world generally make a jest of those who are devout, because they see their devotion goes no further than their prayers, and that when they are over, they live no more unto God till the time of prayer returns again; but live by the same humor and fancy, and in as full an enjoyment of all the follies of life, as other people. This is the reason why they are the jest and scorn of careless and worldly people; not because they are really devoted to God, but because they appear to have no other devotion but that of occasional prayers.

The short of the matter is this: either reason and religion prescibe rules and ends to all the ordinary actions of our life, or they do not. If they do, then it is as necessary to govern all our actions by those rules, as it is necessary to worship God. For if religion teaches us anything concerning eating and drinking or spending our time and money; if it teaches us how we are to use and contemn the world; if it tells us what tempers we are to have in common life, how we are to be disposed toward all people, how we are to behave toward the sick, the poor, the old and destitute; if it tells us whom we are to treat with a particular love, whom we are to regard with a particular esteem; if it tells us how we are to treat our enemies, and how we are to mortify and deny ourselves, then the man must be very weak who can think that these parts of religion are not to be observed with as much exactness as any doctrines that relate to prayers.

Our blessed Savior and His apostles are wholly taken up in doctrines that relate to common life. They call us to renounce the world, and differ in every temper and way of life, from the spirit and way of the world: to renounce all its goods, to fear none of its evils, to reject its joys, and have no value for its happiness; to be as newborn babes, that are born into a new state of things, to live as pilgrims in spiritual watching, in holy fear, and heavenly aspiring after another life; to take up our daily cross, to deny ourselves, to profess the blessedness of mourning, to seek the blessedness of poverty of spirit; to forsake the pride and vanity of riches, to take no thought for the morrow, to live in the profoundest state of humility, to rejoice in worldly sufferings, to reject the lust of the flesh, the lust of the eyes, and the pride of life; to bear injuries, to forgive and bless our enemies, and to love mankind as God loveth them; to give up our whole hearts and affections to God, and strive to enter through the strait gate into a life of eternal glory.

This is the common devotion which our blessed Savior taught, in order to make it the common life of all Christians. Is it not therefore exceeding strange that people should place so much piety in the attendance upon public worship, concerning which there is not one precept of our Lord's to be found, and yet neglect these common duties of our ordinary life, which are commanded in every page of the gospel? I call these duties the devotion of our common life, because if they are to be practiced, they must be made parts of our common life, for they can have no place anywhere else.

If contempt of the world and heavenly affection is a necessary temper of Christians, it is necessary that this temper appear in the whole course of their lives, in their manner of using the world, because it can have no place anywhere else. If self-denial be a condition of salvation, all who would be saved must make it a part of their ordinary life. If humility be a Christian duty, then the common life of a Christian is to be a constant course of humility in all its kinds. If poverty of spirit be necessary, it must be the spirit and temper of every day of our lives. If we are to relieve the naked, the sick, and the prisoner, it must be the common charity of our lives, as far as we can render ourselves able to perform it. If we are to love our enemies, we must make our common life a visible exercise and demonstration of that love. If contentment and thankfulness, if the patient bearing of evil, be duties to God, they are the duties of every day and in every circumstance of our life. If we are to be wise and holy as the newborn sons of God, we cannot be so otherwise than by renouncing everything that is foolish and vain in every part of our common life. If we are to be in Christ new creatures, we must show that we are so by having new ways of living in the world. If we are to follow Christ, it must be in our common way of spending every day.

Thus it is in all the virtues and holy tempers of Christianity; they are not ours unless they be the virtues and tempers of our ordinary life. So that Christianity is so far from leaving us to live in the common ways of life, conforming to the folly of customs, and gratifying the passions and tempers which the spirit of the world delights in, it is so far from indulging us in any of these things, that all its virtues which it makes necessary to salvation are only so many ways of living above and contrary to the world in all the common actions of our life. If our common life is not a common course of humility, self-denial, renunciation of the world, poverty of spirit, and heavenly affection, we do not live the lives of Christians.

It is notorious that Christians are now not only like other men in their frailties and infirmities; this might be in some degree excusable, but the complaint is, they are like heathens in all the main and chief articles of their lives. They enjoy the world, and live every day in the same tempers, and the same designs, and the same indulgences, as those who know not God, nor of any happiness in another life. Everybody who is capable of any reflection must have observed that this is generally the state even of devout people, whether men or women. You may see them different from other people, so far as to times and places of prayer, but generally like the rest of the world in all the other parts of their lives. And consequently, those who add Christian devotion to such a life must be said to pray as Christians, but live as heathens.

All trouble and uneasiness is founded in the want of something or other. Would we know the true cause of our troubles and disquiets, we must find out the cause of our wants, because that which creates and increases our wants does in the same degree create and increase our troubles and disquiets. God Almighty has sent us into the world with very few wants. Meat and drink and clothing are the only things necessary in life; and as these are only our present needs, so the present world is well furnished to supply these needs.

If a man had half the world in his power, he can make no more of it than this. As he wants it only to support an animal life, so it is unable to do anything else for him, or to afford him any other happiness. This is the state of man, born with few wants into a large world very capable of supplying them. So that one would reasonably suppose that men should pass their lives in content and thankfulness to God, or at least that they should be free from violent disquiets and vexations, as being placed in a world that has more than enough to relieve all their wants. But if to all this we add that this short life, thus furnished with all that we want in it, is only a short passage to eternal glory, where we shall be clothed with the brightness of angels and enter into the joys of God, we might still more reasonably expect that human life should be a state of peace and joy and delight in God. Thus it would certainly be if reason had its full power over us.

But, alas! Though God and nature and reason make human life thus free from wants and so full of happiness, yet our passions, in rebellion against God, against nature and reason, create a new world of evils, and fill human life with imaginary wants and vain disquiets. The man of pride has a thousand wants, which only his own pride has created; and these render him as full of trouble as if God had created him with a thousand appetites without creating anything that was proper to satisfy them. Envy and ambition have also their endless wants, which disquiet the souls of men, and by their contradictory motions render them as foolishly miserable as those who want to fly and creep at the same time.

Let any complaining, disquieted man tell you the ground of his uneasiness, and you will plainly see that he is the author of his own torment, that he is vexing himself at some imaginary evil which will cease to torment him as soon as he is content to be that which God and nature and reason require him to be. If you should see a man passing his days in disquiet because he could not walk upon the water, or catch birds as they fly by him, you would readily confess that such a one might thank himself for such uneasiness. But now if you look into all the most tormenting disquiets of life, you will find them all thus absurd, where people are only tormented by their own folly, and vexing themselves at such things as no more concern them, nor are any more their proper good, than walking upon the water or catching birds.

If you should see a man that had a large pond of water, yet was living in continual thirst, not suffering himself to drink half a draught for fear of lessening his pond; if you should see him wasting his time and strength in fetching more water to his pond; always thirsty, yet always carrying a bucket of water in his hand, watching early and late to catch the drops of rain, gaping after every cloud, and running greedily into every mire and mud in hope of water, and always studying how to make every ditch empty itself into his pond; if you should see him grow old and gray in these anxious labors, and at last end a care-filled, thirsty life by falling into his own pond; would you not say that such a one was not only the author of all his disquiets, but was foolish enough to be reckoned among idiots and madmen? But foolish and absurd as this character is, he does not represent half the follies and absurd disquiets of the covetous man. Look where you will, you will see all worldly vexations are very like the vexation of his who was always in mire and mud in search of water to drink, when he had more at home than was sufficient for a hundred horses.

Coelia[1] is always telling you how provoked she is, what intolerably shocking things happen to her, what monstrous usage she suffers, and what vexations she meets with everywhere. She tells you that her patience is quite worn out, and there is no bearing the behavior of people. Every assembly that she is at sends her home provoked; something or other has been said or done that no reasonable, well-bred person ought to bear. Poor people who want her charity are sent away with hasty answers, not because she has not a heart to part with any money, but because she is too full of some trouble of her own to attend to the complaints of others. Coelia has no business upon her hands but to receive the income of a plentiful fortune; but yet, by the doleful turn of her mind, you would be apt to think that she had neither food nor lodging. If you see her look more pale than ordinary, if her lips tremble when she speaks to you, it is because she is just come from a visit, where Lupus took no notice at all of her, but talked all the time to Lucinda, who has not half her fortune. When cross [adverse] accidents have so disordered her spirits that she is forced to send for the doctor to make her able to eat, she tells him, in great anger at Providence, that she never was well since she was born, and that she envies every beggar that she sees in health. This is the disquiet life of Coelia, who has nothing to torment her but her own spirit.

If you would inspire her with a Christian humility, you need do no more to make her as happy as any person in the world. This virtue would make her thankful to God for half so much health as she has had, and help her to enjoy more for the life to come.

Most people suppose that the strict rules and restraints of an exalted piety are such contradictions to our nature as must needs make our lives dull and uncomfortable. This objection supposes that the happiness of life consists in a mixture of virtue and vice, a mixture of ambition and humility, charity and envy, heavenly affection and covetousness. All of which is as absurd as to suppose that it is happy to be free from excessive pains, but unhappy to be without more moderate pains; or that the happiness of health consists in being partly sick and partly well. But piety requires us to renounce no ways of life where we can act reasonably, and offer what we do to the glory of God.

Let us suppose a person [is] placed somewhere alone by himself in the midst of a variety of things which he does not know how to use; that he has by him bread, wine, water, golden dust, iron, chains, gravel, garments, fire, etc. Let it be supposed that he has no knowledge of the right use of these things, nor any direction from his senses how to quench his thirst, or satisfy his hunger, or make any use of the things about him. Let it be supposed that in his drought he puts golden dust into his eyes; when his eyes smart he puts wine into his ears; that in his hunger he puts gravel into his mouth; that in pain he loads himself with the iron chains; that, feeling cold, he puts his feet in the water; that being frightened at the fire, he runs away from it; that being weary he makes a seat of his bread.

Let it be supposed that through his ignorance of the right use of the things that are about him he will plainly torment himself whilst he lives, and at last die, blinded with dust, choked with gravel, and loaded with irons. Let it be supposed that some good being came to him and showed him the nature and use of all the things that were about him, and gave him such strict rules of using them as would certainly, if observed, make him the happier and deliver him from the pains of hunger, thirst, and cold. Now, could you with any reason affirm that those strict rules had rendered that poor man's life dull and uncomfortable? Now this is in some measure a representation of the strict rules of the Christian faith. They only relieve our ignorance, save us from tormenting ourselves, and teach us to use everything about us to our proper advantage.

Man is placed in a world full of a variety of things. His ignorance makes him use many of them as absurdly as the man who put dust in his eyes to relieve his thirst, or put on chains to remove pain. But a state of glory will be given to all those who make a right use of the things of this present world, who do not blind themselves with golden dust, or eat gravel, or groan under loads of iron of their own putting on; but use bread, water, wine, and garments for such ends as are according to nature and reason, and who with faith and thankfulness worship the kind Giver of all that they enjoy here, and hope for hereafter.

If the Christian faith forbids all instances of revenge without any exception,[2] it is because all revenge is of the nature of poison; and though we do not take so much as to put an end to life, yet if we take any at all, it corrupts the whole mass of blood and makes it difficult to be restored to our former health.

If it commands a universal charity, to love our neighbor as ourselves, to forgive and pray for all our enemies without any reserve, it is because all degrees of love are degrees of happiness that strengthen and support the divine life of the soul, and are as necessary to its health and happiness as proper food to the health and happiness of the body.

If it commands us to live wholly unto God and to do all to His glory, it is because every other way is living wholly against ourselves, and will end in our own shame and confusion of face. All that we have, all that we are, all that we enjoy, are only so many talents from God. If we use them to the ends of a pious and holy life, our five talents will become ten, and our labors will carry us into the joy of our Lord. But if we abuse them to the gratification of our own passions, sacrificing the gifts of God to our own pride and vanity, we shall live here in vain labors and foolish anxieties, shunning Christianity as a melancholy thing, accusing our Lord as a hard master, and then fall into everlasting misery.

We may for a while amuse ourselves with names, and sounds, and shadows of happiness. We may talk of this or that greatness and dignity; but if we desire real happiness, we have no other possible way to it. How ignorant, therefore, are they of the nature of man, and the nature of God, who think a life of strict piety and devotion to God to be a dull uncomfortable state; when it is so plain and certain that there is neither comfort nor joy to be found in anything else!

We may see still more of the happiness of a life devoted unto God by considering the poor contrivances for happiness, and the contemptible ways of life which they are thrown into, who are not under the directions of a strict piety, but are seeking after happiness by other methods which the world has invented. I say invented, because those things which make up the joy and happiness of the world are mere inventions which have no foundation in nature and reason. As for instance, when a man proposes to be happy in ways of ambition, by raising himself to some imaginary heights above other people. This is as mere a cheat of our own making as if a man should intend to make himself happy by climbing up a ladder.

If a woman seeks for happiness from fine colors or spots upon her face, from jewels and rich clothes, this is as merely an invention of happiness, as contrary to nature and reason as if she should propose to make herself happy by painting a post, and putting the same finery upon it.

Who can help blessing God for the means of grace and for the hope of glory[3] when he sees what variety of folly they sink into, who live without it? Great devotion and holiness is not to be left to any particular sort of people, but to be the common spirit of all who desire to live up to the terms of common Christianity. For it is as much a law of Christ to treat everybody as your neighbor, and to love your neighbor as yourself, as it is a law of Christianity to abstain from theft. Our blessed Lord recommended His love to us as the pattern and example of our love to one another. "A new commandment," He says, "I give unto you, that you love one another, as I have loved you. By this shall all men know that you are My disciples, if you love one another."[4]

The newness of this precept did not consist in this, that men were commanded to love one another; for this was an old precept, both of the law of Moses and of nature. But it was new in this respect, that it was to imitate a new and (till then) unheard of example of love. It was to love one another as Christ had loved us. There is no principle of the heart more acceptable to God than a universal fervent love to all mankind, wishing and praying for their happiness, because there is no principle of the heart that makes us more like God, who is love and goodness itself, and created all beings for their enjoyment of happiness. The greatest idea that we can frame of God is when we conceive Him to be a being of infinite love and goodness, using an infinite wisdom and power for the common good and happiness of all His creatures.

An ill-natured man among God's creatures is the most perverse creature in the world, acting contrary to that love by which He Himself subsists, and which alone gives subsistence to all that variety of beings that enjoy life in any part of the creation. If we have any temper of our hearts that makes us envious, or spiteful, or ill-natured toward any one man, the same temper will make us envious, and spiteful, and ill-natured toward a great many more. If, therefore, we desire this divine virtue of love, we must exercise and practice our hearts in the love of all, because it is not Christian love till it is the love of all.

God Almighty, besides His own great example of love, which ought to draw all His creatures after it, has so provided for us, and made our happiness so common to us all, that we have no occasion to envy or hate one another. As we cannot be happy but in the enjoyment of God, so we cannot rival or rob one another of this happiness. For as one allowed instance of injustice destroys the justice of all our other actions, so one allowed instance of envy, spite, and ill-will renders all our other acts of benevolence and affection worth nothing. How silly would it be to envy a man that was drinking poison out of a golden cup! And yet, who can say that he is acting wiser than this when he is envying any instance of worldly greatness? How envied was Alexander when, conquering the world, he built towns, set up his statues, and left marks of his glory in so many kingdoms! And how despised was the poor preacher St. Paul when he was beaten with rods![5] And yet how strangely was the world mistaken in its judgment. How much to be envied was St. Paul! How much to be pitied was Alexander!

Our power of doing external acts of love and goodness is often very narrow and restrained. There are, it may be, but few people to whom we can contribute any worldly relief. But though our outward means of doing good are often thus limited, yet if our hearts are but full of love and goodness, we get as it were an infinite power, because God will attribute to us those good works and acts of love and tender charities which we sincerely desired, and would gladly have performed, had it been in our power. You cannot heal all the sick, relieve all the poor; you cannot comfort all in distress, nor be a father to all the fatherless. You cannot, it may be, deliver many from their misfortunes or teach them to find comfort in God.

But if there is a love and tenderness in your heart, that delights in these works, and excites you to do all that you can; if your love has no bounds, but continually wishes and prays for the relief and happiness of all who are in distress, you will be received by God as a benefactor to those who have had nothing from you but your goodwill and tender affections.

Now there is nothing that so much exalts our souls as this heavenly love. It cleanses and purifies like a holy fire, and all ill-tempers fall away before it. Everything that is good and holy grows out of it, and it becomes a continual source of all holy desires and pious practices. By love I do not mean any natural tenderness which is more or less in people according to their constitutions, but I mean a larger principle of the soul, founded in reason and piety, which makes us tender, kind, and benevolent to all our fellow-creatures, as creatures of God and for His sake. It is this love that loves all things in God, as His creatures, as the images of His power, as the creatures of His goodness, as parts of His family, as members of His society, that becomes a holy principle of all great and good actions.

The love, therefore, of our neighbor is only a branch of our love to God. If I hate or despise any one man in the world, I hate something that God cannot hate, and despise that which He loves. And can I think that I love God with all my heart whilst I hate that which belongs only to God, which has no other master but Him, which bears His image, is part of His family, and exists only by the continuance of His love toward it? It was the impossibility of this that made St. John say, "That if any man saith, he loveth God, and hateth his brother, he is a liar."[6]

All hatred of sin which does not fill the heart with the softest, tenderest affections toward persons miserable in it, is the servant of sin. And there is no temper which even good men ought more carefully to watch and guard against than this. For it is a temper that lurks and hides itself under the cover of many virtues and, by being unsuspected, does the more mischief. A man naturally fancies that it is his own exceeding love of virtue that makes him not able to bear with those that lack it. And when he abhors one man, despises another, and cannot bear the name of a third, he supposes it all to be a proof of his own high sense of virtue and just hatred of sin. And yet—if this had been the spirit of the Son of God, if He had hated sin in this manner, there would have been no redemption of the world. If God had hated sinners in this manner day and night, the world itself would have ceased long ago.

To see this in a clearer light, let us suppose a person to have appointed times for praising God with psalms and hymns, and to be strict in the observation of them; let it be supposed also that in his common life he is restless and uneasy, full of murmurings and complaints at everything, never pleased but by chance, as his temper happens to carry him, but murmuring and repining at the very seasons, and having something to dislike in everything that happens to him. Now, can you conceive anything more absurd and unreasonable than such a character as this? Is such a one to be reckoned thankful to God? Is it not certain that such forms of praise must be abhorred as an abomination?

But the absurdity which you see in this instance is the same in any other part of our life. Bended knees, whilst you are clothed with pride; heavenly petitions, whilst you are hoarding up treasures upon earth; holy devotions, whilst you live in the follies of the world; prayers of meekness and charity, whilst your heart is the seat of spite and resentment; hours of prayer, whilst you give up days and years to idle diversions and foolish pleasures: these are as absurd and unacceptable to God as thanksgivings from a person who lives in repinings and discontent. Unless the common course of our lives be according to the common spirit of our prayers, our prayers are so far from being a real or sufficient degree of devotion that they become an empty lip-labor or, what is worse, a notorious hypocrisy.

Ponder these great truths: that the Son of God was forced to become man, to be partaker of all our infirmities, to undergo a poor, painful, miserable, and contemptible life, to be persecuted, hated, and at last nailed to a cross, that by such sufferings He might render God propitious to that nature in which He suffered.

That all the bloody sacrifices and atonements of Jewish law were to represent the necessity of this great sacrifice, and the great displeasure that God bore to sinners.

That the world is still under the curse of sin, and certain marks of God's displeasure at it, such as famines, plagues, tempests, sickness, diseases, and death.

That all the sons of Adam are to go through a painful, sickly life, crucifying the lusts of the flesh, in order to have a share in the atonement of our Savior's death.

That all their self-denials, all their tears and repentance, are made available only by that great intercession which He is still making for them at the right hand of God.

Now consider these great truths: that this mysterious redemption, all these sacrifices and sufferings both of God and man, are only to remove the *guilt* of sin; and then let this teach you with what tears and contritions you ought to *purge* yourself from it. You may fairly look upon yourself to be the greatest sinner that you know in the world. For though you may know abundance of people to be guilty of some gross sins with which you cannot charge yourself, yet you may justly condemn yourself as the greatest sinner that you know. And that for these following reasons:

First, because you know more of the folly of your own heart than you do of other people's, and can charge yourself with various sins that you only know of yourself, and cannot be sure that other sinners are guilty of them. So that, as you know more of the folly, the baseness, the pride, the deceitfulness and negligence of your own heart, than you do of anyone's else, so you have just reason to consider yourself as the greatest sinner that you know; because you know more of the greatness of your own sins than you do of other people's.

Second, the greatness of our guilt arises chiefly from the greatness of God's goodness toward us, from the particular graces and blessings, the favors, the lights and instructions that we have received from Him. Now, just as these graces and blessings, and the multitude of God's favors toward us, are the great aggravation of our sins against God, so they are known only to ourselves. And therefore every sinner knows more of the aggravation of his own guilt than he does of other people's, and consequently he may justly look upon himself to be the greatest sinner that he knows.

How good God has been to other sinners; what light and instruction He has vouchsafed to them, what blessings and graces they have received from Him, you cannot tell. But you know yourself, and therefore are able to charge yourself with greater ingratitude than you can charge other people. So you are not to consider or compare the outward form or course of your life with that of other people, and then think yourself to be less sinful than they because the outward course of your life is less sinful than theirs. And this is the reason why the greatest saints in all ages have condemned themselves as the greatest sinners, because they knew some aggravations of their own sins which they could not know of other people's.

In order to know your own guilt, you must consider your own particular circumstances, your health, your sickness, your youth, your age, your particular calling, the happiness of your education, the degrees of light and instruction that you have received, the good men that you have conversed with, the admonitions that you have had, the good books that you have read, the numberless multitude of divine blessings and favors that you have received, the good motions of grace that you have resisted, the resolutions of amendment that you have so often broken, and the checks of conscience that you have disregarded. For it is from these circumstances that everyone is to state the measure and greatness of his own guilt. And as only you know these circumstances of your own sins, so you must necessarily know how to charge yourself, more so than charge other people.

God Almighty knows greater sinners, it may be, than you are, because He sees and knows the circumstance of all men's sins. But your own heart, if it is faithful to you, can discover no guilt so great as your own, because it can only see in you those circumstances on which the great part of the guilt of sin is founded. You may see sins in other people that you cannot charge upon yourself; but then you know a number of circumstances of your own guilt that you cannot lay to their charge. And perhaps that person that appears so odious in your eyes, would have been much better than you are, had he been in your circumstances and received all the same favors from God that you have. This is a very humbling reflection: that in your situation he might have been much truer to his duty than you are.

I have now only to add a word or two in recommendation of a life governed by the spirit of devotion. In this polite age of ours we have so lived away the spirit of devotion that many seem afraid even to be suspected of it, imagining great devotion to be great bigotry; that it is founded on ignorance and poorness of spirit, and that little, weak, and dejected minds are generally the greatest proficients in it. People of fine parts and learning, or of great knowledge in worldly matters, may perhaps think it hard to have their want of devotion charged upon their ignorance. But if they will be content to be tried by reason and Scripture, it may soon be made to appear that a want of devotion, wherever it is, either among the learned or unlearned, is founded on gross ignorance, and the greatest blindness and insensibility that can happen to a rational creature. And that devotion is so far from being the effect of a little and dejected mind, that it must and will be always highest in the most perfect natures.

Who reckons it a sign of a poor, little mind for a man to be full of reverence and duty to his parents, to have the truest love and honor for his friend, or to excel in the highest instances of gratitude to his benefactor? Are not these tempers in the highest degree in the most exalted and perfect minds? And yet what is high devotion but the highest exercise of these tempers of duty, reverence, love, honor, and gratitude to the amiable, glorious parent, friend and benefactor of all mankind? So long as duty to parents, love to friends, and gratitude to benefactors are thought great and honorable tempers, devotion, which is nothing else but duty, love, and gratitude to God, must have the highest place among our highest virtues.

If a prince, out of his mere goodness, should send you a pardon by one of his slaves, would you think it a part of your duty to receive the slave with marks of love, esteem, and gratitude for his great kindness in bringing you so great a gift, and at the same time think it a meanness and poorness of spirit to show love, esteem, and gratitude to the prince, who of his own goodness freely sent you the pardon? And yet this would be as reasonable as to suppose that love, esteem, honor, and gratitude are noble tempers and instances of a great soul when they are paid to our fellow creatures, but the effects of a poor, ignorant, dejected mind when they are paid to God.

Devotion, therefore, is the greatest sign of a great and noble genius. It supposes a soul in its highest state of knowledge, and none but little and blinded minds, that are sunk into ignorance and vanity, are destitute of it. There is nothing that shows so great a genius, nothing that so raises us above vulgar spirits, nothing that so plainly declares a heroic greatness of mind, as great devotion. All worldly attainments, whether greatness, wisdom, or bravery, are but empty sounds, and there is nothing wise, or great, or noble in a human spirit, but rightly to know, and heartily worship and adore the great God who is the support and life of all spirits, whether in Heaven or on earth.

NOTES

1. Coelia, Lupus, and Lucinda are three imaginary persons among many whom Law used in his *Serious Call* to illustrate different human characteristics.
2. Cf. Romans 12:19.
3. A reference to the prayer of "General Thanksgiving" in the Anglican *Book of Common Prayer,* 1662 edition.
4. John 13:34, 35.
5. 2 Corinthians 11:25.
6. 1 John 4:20.

Nicolaus Ludwig, Count von Zinzendorf

The first characteristic of importance to recognize about Nicolaus Lud-
wig, Count von Zinzendorf und Pottendorf (1700-1760), is the sin-
cerity and depth of his Christian faith. In the course of history few
have matched the lifelong ardor and devotion Zinzendorf expressed
toward the Person of the Lord Jesus Christ. "I have one passion," he
once declared. "It is He!"

Second in importance, perhaps, is the fact that Zinzendorf was a
European nobleman, scion of an ancient Austrian house, and the son of
a high official of the Saxon electoral court. In his relations with fellow
Christians in Europe and America, as well as with the world at large,
he always dealt from a position of power, and was usually surrounded
by a retinue. His interviews with John Wesley and Henry Muhlenburg,
records of which have been preserved, breathe a knowledge of theology
mixed with a touch of hauteur.

Yet there was a sweetness and kindliness in the man, and a sacrifi-
cial purpose, that lifted him above class distinctions and made him the
inspiration of one of the greatest missionary enterprises in the chroni-
cles of the church.

Zinzendorf was born in Dresden of Lutheran parents who had fled
to Saxony to escape Roman Catholic persecution in Austria. His father
died soon after the birth, his mother remarried, and he was brought up
by uncles and a pietistic grandmother, Katherine von Gersdorff. From
1710 to 1716 he studied at the Halle Padagogium, where he was teased
by his classmates and tyrannized by his teachers. Nevertheless his
devotional life was strengthened. His relatives insisted on his studying
law at Wittenberg University with a view to a diplomatic career.

He entered civil service in Saxony at age twenty-one, but a disap-
pointing love affair made him decide to settle on his estate at Berthels-
dorf, seventy miles east of Dresden, and become a Christian landowner
promoting "heart religion." Meanwhile, German-speaking Moravians
and Bohemians were seeking refuge in Saxony from continued persecu-
tion. They were descendants of the "Unitas Fratrum," once led by John

Hus. Zinzendorf offered them sanctuary in a corner of his estate, where they founded a village and named it Herrnhut ("The Watch of the Lord"). At first he paid slight attention to them, but in 1727 he resigned from government and became their spiritual leader and eventually their bishop.

While attending the coronation of the Danish king in Copenhagen, Zinzendorf met a West Indian Negro. He returned to Herrnhut aflame with missionary enthusiasm, and the community soon became an intense training ground for foreign mission endeavor. April 13, 1727 has generally been reckoned the date when the Moravian church was reborn. Young men and women began going out as missionaries to the West Indies, Greenland, the Baltic states, India, Labrador, Georgia, North Carolina, Surinam, Guiana, Egypt, South Africa, and Alaska. Natives and Negro slaves were won to Christ, and churches were founded which still exist.

Zinzendorf established a base in Bethlehem, Pennsylvania, and spent much time in the American colonies. He also lived in England for six years, and saw Parliament enact a law officially recognizing the "Moravian Episcopal Church." At the same time Zinzendorf maintained his Lutheran connections in Germany. Says historian Richard Pierard, "Zinzendorf's importance lies in the creation of a missionary, service-oriented free church based upon a common experience of salvation and mutual love, and the emphasis upon deep, emotional religious expression, especially in his hymns, prayers, and poems, which infused new life into Protestant orthodoxy."

This message of "Saving Faith" was one of Nine Public Lectures on Important Subjects in Religion, delivered in Fetter Lane Chapel, London, in 1746, and newly translated and edited by George W. Forell. They were published by the University of Iowa Press, Iowa City, 1973, and are used by permission.

THIRTEEN

Saving Faith
by Nicolaus Ludwig Count von Zinzendorf

In many places in the Holy Scriptures faith is called love; and this is so not only in the New Testament, but occurs already in the Old Testament. For when God wants to praise Abraham for following and believing Him through thick and thin, then God says to him, "Now I know that you love God."[1] It is necessary that we mark this well, for otherwise the whole thirteenth chapter of the First Letter to the Corinthians would be an unintelligible chapter, since Paul explicitly says, "Even if one believes, he will not be saved, if he does not love."[2]

Now, the Savior states positively that he who believes shall be saved,[3] and Paul says, nevertheless, that even though one believes, he will not be saved if he does not love. Hence it is quite clear that the Holy Scripture wants to point out to us that there is no saving faith which is not simultaneously love for Him who laid down His life for us, for Him who has created us, without whom we cannot live and exist for one moment.

In order to make myself clear I will call faith *fiducia implicita* and *explicita* (faith implicit and explicit). Faith as it is in our own selves shall be called implicit faith, and faith which is manifested to others, which unfolds itself, shall be called explicit faith. Both of them, when they are together, are such that they make the man who has them unspeakably happy and even here manifest eternal life.

But in any event if they cannot be together, then it is sufficient if only the first is there, implicit faith, the undisclosed but conscious believing within the heart. And this faith within the heart which one has within himself I also view from two perspectives: the first is "faith-in-distress" and the second "faith-in-love."

No man can create faith in himself. Something must happen to him which Luther calls "the divine work in us," which changes us, gives us new birth, and makes us completely different people in heart, spirit, mind, and all our powers. This is *fides*, faith, properly speaking. If this is to begin in us, then it must be preceded by distress, without which men have no ears for faith and trust.

The distress which we feel is the distress of our soul when we become "poor," when we see we have no Savior, when we become palpably aware of our misery. We see our corruption on all sides and are really anxious because of it. Then afterward it happens as with patients who have reached the point of crisis. They watch for help, for someone who can help them out of their distress, and accept the first offer of aid without making examination or investigation of the person who helps them.

That is the way it went once with the woman whom the Savior healed. For twelve years she had gone to see all kinds of physicians and had endured much from them. And finally she came upon Him too and said, "If only I would touch that man's clothes, it would help me; even if I could not get to the man Himself, if I could only get hold of a bit of His garment, then I would be helped."[4]

This is faith-in-distress. And here I can never wonder enough at the blindness and ignorance of those people who are supposed to handle the divine word and convert men, those abortive so-called Christians who think that if they have [people] memorize the catechism or get a book of sermons into their heads or, at the most, present all sorts of well-reasoned demonstrations concerning the divine being and attributes, thus funneling the truths and knowledge into their heads, that this is the sovereign means to their conversion. But this is such a preposterous method that if one wanted to convert people that way, reciting demonstrations to them, then it is just as if one wanted to go against wind and current with full sails, or as if one, on the contrary, would run one's boat into an inlet so that one could not find one's way out again.

That knowledge of divine things which is taken to be faith is only an adjunct of faith. It puffs up and nothing comes of it. And if one has all of it, says Paul, and does not also have love, and even if one can preach about it to others, still it is nothing more than if a bell rings in the church. As little as the bell gets out of it, as little as it is benefited by the fact that it hangs there and rings, just so little does the fact that a teacher makes the most cogent demonstrations benefit him as far as his own salvation is concerned.

But what results from this faith-in-distress, from this blind faith which one has out of love for his own salvation? Thankful love results from it. Long ago Manoah and his wife loved a man who came to them. They did not know him, for they said, "What is your name? We do not know you, but we love you. We should like to know who you are, so that we might honor you when what you have said to us comes true."[5]

So it is exactly with the faith-in-distress; it has to do completely with an unknown man, yet with a man of whom one's heart says, "He likes to help, He likes to comfort, and He can and will help. My heart tells me that it is He of whom I heard in my youth. They called Him the Savior, the Son of God, the Lord Jesus. He must help me. Oh, if He would only come to my aid! If He would only take my soul into His care, so that it would not perish! *Kyrie Eleison!* Lord, have mercy!"

Faith-in-distress has the infallible promise that the one having faith shall be helped. He shall obtain grace. No one shall come in vain or ask in vain. The thief on the cross cried out of his faith-in-distress, "Lord, remember me when you come into Your Kingdom. I love You as an unknown Lord of whom I know nothing and whom I have never known. But now I hear that You have a Kingdom and that You are hanging here because You have said You are a King. It may be true. I believe You. Now when You come to the place where Your Kingdom is, do think of me, do remember me then!"

The Lord instantly agreed: "Today you will be with Me in Paradise."[6] Had the thief been so inclined [to Jesus] in prison, then one doubt or another would probably have developed; but because he had no time, it went very well. People who are healthy and prosperous, who can be distracted or deliberate, who can eat, drink, sleep, and go to work, will probably have second thoughts which will disturb their faith.

Such disruptions do not consist in doubts as to whether there is a Savior, or whether this invisible Jesus of whom one has heard could rescue souls from their destruction. Rather, the question will be really whether He wants to help such a sinner, who is such a thoroughly miserable and wretched creature. Sin begins to dawn on one only after faith, after trust, after the yearning and longing for help, for rescue, when one has time for reflection, when the distress is not too pressing. When distress and help do not succeed each other so quickly that one cannot think of anything in between, then doubt comes, saying, "I am too great a sinner." But doubt is no sooner there, than it is really refuted by the actual forgiveness of sins. "Take heart, my son, your sins are forgiven."[7]

All this is God's work in us, implicit faith, which has to do with the heart alone. It is within the heart, and one has nothing to demonstrate to anyone else. Here at the very moment when one knows and feels himself to be so wretched, grace and forgiveness of sins is preached into his heart. This happens with infallible certainty and without concern that it could come to nothing. Man emerges at once out of the deepest sorrow and dismay over himself into blessed rest and contentment. At the same time he experiences love and thankfulness and attachment to Him who died for his soul, who gained eternal life for him with His blood. Whether he had thought more or less about the matter, or knew more or less, does not matter. From that very hour he loves Him as his highest good, and the Savior can say to him, "You do indeed truly love Me, and I have forgiven you a great many sins. I have rescued you from genuine misery, it is true. Now you stand there and feel ashamed for all eternity, and can hardly get over your astonishment at how much I have forgiven you."

Peter experienced something of this. In the Savior's affairs he was not just a natural, unconverted, unfamiliar man (which indeed is in itself sin enough). Rather he was a deliberate abjurer—what today is called a renegade. He would rather not know his Lord; he was ashamed of his Lord; he denied his Lord three times. And a few days later his Lord came up and rose from the dead and was loved by those people who had followed Him to death itself; by the women who had helped to place Him into the grave, and who came back out of love at early dawn and looked for Him. "Ah," says the Savior to them, "you dear children, I beg of you not to delay here with Me, but go and tell My Peter that I am here again."[8]

This must have been an astonishing message to Peter. Was this all his punishment, to be notified that his Lord is risen again? And if so, should he have been the first to be comforted, to have his heart revived? When the Savior said to him afterward, "Do you love Me more than these do?" Peter said, "You know all things. You know how much I love You."[9] And at that time Peter really did love [Jesus] more than all the others. Before he had loved Him in his imagination. He had honored Him, and out of esteem for Him had rashly claimed to be ready to suffer death for Him rather than forsake Him. Peter did make a bold beginning, but he got stuck, because his love was dry and intellectual. But when the Savior forgave him everything, when He acquitted him of his sins, when He declared a renegade to be His apostle, then Peter could hold back no longer. If anyone said anything about his Lord to him, tears filled his eyes, and his body and soul were humbled. Already in the high priest's palace the bare presentiment of the character of his Lord had made his eyes fountains of tears.

All this is still implicit faith, the faith which is God's work in the heart, in the midst of our stillness, where we and He have to do with each other alone, where nothing comes between us and Him—no man, no book, no knowledge, no learning, not even the most necessary truths—but only the distress, the sinner's shame, and the faithfulness of the Shepherd.

Now I come to the other faith which I have called explicit faith, the faith which unfolds and manifests itself. And this faith is also of two kinds: faith while one is still learning about the Savior, and faith when one expounds and teaches the Savior to others.

The people who had seen the risen Lord, who had loved Him so tenderly, went away with fear and joy and told no one anything. They knew now that He was not a mere man. They knew that something more profound, indeed something inexpressible, lay behind the man; but they lacked the words, the fitting expressions. They were conscious enough that their Creator was their Savior.

Thomas, when he had to do only with the eleven [disciples] and the Savior, could cry out without reflection, "My Lord and my God!"[10] But if they would have gone to tell the people that the Savior was God, that He had redeemed the whole world, then they would not have had words for it. This they could not yet explain, for this was for them not unraveled for speaking. They could not bring it into a discourse nor make it plain. It did shine through all their expressions, but not in any orderly fashion.

One has only to compare the first sermons of the apostles with the subsequent ones. One has only to read Paul's epistles which he wrote at the beginning and contrast them with the others that came out later. One only has to read John's letters and after that his Gospel, with which he concludes. Then one will see how the apostles' faith itself evolved, how the solid ideas of God the Creator as a human being successively developed. They obtained one important demonstration of grace and power after another in their addresses. They had grace not only for confessing in the face of all the world, but also for learning to prove what they preached and for finding words to make themselves clear on these subjects.

One of the greatest pleasures is to read the Bible according to the epochs, periods, and stages by which the preaching of the gospel has from time to time been growing and ascending. If one starts with the thirties, after the Savior's birth, down to the nineties, and keeps this development in sight and meditates upon it in a simple and childlike way, one can see what Paul means by saying, "that your love may abound more and more, with knowledge and all discernment,"[11] and that thereafter "you may make such progress that you will measure the length, breadth, depth, and height of things."[12] You will also be able to speak as plainly of the profoundest mysteries of God your Lord as if they were catechism questions.

Then you will have to stand and say at last, "It is good that Jesus is my Creator and my God, that He is the God over everything. But what an observation this is, that my Creator has laid down His life for me!" All your theology, all your theosophy, insight, and knowledge will be caught up in this as the central point. All of this will run together into the wounded heart of Jesus. It will disappear and be lost in love. Nothing greater, nothing higher can be thought of. John, full of the eternal power and majesty of his God, full of the Cause of Causes, full of the *logos* of the Godhead who was in the beginning with God and was Himself God;[13] [I say,] John, full of these stupendous ideas, writes, "Jesus Christ has loved us and washed us of our sins with His blood."[14] And when John portrays the majestic hours in Heaven, the great disclosures of the heavenly revelations; when he describes the temple of God open in Heaven and the ark of the covenant; when thunder and lightning and the trumpets of angels are heard, and hosts which no one can number are seen: then their song is, "You have bought us with Your blood!"[15]

This is the great subject matter. This is the chief object of faith. "I know nothing but that You have died for me out of love. You have laid down Your life for me. I know that if You had not died for me, I should have been lost. I should have sunk into the bottom of Hell, had You not extinguished Hell for me, had You not (as Dr. Luther says) drunk up death."

This is the first part of explicit faith. One knows in his inmost person with whom he deals. One knows Him from head to foot, in heart and body. One knows Him in His most profound nature as it is now and was then. And when one has thought and felt this long enough and has become a scribe instructed for the Kingdom of Heaven, then one takes out one truth after the other, presents it, and demonstrates it with reasons grounded deep within oneself, which grasp the hearers' hearts. For if one would speak to those who know and love the Savior about His glory and majesty, then they say, "There is no doubt about that; that is clear enough to me, and I have no hesitation here. But the trembling of God shakes my soul. His [Jesus'] suffering, His death, His *angst*, His atoning battle which He endured for me, the fact that He had to be absolved through the Holy Spirit, that with Him all my sin is forgiven, that with Him I have leave to be eternally blessed—*this* is the reality for which no word, no expression, is adequate." One's feeling of this cannot be made plain to someone who does not have it himself. It all gets stuck or comes out only half and half. These are the unspeakable things.

> When that Heart confronts my eye
> in all His godly greatness,
> then I think, "I die!"
> Then I think: Good-bye,
> you self-empowered repenting.
> Like wax before the fire, I
> want to melt in Jesus' suffering.

When a person has this faith, this faith-in-distress, this faith made doubtful by reason of great unworthiness, this faith which has fallen in love through the real help, through the blessed happiness and grace which the heart has obtained, is that not beautiful? When a person has within himself the meditations of faith and the lasting feeling, the searching in Jesus even up to His eternal Godhead, finding His Father and His Spirit, and all this coming from His side, out of His heart, is that not beautiful?

And when at last he obtains and experiences as a gift the learned faith which preaches from the wounds of Jesus to his Creator's power and from his Creator's power into the side of

Jesus, into His wounded heart, and which makes everybody convinced and brings them to an evident certainty, is not that beautiful? Is not that a great blessedness? Does it not make a blessed man who, as Paul says, believes all this from his heart[16] and can say and confess it with complete assurance? His faith so flows from his heart that he can thus pour himself out before mankind.

If a minister preaches and has nothing in his heart, then it is neither fish nor fowl; it lacks the authority, the *exousia*. The man does not speak as one who understands what he is talking about, as one who is at home there, as one who is steeped in the subject. Rather, he describes the four square corners of a round tower. He betrays by his description that he has not been at the place about which he is speaking.

But if someone does speak distinctly, convincingly, solidly, and truly of something which he has not experienced, he is a prophet. He is to be looked upon either as in an extraordinary state for this specific occasion or as an extraordinary person for all time, as a special servant used by God in an extraordinary way for a specific purpose. For this purpose he is to be venerated, which does not depend on his inner condition.

It is an extraordinary case when people can speak of heavenly and divine things without having experienced them in their hearts. The Apostle Paul speaks of some such thing incessantly in the thirteenth chapter of First Corinthians. What is that thing called? He repeats it so often that one sees it is very important to him. He would like everybody to know it inside and out. It is what really matters. If it is in order, the rest will turn out all right. "This is love," he says. "Love."

Now, were this expounded in the terminology which is customary in Christendom, then it would turn out as it has with most people. When they speak of love, they mean by it a goodness which is well-meaning toward the neighbor, serves him gladly, and helps him out of distress. I have seen in the commentaries of most theologians that when they come to this text, "If I give away all I have to the poor, and if I deliver my body to be burned, but have not love, I gain nothing,"[17] they explain it this way. They say, "If someone did this and yet did not do it out of heartfelt love toward his neighbor, but rather out of pride, out of vanity of mind, in order to be seen, he would gain nothing by it."

From this it can clearly be seen that they understand the entire chapter to be about that virtue which in everyday life is called love. It means to be loving and kindhearted, to have a good disposition, to wish one's neighbor nothing bad, but rather to be helpful to him and work for his advantage, to have a sympathetic heart toward him. In this manner they expound it without much ado.

It was a great moment for me when I saw that one single commentator among all the rest thought of bringing that place in the Song of Songs to bear on 1 Corinthians 13: "You have ravished my heart with a glance of your eyes"; also, "O that he would kiss me with the kisses of his mouth," "your name is oil poured out."[18] Such little crumbs are like balsam when one discovers a person whose eyes are beginning to open and who, rather shyly, so that he will not become entangled in vexations and a theological brawl, comes out with a reference and cites a text which the reader himself may trace afterward. This is indeed a real joy.

I am not afraid to maintain publicly and candidly that the apostle, in this thirteenth chapter of the First Letter to the Corinthians, means nothing the least bit different in his entire discourse from what we call saving faith. This he calls love, and distinguishes it in the last verse of the chapter from faith purely for the reason that as soon as one has a faithful heart toward the Savior, one must trust in certain things and promises which one sees neither now nor then, but must expect. These things, when they are fulfilled, take away that part of saving faith which consists in hoping and expecting, and leave nothing behind except that part which consists in love and faithfulness.

O dear friends, do not imagine that we know the Savior. We begin to know Him only when we have loved Him very tenderly, when we have loved Him first above all things, when for us nothing in the world is in competition with Him; when we have forgotten ourselves, our health, our life, our possessions and goods, our enjoyment on account of Him. Our whole life consists in the increasing and growing in knowledge of Him, so that we know Him better today than yesterday, and in a year know Him a year better; in twenty years twenty years better, and in eternity an eternity better than now. This is the great science. In Him and His Person lies hidden a treasure of wisdom and knowledge which cannot be fathomed or exhausted.

Paul says that nobody can call Jehovah Jesus unless he has been inspired by the Holy Spirit.[19] It is not possible, he says. Whoever can say, "Jehovah Elohim, who has created mankind and all things, whose handiwork we are, who is exalted above all heavens, is my Savior, is my infant Jesus in the womb, in the cradle, and in the temple, is the carpenter from Nazareth who spent His life in sweat and labor at His handicraft until He was thirty years old; the teacher come from God whom the Devil plagued for forty days in the wilderness, who began to establish His little church with twelve, with seventy, and with five hundred, and upon the cross selected the first two elders of His church, His mother and His beloved John: this is the very Creator, the architect of the universe, of the sun and the moon and all the stars, and of all conceivable worlds"—whoever can declare this with feeling and understanding:

> I believe a point in time will be
> when Christ my Creator will come to me
> to wed me body and soul,

such a person is an angelic, heavenly, and divine man (this is Paul's and John's expression). This cannot happen without the Holy Spirit. This no one can do who is not filled with the Holy Spirit.

Now, what is more customary in the Christian world than this? The Catholic and Lutheran churches make up the majority of European Christians; and although in other denominations the Savior is handled in another way and things are moving toward a purely philosophical conception (and although even some Lutherans, who want to give themselves airs, are beginning to choose this dry way which will in the end make the Savior into a Confucius), this nevertheless is certain, that the greatest number of our denominations still have the Creator as Savior on their lips. They still sing,

> The blest Creator of all creation
> assumed a servant's low condition
> to win the flesh. . . .

This is at the same time a Catholic and a Lutheran verse; this the two denominations have in common. Are therefore all these people men of God? Are all of these men saved? There are thousands of people in the world who, when they hear the Savior proclaimed, pay attention just as if they were reading a newspaper report about people who are five hundred or a thousand miles away from them. They are not concerned; in a few days they have forgotten what it was. Why? It was not important to them.

But he with whom the Holy Spirit has had to do, whose heart the Holy Spirit has reached, whose heart the Holy Spirit has unlocked, from whose heart He has rolled away the stone—when such a heart hears of the Savior, the Reconciler, when it hears that his Creator is his Savior, it is for such a soul as if someone received news of his son, his father, his brother. It is as if a wife received news of her husband, and they have reason to believe that it is true. One finds everything coming alive. It is the consequence of the love which is in the heart toward the matter.

But how does one become involved in this love? It is "poured out into our hearts through the Holy Spirit which has been given to us."[20] When the Holy Spirit comes into the heart, He melts the heart; then the eyes fill with tears, then body and soul rejoice. This happened to Cornelius; this happened to Queen Candace's treasurer. They felt this joy and tasted this blessedness, but they did not know what name to give it. Then it was said to Cornelius, "Now send for Simon; he will explain it to you. He will tell you what has been done in your heart; he will name the man to whom you are to attribute all of this."[21]

And to Queen Candace's treasurer, the Savior Himself sent Philip. As soon as the man wanted to know it, Philip had to climb up into the chariot to him and only name the Lamb for him which had taken hold of his soul, which had already seized his bones.[22] Philip said, "This is His Name, it is He." And then there was no question about baptism; it was immediately ready. It did not take several weeks of preparation first. There was no need to memorize a book. There was no need for answering twenty-four or thirty questions. Rather, "Who will prevent you from being baptized? Do you believe? Is that man important to you? Do you believe all the good said about Him, and believe it gladly?" "Oh, yes, with all my heart." Then everything was well, and the blood of the covenant was poured over him. Then that grace was made known to him which so many thousands of souls have in common with him, who also gladly receive the Word, are baptized, and received into the community at the hour of awakening.

I would like this love to be the only pleasant and blessed reality, the pearl toward which all souls extend their desires, so that they might win it and forget everything else, so that each soul would ask itself honestly and candidly, Do you have this love? Can you feel it? Can you say as you are going to a church, a meeting, as you go here and there, can you believe that you love something? Is your heart so disposed? Do you like that which has been explained to you, and do you care about it? Do you feel a condition which you have not had before? Has something happened to you which you need explained, if you cannot explain it yourself? Do you have a little verse in the Bible, a stanza from a hymn, something for which you need a good friend who can say to you, "The same thing happened to me"?

Not every man is so foolish that he restricts the communion of saints, the invisible church, to the case of the person who, belonging to the Anglican, the Lutheran, or any other church, travels to Paris and there remains in his spirit in communion with his Anglican or Lutheran church. There are indeed such absurd teachers who restrict it to this, but they are not so respected that they are able to adulterate the general interpretation, which is that in all nations, and even in the erroneous religious denominations themselves, God has His own people. "The Lord knows His own."[23]

It would be right if every one of us would base all his association with people, all love toward people, all brotherly love solely on this principle—that these others are also my Lord's people; they are my brothers and sisters; we are the children of one Father; they all have the same blessed happiness that I have; they enjoy what I enjoy; they are just as favored as I am and just as redeemed; they are destined for the same glory to which I am called through grace. When souls advance in the experience, in the insight, in the feeling and love of the Savior, such affection and intimacy would grow in its extensiveness. But as high as Heaven is from the earth, so far must the preference which a person gives his Lamb, his Husband, his Creator, the Surety crucified for our debt, his Redeemer and Savior, transcend everything which one owes all one's fellow creatures, all one's fellow men, yes, all one's fellow Christians.

Faith is no great art; rather, the first beginnings of faith, the very first faith is an effect of misery. No man except one who has the spirit of Lucifer, who has a satanic pride and blindness so that he does not want to see his physical and spiritual distress, who has been brought to insensibility because he will not feel his daily plague (and that is a Satan's spirit, a Satan's pride), none but such a person is in danger of missing the faith-in-distress.

But what grace, what patience and condescension it is that the Creator, who knows His poor creature better than it knows itself, requires of it no other faith for being saved than the faith-in-distress, the first faith. When my anxiety, my sin, my corruption make me believe, then I think, "He who appears before my heart, who has such a bloody appearance, who is said to have died for me, certainly it will be He. Yes! Yes! It is He!" That makes me blessedly happy. That helps me into the eternal Kingdom.

Whoever does not learn to believe this way, that is, whoever does not have so much misery, so much distress that he must believe, how can that person be helped? He is already judged for this very reason, because he does not feel misery enough to cause him gladly to believe. For even though a man is proud and egotistic in a merely human way, and finally nevertheless does find in himself the fibers of his utter corruption and distress, his excuses cease. He begins to inveigh against himself, to condemn himself.

And as soon as he does this, as soon as he discovers himself lost, then he is so full of anxiety that he does not have to create any for himself. He does not have to imagine any misery. And if this anxiety remains in him and increases and pushes its way into all his business, into his well-being, and he is forced to cry out for help, then he is in faith, in the faith-in-distress, in the midst of saving faith, and does not know himself how he got into it.

"I believe it gladly because I delight in it!" So easy is it to be saved; so completely without excuse remain those who perish through unbelief.

NOTES

1. Zinzendorf sometimes makes ingenious translations of his own from Scripture. Genesis 22:12 actually reads, "Now I know that you fear God . . ."
2. 1 Corinthians 13:2 reads, "And though I have all faith . . . but have not love, I am nothing."
3. Mark 16:16.
4. Cf. Matthew 9:21.
5. "But we love you" is Zinzendorf's addition to Judges 13:17.
6. Luke 23:43.
7. Matthew 9:2.
8. Zinzendorf's version of Mark 16:7.
9. Cf. John 21:15.

10. John 20:28.
11. Philippians 1:9.
12. Cf. Ephesians 3:18.
13. John 1:3.
14. Revelation 1:5.
15. Cf. Revelation 5:9.
16. Romans 10:9.
17. 1 Corinthians 13:3.
18. Song of Solomon 4:9b, 1:2a, 1:3.
19. 1 Corinthians 12:3.
20. Romans 5:5.
21. Cf. Acts 10:32.
22. Cf. Acts 8:35.
23. 2 Timothy 2:19.

Samson Occom

To make available this selection from the writings of Samson Occom (1723-1792) has meant improvising. Not having access to the portions of Occom's unpublished diary in the archives of the Connecticut Historical Society and Dartmouth College, I have relied upon Samson Occom and the Christian Indians of New England, by W. DeLoss Love, Ph.D., a volume published in 1899 by Pilgrim Press. All quotations from the Occom diaries and writings are taken from this work.

However, Dr. Love's study is the fruit of such excellent research, and quotes so judiciously and so liberally from the Occom manuscripts, that the reader should (in my opinion) be able to form a clear estimate of the man from his own words. It should be added that a fresh biography of Occom, the most distinguished Christian Indian of New England history, is overdue, and that in particular his diaries need to be published in full.

Dr. Love appraises Occom's contribution in these words: "If any native has merited the dignity of being called an Indian statesman, that man was Samson Occom. He believed in the efficacy of Christian missions, and in education, particularly in industrial affairs; but he seems to have thought that the civilization of the Indian depended in large measure upon his relation to the land upon which he lived. So long as he roamed at large in the forest, he thought, the native would remain a savage. It was necessary to gather them apart from the white men and on land which they could not sell, where they could be taught industrial pursuits and obtain a living from the soil. He believed in maintaining so far as possible a tribal unity, establishing a form of self-government under the protection of the state."

That, of course, is what happened. But Samson's personal efforts to civilize his countrymen ran into difficulties at home. Mary Occom, his wife, whom Dr. Love calls "an estimable Christian woman," was from the Montauk tribe of Long Island, and she preferred to live by Indian custom. Samson, for his part, wished to live in the English style. One friend wrote in his diary after a visit to their home, "She declined, evening and morning, setting at table. Her dress was mostly Indian, *and when he spoke to her in English, she answered in her native language, although she could speak good English."* As for the seven *children, they suffered from their father's prolonged absences. While some of them eventually rose above the usual level to lead useful lives, others adopted the roving life of the Indian and, as he wrote, brought their father "sorrow upon sorrow."*

Another grave disappointment to Samson was the failure of his teacher and benefactor, Dr. Eleazar Wheelock, to use the funds Samson raised in a two-year visit to Britain for their intended purpose, which was to train and educate Indians. Instead, Wheelock's Indian Charity School became a school for whites and was renamed Dartmouth Academy. It seems Dr. Wheelock became disillusioned and lost confidence in the Indians, and they in him.

The saga of the American Indian has become a major tragedy in the nation's growth, and Samson Occom was one of the first to see it coming. He witnessed the dying of the Connecticut tribes, and predicted that white settlers would crowd the Six Nations out of the Mohawk Valley. And so it came to be; the "Brothertown" village Samson founded at Tuscarora, New York, is now Brothertown, Wisconsin. One critic has remarked that the funeral sermon Occom preached for the murderer Moses Paul in New Haven was in a sense a funeral sermon for his race.

Today there are new stirrings among the Christian Indians of North America. Leaders of the Indian churches believe that their best days lie ahead. Perhaps it was for them Samson Occom wrote the hymn he published in 1774:

> "All hail the Lamb, who once was slain;
> Unnumber'd millions born again
> Will shout Thine endless praise."

Samson Occom, Indian Evangelist Excerpts from His Diary and Other Writings

"I was born a heathen and brought up in heathenism till I was between sixteen and seventeen years of age, at a place called Mohegan, in New London, Connecticut, in New England. My parents lived a wandering life as did all the Indians at Mohegan. They chiefly depended upon hunting, fishing, and fowling for their living, and had no connection with the English, excepting to traffic with them in their small trifles. They strictly maintained and followed their heathenish ways, customs, and religion. Neither did we cultivate our land nor keep any sort of creatures, except dogs which we used in hunting, and we dwelt in wigwams. These are a sort of tent covered with mats made of flags [plants]. And to this time we were unacquainted with the English tongue in general, though there were a few who understood a little of it." So begins the diary of this great Native American Christian.

Samson Occom was born sometime in the year 1723 in a wigwam to Joshua and Sarah Ockham, or Aucom. Efforts had been made to Christianize the Mohegan Indians in years past. In 1714 the Rev. Experience Mayhew of Martha's Vineyard island preached to them in a double wigwam for an hour and a half. He received their thanks, but their response was that they had their own way of worship; and the English were no better for being Christians, as they would cheat the Indians of their land just the same.

Missionary interest in reaching the Indians caused the Rev. Jonathan Barber of Springfield to be appointed in charge of a school for Mohegan children; but continuing controversy over land problems caused the school to die out, as the children would not attend. Samson Occom describes the "civilizing" efforts in these words:

"Once a fortnight in ye summer season a minister from New London[1] used to come up and the Indians to attend. Not that they regarded the Christian religion, but they had blankets given to them every fall of the year, and for these things they would attend. And there was a sort of a school kept when I was quite young, but I believe there never was one that ever learnt to read anything.

"When I was about ten years of age there was a man who went among the Indian wigwams, and wherever he could find the Indian children would make them read, but the children used to take care to keep out of his way. He used to catch me sometimes and make me say over my letters, and I believe I learnt some of them. But this was soon over too, and all this time there was not one amongst us that made a profession of Christianity."

In 1739 the Rev. David Jewett became the minister of the North Church of New London, today the First Congregational Church of Montville. One year later the Great Awakening took place, and the Mohegan Indians were in the midst of it all. George Whitefield, Gilbert Tennent, and James Davenport were in the neighborhood, and Jewett was deeply stirred. Davenport in particular attracted the Indians. Eleazar Wheelock, Davenport's brother-in-law, preached to them. Jewett distributed Bibles, psalters, primers, and catechisms among them. In time several Indians were admitted to fellowship by the church, and among them was Sarah Occom, now a widow.

Samson Occom's account of how the revival affected him personally follows:

"When I was sixteen years of age [1739 or 1740] we heard a strange rumor among the English that there were extraordinary ministers preaching from place to place and a strange concern among the white people. This was in the spring of the year. But we saw nothing of these things till some time in the summer, when some ministers began to visit us and preach the Word of God; and the common people also came frequently and exhorted us to the things of God, which it pleased the Lord, as I humbly hope, to bless and accompany with divine influences to the conviction and saving conversion of a number of us, amongst whom I was one that was impressed with the things we had heard.

"These preachers did not only come to us, but we frequently went to their meetings and churches. After I was convicted I went to all the meetings I could come at, and continued under trouble of mind about six months, at which time I began to learn the English letters, got me a primer, and used to go to my English neighbors frequently for assistance in reading, but went to no school. And when I was seventeen years of age I had, as I trust, a discovery of the way of salvation through Jesus Christ, and was enabled to put my trust in Him alone for life and salvation.

"From this time the distress and burden of my mind was removed, and I found serenity and pleasure of soul in serving God. By this time I just began to read in the New Testament without spelling, and I had a stronger desire still to learn to read the Word of God, and at the same time had an uncommon pity and compassion to my poor brethren according to the flesh. I used to wish I was capable of instructing my poor kindred. I used to think if I could once learn to read I would instruct the poor children in reading, and used frequently to talk with our Indians concerning religion. Thus I continued till I was in my nineteenth year, and by this time I could read a little in the Bible."

The Rev. Dr. Eleazar Wheelock at this time pastored the Second Congregational Church of nearby Lebanon. He is described as "of a middle stature and size, well proportioned, erect, and dignified. His voice was remarkably full, harmonious, and commanding." The Indians particularly felt the power of the personal magnetism which was characteristic of him as a teacher. Among those who went to Lebanon to sit under his ministry was Sarah Occom. Samson, her son, tells what happened:

"At this time my poor mother was going to Lebanon, and having had some knowledge of Mr. Wheelock and learning that he had a number of English youth under his tuition, I had a great inclination to go to him and to be with him a week or a fortnight, and desired my mother to ask Mr. Wheelock whether he would take me a little while to instruct me in reading. Mother did so, and when she came back, she said Mr. Wheelock wanted to see me as soon as possible. So I went up thinking I should be back again in a few days. When I got up there, he received me with kindness and compassion, and instead of staying a fortnight or three weeks, I spent four years with him."

Such were the beginnings of Dartmouth College!

Samson joined Dr. Wheelock's church, built a hut in the woods near the minister's home, and lived on an allowance provided by the Scottish Society for Propagating the Gospel. He conducted evangelistic meetings among Indians at Longmeadow,

Windham, Niantic, Groton, and Long Island. However, his constant application to books overstrained his eyes, and made it impossible to continue his education. It was proposed to send him to Yale College, but when he left Wheelock's family school, his formal education was complete. He was trained in Latin, Greek, French, and Hebrew, but not in the more rarefied treasures of theology. He remained a simple, but totally committed, Christian.

On August 29, 1759, Samson Occom was ordained a Presbyterian minister in East Hampton, Long Island. He took for the text of his "trial sermon" Psalm 72:9, "They that dwell in the wilderness shall bow before him; and his enemies shall lick the dust." At the time he was serving at Montauk, Long Island, as schoolmaster, preacher, and judge. His annual salary from the missionary society was twenty pounds. Meanwhile he had married Mary Fowler, member of an outstanding Indian family living at Montauk. She was, we are told, "intelligent, virtuous, and comely."

From 1760 to 1764 Occom was engaged in a major missionary enterprise to the Six Nations of New York, whose legendary fifteenth-century chief was the famed Hiawatha. The New York correspondents of the Scottish Society for the Propagation of the Gospel, who had earlier sponsored David Brainerd, received word that the Oneida Indians, in particular, had requested that a minister be sent to them. In due time Samson Occom was appointed, and on June 10, 1760, he and his nephew, David Fowler, mounted their horses at Lebanon and set out as the first missionaries to be commissioned by the Christians of Connecticut.

Excerpts from Samson's diary describe the journey:

"Wednesday, June ye 10. Reached Hartford about 9 at night. Lodged at Capt. Daniel Bull's, and were very kindly treated. The man seems to be truly religious, keeps very good order in his house.

"Saturday June ye 13. Went on our way, got within five miles of the City of New York, and turned in to one Mr. Goldsmith's.

"Sabbath June ye 14. Tarried at Goldsmith's. We did not go to the city to public worship for fear of the smallpox, being informed [it was] very rife there. But I never saw a Sabbath spent so by any Christian people in my life as some spent it here. Some were riding in chairs, some upon horseback, others traveling afoot, passing and repassing all day long; and all sorts of evil noises [were] carried on by our [door]. Drunkards were reeling and staggering in the streets, others tumbling off their horses. There were others at work in their farms, and [if] ever any people under the heavens spoke Hell's language, these people did. For their mouths were full of cursings, profaning God's holy Name. I greatly mistake if these are not the sons and daughters of Belial.

"O Thou God of Heaven, Thou yet hast all the hearts of the children of men in Thine hands. Leave me not to practice the works of these people, but help me, O Lord, to take warning and to take heed to myself according to Thy Holy Word, and have mercy upon the wicked. Convince and convert them to Thyself, for Thine own glory.

"I have thought there was no heathen but the wild Indians, but I think now there is some English heathen, where they enjoy the gospel of Jesus Christ too. Yea, I believe they are worse than ye savage heathens of the wilderness. I have thought that I had rather go with the meanest and most despised creature on earth to Heaven, than to go with the greatest monarch down to Hell, after a short enjoyment of sinful pleasures with them in this world. I am glad there is one defect in the Indian language. I believe in all their languages they can't curse or swear or take God's Name in vain in their own tongue."

A letter to the Rev. Eleazar Wheelock, dated June 24, gives an insight into Occom's motivation: "Rev'd Sir. We reached New York ye 15 inst. and to my surprise, the gentlemen had concluded not [to] send me at all [to the Oneidas], and all the reason that they can give is, they are afraid the Indians will kill me. I told them they could not kill me but once, and told them I intended to proceed on my journey and if I perish for want of support, I perish. The people are uncommonly kind to me in this great city. I am invited every day to dine with some gentleman or other. Ministers of all sects and denominations are extremely kind to me."

Occom proceeded to Albany, where he received letters and a pass from General Amherst, who headed the British forces in North America. He then continued on to Lake Oneida and spent nine weeks with the Indians. Their early suspicions were soon disarmed, and they built a house for Occom and his nephew. When he left, the Oneidas presented him with a belt of wampum, and the old king made an address in the Council House, amid a large gathering, in which he said:

"We are glad from the inside of our hearts that you are come here to teach the right way of God. We are also thankful to those who sent you, and above all to God.

"We intend by the help of God to repent of all our sins and all our heathenish ways and customs. We will put them all behind our backs and will never look on them again, but will look strait forward and run after Christianity.

"If we shall try to set up a school, we beg the assistance of the English if they see fit.

"We desire that strong drink may be prohibited, that it may not be brought among us, for we find it kills our bodies and souls, and we will try to hinder it here.

"We desire to be protected on our lands, that none may molest or encroach upon us.

"This belt of wampum shall bind us fast together in perpetual love and friendship."

The president of the Scottish Society's New York correspondents, Rev. David Bostwick, wrote this report to Scotland: "He [Occom] is married to an Indian woman who is also esteemed truly pious, and has six children, with whom he would gladly dwell in the wilderness if he could be supported as a missionary. He well understands the business of farming, having chiefly supported his family by it while he preached to the handful of Indians upon Long Island. He has acquired a tolerable acquaintance with Latin, Greek, and Hebrew, with the sciences, and is really a good divine. His piety is unquestionable, having been manifested by more than ten years' exemplary conduct. His temper is very amiable and Christianlike, full of humility and meekness. His heart is much set on preaching the gospel to the Indians, and he seems willing to spend and be spent, to do or suffer anything for their conversion and salvation. In short, nothing is wanting to fix him there, but a support."

The support did not come, and Samson turned to the Niantic Indians of Connecticut, where he was employed as a missionary at thirty pounds a year. He moved his family from Montauk to Mohegan, and served on home ground until 1765, when he was chosen by George Whitefield to travel to England. The purpose was to raise funds for the evangelizing and educating of the American Indians, a cause dear to the heart of the English evangelist. However, some of the mission bureaucrats objected to the scheme. Occom himself wrote to Wheelock, "The honorable commissioners here are still very strong in their opposition to your scheme. They think it is nothing but a shame to send me over the great water. They say it is to impose upon the good people. They further affirm I was brought up regularly and a Christian all my days. Some say I can't talk Indian. Others say I can't read. In short I believe the old Devil is in Boston to oppose our design, but I am in hopes he is almost superannuated, or in a delirium. I have a struggle in my mind at times, [thinking I may] never see my poor family again, but I verily believe I am called of God by [a] strange Providence, and that is enough."

On November 21, 1765, Occom finally set out for Boston. On December 23 he and a white minister embarked on a packet for England. It is worth mentioning that their ocean passage was twenty guineas, and that the joint owner of the ship, Mr. John Hancock, contributed one-fourth of the fare. The coast of England was sighted on February 2, and four days later they were in London. On Sunday February 16, the Reverend Samson Occom appeared in the pulpit of Whitefield's tabernacle. He was forty-three years of age.

What was he like, this man who came from a Native American tribe to preach the gospel in the most famous pulpit in Britain? Says his biographer, W. DeLoss Love, "His face, while distinctly that of an Indian, had a nobility of expression. His flowing locks reached almost to his shoulders. In attire he was clad in ministerial black, with vest of colonial cut and knee breeches. His sermons were always simple. They had, however, the indescribable scent of the forest in them. He seems to have come under the influence of Whitefield's fervor. This Indian preacher was no novice. He had already been before large audiences in Boston and New York.

"The secret of his power was in the fact that he was himself the embodiment of his cause—a native Indian of no mean tribe, who had risen to the highest station of any Indian preacher in the century. He was in earnest, and never once did he forget the main object of his long journey. Withal, his manners were such as intercourse with some of the best New England families could cultivate, for he had been often a welcome guest in their homes. Calm, dignified and self-possessed, as many an Indian chief was wont to be, he exhibited those qualities which were esteemed in a minister of that day."

Whitefield took Occom to meet the Earl of Dartmouth, for whom the Wheelock Indian school was eventually named, and which became Dartmouth College. He met King George III, who contributed two hundred pounds to the cause. He met the Countess of Huntingdon, the Rev. John Newton, the Archbishop of Canterbury, William Warburton, bishop of Gloucester, and many others. He traveled to Scotland and Ireland. During this time he delivered more than four hundred sermons or addresses, and raised twelve thousand pounds to further the work of Christianizing the Indians of North America. In Edinburgh, Scotland, after addressing the General Assembly of the Church of Scotland, Occam was approached about accepting a doctorate in divinity from the University, but "modestly declined the honor." After two years and one month he sailed for home, to receive the congratulations of his sponsors in Boston.

Enough has now been set forth to indicate the remarkable qualities of the Reverend Samson Occom, and the impact he made upon his generation. The rest of this selection will be devoted to quotations from the man himself, including the sole sermon of the thousands he preached which has been preserved in print. First, let us listen to his views of Negro slavery and slaveholders:

"I will tell who they are, they are the preachers or ministers of the gospel of Jesus Christ. It has been very fashionable for them to keep Negro slaves, which I think is inconsistent with their character and function. If I understand the gospel aright, I think it is a dispensation of freedom and liberty, both temporal and spiritual, and [if] the preachers of the Holy Gospel of Jesus do preach it according to the mind of God, they preach true liberty; and how can such keep Negroes in slavery? And if ministers are true liberty men, let them preach liberty for the poor Negroes fervently and with great zeal, and those ministers who have Negroes set an example before their people by freeing their Negroes. Let them show their faith by their works."[2]

Equally significant was Occom's letter to his "Indian brethren," urging them to remain neutral during the Revolutionary War. We are not told whether this was sent to the Six Nations of New York, or to his own Mohegan tribesmen, but we do know that his fellow Mohegan and classmate at Lebanon, Joseph Johnson, took a copy of Occom's letter to General George Washington at Cambridge, Massachusetts, in February 1776, and that the General read it. Here is the letter:

"Beloved Brethren: I rejoice to hear that you keep to your promise that you will not meddle with the family contentions of the English, but will be at peace and quietness. Peace never does any hurt. Peace is from the God of peace and love, and therefore be at peace among yourselves, and with all men, and the God of peace dwell with you.

"Jesus Christ is the Prince of Peace. He is the Peace Maker. If all mankind in the world believed in Jesus Christ with all their hearts, there would be no more wars; they would live as one family in peace. Jesus Christ said to His disciples just before He left them, 'Peace I leave with you, My peace I give unto you, not as the world giveth give I unto you,' and again, 'A new command I give unto you, that you love one another.'[3]

"Now consider, my beloved brethren, who is the author of these bloody wars. Will God set his people to kill one another? You will certainly say No. Well, who then makes all this mischief? Methinks I hear you all say, the Devil, the Devil—so he is, he makes all the contentions as he sows the seeds of discord among the children of men and makes all the mischief in the world. Yet it is right for the peaceable to defend themselves when wicked people fall upon them without reason or cause. Then they can look up to Heaven to their God and He will help them.

"I will now give you a little insight into the nature of the English quarrels over the great waters. They got to be rich, I mean the nobles and the great, and they are very proud and they keep the rest of their brethren under their feet. They make slaves of them. The great ones have got all the land and the rest are poor tenants; and the people in this country [America] live more upon a level and they live happy, and the former kings of England used to let the people in this country have their freedom and liberty. But the present King of England wants to make them slaves to himself, and the people in this country don't want to be slaves. And so they are come over to kill them, and the people here are obliged to defend themselves. They don't go over the great lake to kill *them.*

"And now I think you must see who is the oppressor and who are the oppressed, and now I think, if you must join on one way or other you can't join the oppressor, but will help the oppressed. But let me conclude with one word of advice. Use all your influence to your brethren, so far as you have any connections, to keep them in peace and quietness, and not to intermeddle in these quarrels among the white people. The Lord Jesus Christ says, 'Blessed are the peacemakers, for they shall be called the children of God.'[4] This with great love is from your true brother, Samson Occom."

During his stay in Britain, Occom was offered episcopal ordination shortly after he arrived, and refused it. This refusal caused considerable dissatisfaction among the Anglican clergy, and helps to explain their coolness to his appeals for funds for the Indian work. Here is Occom's reaction after he returned to Mohegan territory, expressed in his own words:

"Now I am in my own country, I may freely inform you of what I honestly and soberly think of the bishops, lord bishops, and archbishops of England. In my view, they don't look like gospel bishops or ministers of Christ. I can't find them in the Bible. I think they a good deal resemble the anti-Christian popes. I find the gospel bishops resemble, in some good measure, their good Master, and they follow Him in the example He has left them. They discover meekness and humility, are gentle and kind unto all men, ready to do good unto all. They are compassionate and merciful unto the miserable, and charitable to the poor.

"But I did not find the bishops of England so. Upon my word, if I never spoke the truth before, I do now. I waited on a number of bishops, and represented to them the miserable and wretched situation of the poor Indians who are perishing for lack of spiritual knowledge, and begged their assistance in evangelizing these poor heathen. But if you can believe me, they never gave us one single brass farthing. It seems to me that they are very indifferent whether the poor Indians go to Heaven or Hell. I can't help my thoughts; and I am apt to think they don't want the Indians to go to Heaven with them."

The sermon by Occom that has come down to us was preached in the brick meeting-house of the First Church in New Haven on September 2, 1772. A condemned murderer, a twenty-nine-year-old Indian named Moses Paul, had requested the sermon. It was preached before "a great concourse of people whose curiosity was as much excited to hear Mr. Occom preach as to see the execution," according to a newspaper account. The condemned man, surrounded by guards, was brought into the church and the service began, while a large crowd stood outside. His crime was committed outside a tavern in Bethany the previous December, the murderer acting in spite with a club on a stranger after being refused a drink and being ejected from the place for being disorderly.

Occom took for his text Romans 6:23, "For the wages of sin is death, but the gift of God is eternal life through Jesus Christ our Lord." He developed two propositions: "that sin is the cause of all the miseries that befall the children of men, both as to their bodies and souls for time and eternity," and "that eternal life and happiness is the free gift of God through Jesus Christ our Lord." He addressed in turn the criminal, the ministers, and the assembled Indians. What follows are his remarks to the Indians present:

"My poor kindred, you see the woeful consequences of sin by seeing this, our poor miserable countryman, now before us, who is to die this day for his sins and great wickedness. And it was the sin of drunkenness that has brought this destruction and untimely death upon him. There is a dreadful woe denounced from the Almighty against drunkards, and it is this sin, this abominable, this beastly and accursed sin of drunkenness, that has stripped us of every desirable comfort in this life. By this we are poor, miserable, and wretched. By this sin we have no name nor credit in the world among polite nations. For this sin we are despised in the world, and it is all right and just, for we despise ourselves more; and if we do not regard ourselves, who will regard us? And it is for our sins, and especially for that accursed, that most hateful sin of drunkenness, that we suffer every day.

"For the love of strong drink we spend all that we have, and everything we can get. By this sin we cannot have comfortable houses, nor anything comfortable in our houses; neither food nor raiment nor decent utensils. We are obliged to put up any sort of shelter just to screen us from the severity of the weather; and we go about with very mean, ragged, and dirty clothes, almost naked. And we are half-starved, for most of the time obliged to pick up anything to eat. And our poor children are suffering every day for want of the necessaries of life. They are very often crying for want of food, and we have nothing to give them. And in the cold weather they are shivering and crying, being pinched with the cold—all this for the love of strong drink.

"And this is not all the misery and evil we bring on ourselves in this world; but when we are intoxicated with strong drink, we drown our rational powers, by which we are distinguished from the brutal creation. We unman ourselves, and bring ourselves not only level with the beasts of the field, but seven degrees beneath them. Yea, we bring ourselves level with the devils. I do not know but we make ourselves worse than the devils, for I never heard of drunken devils.

"My poor kindred, do consider what a dreadful abominable sin drunkenness is. God made us rational creatures, and we choose to be fools. Do consider further, and behold a drunkard, and see how he looks when he has drowned his reason. How deformed and shameful does he appear? He disfigures every part of him, both soul and body, which was made after the image of God. He appears with awful deformity, and his whole visage is disfigured. If he attempts to speak he cannot bring out his words distinct, so as to be understood. If he walks he reels and staggers to and fro, and tumbles down. And see how he behaves! Now he is laughing, and then he is crying; he is singing, and the next minute he is mourning. He is all love to everyone, and anon he is raging, and for fighting and killing all before him, even the nearest and the dearest relations and friends. Yea, nothing is too bad for a drunken man to do. He will do that which he would not do for the world, in his right mind.

"Further, when a person is drunk, he is just good for nothing in the world. He is of no service to himself, to his family, to his neighbors or his country; and how more unfit is he to serve God! Yet he is just as fit for the service of the Devil.

"Again, a man in drunkenness is in all manner of dangers. He may be killed by his fellowmen, by wild beasts, and tame beasts. He may fall into the fire, into the water, or into a ditch; or he may fall down as he walks along, and break his bones or his neck. He may cut himself with edged tools. Further, if he has any money or anything valuable, he may lose it all, or may be robbed, or he may make a foolish bargain and be cheated out of all he has.

"I believe you know the truth of what I have just now said, many of you, by said experience; yet you will go on still in your drunkenness. Though you have been cheated over and over again, and you have lost your substance by drunkenness, yet you will venture to go on in this most destructive sin. O, fools, when will ye be wise? We all know the truth of what I have been saying, by what we have seen and heard of drunken deaths. How many have been drowned in our rivers, and how many have been frozen to death in the winter seasons! Yet drunkards go on without fear and consideration. Alas, alas! What will become of all such drunkards? Without doubt they must all go to Hell, except they truly repent and turn to God.

"Drunkenness is so common amongst us that even our young men and young women are not ashamed to get drunk. Our young men will get drunk as soon as they will eat when they are hungry. It is generally esteemed amongst men more abominable for a woman to be drunk than a man; and yet there is nothing more common amongst us than female drunkards. Women ought to be more modest than men. The Holy Scriptures recommend modesty to women in particular; but drunken women have no modesty at all. It is more intolerable for a woman to get drunk, if we consider further, [because] she is in great danger of falling into the hands of the sons of Belial, or wicked men, and being shamefully treated by them.

"And here I cannot but observe that we find in the Sacred Writ a woe denounced against men who put their bottles to their neighbors' mouths to make them drunk, that they may see their nakedness,[5] and no doubt there are such devilish men now in our own day, as there were in the days of old.

"And to conclude, consider, my poor kindred, you that are drunkards, into what a miserable condition you have brought yourselves. There is a dreadful woe thundering against you every day, and the Lord says that drunkards shall not inherit the Kingdom of God.[6]

"And now let me exhort you all to break off from your drunkenness, by a gospel repentance, and believe on the Lord Jesus and you shall be saved. Take warning by this doleful sight before us, and by all the dreadful judgments that have befallen poor drunkards. O, let us all reform our lives, and live as become dying creatures in time to come. Let us be persuaded that we are accountable creatures to God, and we must be called to an account in a few days.

"You that have been careless all your days, now awake to righteousness, and be concerned for your poor and never-dying souls. Fight against all sins, and especially the sin that easily besets you, and behave in time to come as becomes rational creatures. And above all things, receive and believe on the Lord Jesus Christ, and you shall have eternal life. And when you come to die, your souls will be received into Heaven, there to be with the Lord Jesus in eternal happiness, and with all the saints in glory; which God of His infinite mercy grant, through Jesus Christ our Lord. Amen."

The newspaper report said, "The Rev. Mr. Occom attended the criminal to the place of execution, where he made a short but well-adapted prayer to the occasion. The criminal behaved with decency and steadiness, and appeared to be in the exercise of fervent prayer all the way from the gaol to the gallows. He took a most affectionate leave of his countrymen the Indians, many of whom were present, and exhorted them to shun those vices to which they are so much addicted, viz. drunkenness, revenge, etc."

Occom's sermon went through nineteen editions, was reprinted in London, and translated into Welsh. Thirty-five years after his death it was still in great demand. It may well have been the most powerful temperance sermon ever preached.

Little attempt has been made in this sketch to convey the lifelong interest Occom took in the spiritual welfare of his fellow countrymen; how he visited in hundreds of homes, gave medical help, baptized, married, and buried, established villages, and also ministered lovingly to white people on the frontier. Two excerpts from his diary may be cited to give some idea of his labors. The first describes a visit during one of his "peregrinations" as he called them, along the Mohawk River in October and November, 1785:

"Sabbath, Oct. 30. Had a meeting in David Fowler's house, and a number of Stockbridgers came to meeting to the distance of six miles. They had eleven horses and there was a number of foot people, and there was a solemn assembly. The people attended the Word with affection, many of them. I spoke from Matthew 4:10. In the afternoon I spoke from [Psalm] 32:1.[7] In the evening we had singing a long while, and then gave them a word of exhortation and concluded with prayer.

"Monday, Tuesday and Wednesday nothing happened remarkable, only rainy and snowy weather, and I was much confined [by] my wrenched back.

"Thursday, Nov. 3. Towards night we attended upon the ancient ordinance of marriage, the first that ever was celebrated by our people in their New Settlement in this wilderness. The couple to be married and the young people formed in a neighboring house and came to the house of wedding in a regular procession according to their age and were seated accordingly. The old people also seated themselves regularly, and a great number of Stockbridgers came from their town to attend the wedding, but many of them were too late.

"When I got up, I spoke to them some time upon the nature of marriage, the honorableness and lawfulness of it, whereby we are distinguished from the brutal creation. Said some of the first marriage in Eden, and of the marriage where Christ and His disciples were invited, and the honor He did to it by working the first miracle He wrought in the world, in turning water into wine. And then we prayed. After prayer I ordered them to take each other by the right hand alternately, and then I declared them in the face of the assembly to be a lawful husband and wife, according to the law of God. And then prayed. Prayer being ended, marriage salutations went round regularly, and concluded by singing a marriage hymn. Then the people sat down, and Jacob Fowler,[8] who was appointed master of ceremonies at this marriage, gave out some drink around the company, and then supper was brought, set in order on a long board, and we sat down to eat, and had toddy well sweetened with wild sugar made of sugar trees in the wilderness. And after supper we spent the evening in singing psalms, hymns, and spiritual songs. And after that everyone went home peaceably without any carousing or frolicking.

"Friday, Nov. 4. The young people put on their best clothes, and went to a neighbor's house, all on horseback, and they appeared agreeable and decent, and they had no carousing. They had some pleasant chat and agreeable conduct, some singing of psalms, hymns, and spiritual songs. Some time in the afternoon they dined together, and after dinner everyone went home quietly. So the wedding ended, and it was conducted, carried on, and finished with honor and great decency; and the Lord help this people to go on regularly in all their concerns."

The name of this new settlement—for the record—was "Eeyamquittoowauconnuck."

Finally, we shall glimpse the evangelist in action in the fall of 1786. This excerpt from his diary records his journey to Oneida, where he now lived, from Mohegan.

"Tuesday, Oct. 24. Our men went to Canaserake to fishing, and I set off for home. Stopped at the Old Town, and intended to pass along, but they desired me to stay to have a meeting in the evening, and I consented. In the evening they collected together I believe most all the old people, and many young people. I expounded upon 2 Corinthians 13:11 ['Finally, brethren, farewell. Be perfect, be of good comfort, be of one mind, live in peace; and the God of love and peace shall be with you'] and there was deep attention with flow of tears. After I had done, two or three spoke in their own tongue, rehearsing what I had delivered, and the chief man asked me as I was about to leave them, how they should go on in their religious concerns. I told them as they were not formed into [a] church state, they should enter into Christian fellowship and put themselves under watch care of one another, and carry on the public worship of God in singing, praying and reading the Word of God, and some exhortation, and some explanation of the Word of God, and maintain family worship constantly. . . ."

Samson Occom lived five more years, and died in his sixty-ninth year at his home in Tuscarora, near Oneida, New York, in July 1792. Over three hundred Indians, and many whites, attended the funeral. They were his pupils, his parishioners, and his own kindred. We shall let his biographer, Dr. Love, tell the rest: "They returned to the house of mourning from the place where they had found a cathedral under the arches of the woodland. As the summer's sun was declining in the west, at their customary hour, the body of this Indian Moses was lifted, not by angels, but by the strong arms of his faithful friends, the New England aborigines, and borne up the hill, and laid beside his own dust—a king like those of the Scriptures to rest in the inheritance of David."

NOTES

1. The man was the Rev. Jonathan Barber (see page 247).
2. Cf. James 2:18.
3. John 13:34.
4. Matthew 5:9.
5. This seems to be a reference to Genesis 9:20-22 and Leviticus 18:6-19.
6. 1 Corinthians 6:10.
7. "It is written, thou shalt worship the Lord thy God, and him only shalt thou serve" (Matthew 4:10). "Blessed is he whose transgression is forgiven, whose sin is covered" (Psalm 32:1).
8. Jacob Fowler was Occom's nephew.